THE LITERARY REVIEW

AN INTERNATIONAL
JOURNAL OF
CONTEMPORARY
WRITING

FALL 2009
VOL.53 / NO.1

EDITOR
Minna Proctor

EDITOR EMERITUS
Walter Cummins

EDITOR-AT-LARGE
René Steinke

POETRY EDITORS
Renée Ashley
David Daniel

BOOKS EDITOR
Jena Salon

ASSISTANT EDITOR
Melody Feldman

EDITORIAL COORDINATOR
Louise Dell-Bene Stahl

PRODUCTION EDITOR
Kate Munning

EDITORIAL ASSISTANTS
Cassie Hay
Ryan Romine

EDITORIAL INTERNS
Emily Burns
Helena Davis
Ryan Elwood
Megan Kellerman

WEBMASTER
Mike Neff

DESIGN
Half and Half Studio

READERS
Gloria Amodeo
Pete Barlow
Vicki Brand
Janet Calcaterra
Dan Capriotti
Dana Connolly
Becky Firesheets
Hilary Ford
Kimberlee Gertsmann
Jerisha Gordon
Pamela Harris
Racquel Henry
Marquita Hockaday
Elise Johansen
Kerstin Lieff
Michele Lesko
Andrew W. McKay
Chloé Yelena Miller
Theresa Miller
Richard O'Brien
Drew Riley
Kurt Simmons
Ian Stone
Steven Taylor
Ethan Tinkler
Lisa Voltolina
Anne Harding Woodworth

CONTRIBUTING EDITORS
John E. Becker
Martin Green
Jody Handerson
Harry Keyishian
Marjorie Deiter Keyishian
Michael Morse
William Zander

ADVISORY EDITORS
Esther Allen
Beth Bjorklund
Lane Dunlop
H.E. Francis
Thomas E. Kennedy
Bharati Mukherjee
J.P. Seaton
Sudeep Sen
Charles Simic
Ilan Stavans

BOARD OF DIRECTORS
David Daniel
Martin Donoff
Minna Proctor
Marilyn Rye

FOUNDERS
Charles Angoff
Clarence Decker
Peter Sammartino

PUBLISHED QUARTERLY
SINCE 1957
BY FAIRLEIGH DICKINSON
UNIVERSITY

285 MADISON AVENUE
MADISON, NJ T07940

THELITERARYREVIEW.ORG

All correspondence should be addressed to *The Literary Review*, USPS (587780), 285 Madison Avenue, Madison, NJ 07940 USA. Telephone: (973) 443-8564. Email: tlr@fdu.edu. Web: www.theliteraryreview.org. Periodical postage paid at Madison, NJ 07940 and at additional mailing offices. Subscription copies not received will be replaced without charge only if claimed within three months (six months outside U.S.) from original date of mailing. postmaster, send address changes to *The Literary Review*, 285 Madison Avenue, Madison, NJ 07940.

Manuscripts are read September through May. We only consider online submissions of poetry, fiction and creative non-fiction. For more information go to www.theliteraryreview.org/submit.html.

SUBSCRIPTIONS
One year: $18 domestic, $21 international; Two year: $30 domestic, $36 international.
Single issues: $7 domestic, $8 international.
Visa, MasterCard and American Express are accepted.

The Literary Review is a member of CLMP and CELJ. It is indexed in Humanities International Complete, Arts and Humanities Citation Index, MLA International Bibliography, Index of American Periodical Verse, Annual Index of Poetry in Periodicals, and the Literary Criticism Register. Microfilm is available from National Archive Publishing Company, P.O. Box 998, Ann Arbor, MI 48106. Reprints are available from the Institute for Scientific Information, 3501 Market Street, Philadelphia, PA 19104. CD-ROM versions are available from Ebsco Publishing, 83 Pine Street, P.O. Box 2250, Peabody, MA 01960-7250, and poetry can be accessed on CD-ROM through Poem Finder, available from Roth Publishing, Inc., 185 Great Neck Rd., Great Neck, NY 11021. The full text of *The Literary Review* is also available in the electronic versions of the Humanities Index from the H.W. Wilson Company, 950 University Avenue, Bronx, NY 10452. Selections from *The Literary Review* are available online on the Infonautics Electric Library, www.bigchalk.com.

PRINTING BY WESTCAN PRINTING GROUP
78 HUTCHINGS STREET, WINNIPEG, MB R2X 3B1, CANADA

COPYRIGHT ©2009
FAIRLEIGH DICKINSON UNIVERSITY
A QUARTERLY PUBLICATION
PRINTED IN CANADA

ISBN: 978-0-9841607-3-0 0-9841607-3-6

PERMISSIONS
69: "An Almost Guinea Fowl" is from the collection *Landscape with Dog and Other Stories*, publishing November 2009 with Clockroot Books, Northampton, MA. Reprinted here by permission of the author.

COVER ARTIST

WALTER MARTIN AND PALOMA MUÑOZ
WISH AND WEIGHT

As a writer, an artist and a semi-crazed, menopausal older woman, I've had my share of therapy. If one could illustrate that innate, morbid curiosity which draws us to examine those dark, quirky and often profoundly disturbing aspects of life, one might end up with something like the work of Walter Martin and Paloma Muñoz, featured on our cover this issue.

"Wish and Weight" is part of an ongoing series that was recently featured in the exhibition "Islands," at the P.P.O.W. Gallery in New York City. A disconsolate man stands alone in a forest on a snowy night. His outsized head rests against a leaf-bare tree, the lurid orange of his sweater and hair starkly contrasts the gloomy despair. His head is so big, so weighty, so unbearably too much.

For the Travelers series, Martin and Muñoz have created a progression of miniature dioramas and snowy globes, each one with the tongue-in-cheek charm of a Brueghel snow scene combined with deeply unsettling images; minute suicides, murders, eminent and present disasters—all dancing in that surprisingly narrow margin between serenity and despair. Whether peering in at these tiny, dark allegories or viewing the large macro-photographs of the work, I can't help but identify with the figures in each tiny, perfect world, captured in that single, breathless moment when the dream becomes a nightmare.

Martin and Muñoz have been collaborating since 1994. Their time, and a wealth of tiny supplies, is divided between residences in the south of Spain, a converted guitar factory in Brooklyn and their home in rural Pennsylvania. Their work is exhibited worldwide and is included in the collections of Museo Nacional Centro de Arte Reina Sofia in Madrid, La Caixa in Barcelona, Spain, and the KIASMA Museum of Contemporary Art in Helsinki, Finland. The Travelers series was published as a book last year by Aperture.

—Jody Handerson

WISH AND WEIGHT © 2007 COPYRIGHT WALTER MARTIN & PALMOA MUÑOZ. COURTESY OF THE ARTISTS AND PPOW, NY

EDITOR'S NOTE

From the moment we announced the *Therapy!* issue, we knew that it would be a hugely popular theme. Not with readers, mind you, but with writers. Indeed, we had no shortage of contributors addressing their submission "To The Editors, For the therapy issue . . ." The allure of pure madness aside, as well as the attendant delusion that asylum is a larval spa vacation, writers tend to cast themselves on the neurotic end of the sanity spectrum. As poetry editor, Renée Ashley, hollered at me from the other end of a long hallway—in response to my request last summer that she give me some of her own work to publish—"there's no real choice, Minna, it has to be for *Therapy!* That's where I fit in best."

We are all casting our dreams as word pictures, building castles for our inner child, and, as Frank Bidart (interviewed in these pages) would say, *still* wrestling with Mother.

The inception of this theme came from a student thesis paper delivered at the summer session of Fairleigh Dickinson's MFA program. "Is therapeutic poetry, therapy, or poetry?" she asked. And then proceeded to present a selection of poems about incest, some of which were great works of art and others of which were piteous, yes, but had the aethestic vigor of a shopping list. We then made the assumption that it would be a delightful and worthwhile endeavor to find the therapy in the art, rather than the other way around. Which engendered responses from our contributors, like that from Mary Rose O'Reilley: "Carl Jung could curl up in the bathtub with these poems til the waters rose, though none are explicit about therapy."

Perfect!

And so, what to do with a theme that articulates the underlying mood of most creative expression, while avoiding the shopping lists and the bearded doctors settling back into plush leather armchairs? Go nuts, of course, and just include everything else.

Curl up in a bathtub and enjoy our selections. We promise, you will not be cured.

Minna Proctor
Madison, New Jersey

THERAPY! FALL 2009 VOL.53 / NO.1

Contents

POETRY

7–11
Peter Kocan
The Carol Singers; The Beauty; On an Invitation to Revisit; Cured

30–36
Bruce Cohen
A Rare Condition; Art Therapy; Divine Wow:

37–42
Gillian Parrish
tilth; might come to rest

48–50
Robert Nazarene
On the Whereabouts of a Mouse Studying to Be a Rat; Joi de Vivre

67–68
Yonatan Maisel
Self-Esteem, by-Proxy: On How Your Downfall Quells My Angst

95–97
Karina Borowicz
"Mystery Piano Found Deep in Cape Cod Woods"; Long Time; Neon

122–129
Catherine Doty
The First Time I Was Told To Fuck Myself; Breathing Under Water; Behind Bars; Sweet Ants

138–146
Mary Rose O'Reilley
The Last; Reading Anna Karenina on the Empire Builder; Confession

175–178
Renée Ashley
Where Does the Mind Go When It Refuses To Leave; Contemplation within the Framework of the Dream; My Father Is Ashes; All My Suicides Have Been Men

FICTION

12–23
Linda Davis
The True Definition of Fat

43–47
Lawrence Cady
Help Me, Christina

51–66
Chris Gavaler
The Marriage of the Strawman and the Patchwork Girl

69–77
GREECE
Ersi Sotiropoulos
Karen Emmerich, translator
An Almost Guinea Fowl

78–82
Kyle McManus
Other People's Boredom

83–94
Jeff Hart
The Amazing Dreamer Stays Awake

98–109
Robert Repino
We Have the Answer to the Apocalypse

110–121
Faye Reddecliff
The River

130–137
Ron Savage
The Cave at Elgon

147–160
Polly Buckingham
Monster Movie

161–169
Jamie McCulloch
Roman Holiday

170–174
Martin Ott
Sugar, Wine, Smoke and Glue

179–190
Matthew Salesses
The Last Seal Pup

ESSAY

24–29
Rand B. Lee
Girl, Breastless, Dancing

BOOKS

191–198
H. L. Hix
In Conversation with Frank Bidart

199–202
Stephen Elliott
The Adderall Diaries: A Memoir of Mood, Masochism, and Murder
Reviewed by Jena Salon

203–205
Valeria Parrella
From Grace Received
Reviewed by Cassie Hay

206–211
Mahmoud Darwish
If I Were Another
Reviewed by Paul-Victor Winters

212–213
Eula Biss
Notes from No Man's Land: American Essays
Reviewed by Marion Wyce

214–216
Inger Christensen
Azorno
Reviewed by Christine Condon

217–219
Guillermo Rosales
The Halfway House
Reviewed by Abigail Deutsch

CONTRIBUTORS

220–222

POETRY

Peter Kocan
The Carol Singers

One Christmas Eve carol singers came
From the local church, three car loads
With an organ mounted on a truck.
The organ's earnest note was heavy
With their good intentions.

They stayed fifteen minutes outside
Each ward. A few curious patients
Came out to listen and receive
Embarrassed gifts and blessings.
A few stars leaned down, as though to hear.

But mostly the singers spoke
To blank doors shut tight on depths
Where no song penetrates. Still they sang,
And moved on, and sang again,
Carrying their disappointment.

Against blinded windows and hard
Roofs and walls of the hospital,
Against all that deep darkness,
Their carols wafted, offering news
Of some miraculous event.

The Beauty

I don't know her name. Neither does she.
I secretly christened her "The Beauty"
After seeing her in that little group
Of retard women trailing like sheep

Behind a nurse. Daily they're taken out
And led to the canteen for a treat,
Then shepherded round for exercise.
At morning and evening they pass.

The first time I didn't understand.
I just saw her wandering behind
The hags, and then pausing absently,
Her mind elsewhere. And when she turned to me

A vague smile, a blue-eyed open glance,
I took it for serene intelligence,
Until the nurse came scowling back
To hurry the moron with a kick.

On an Invitation to Revisit

Why go back? Certainly the earth
And water would be as they were,
And the wind, playing the same tunes
On a thousand old instruments
Of stick and stone I remember.

And I've no doubt the sky would be
The same old famous masterpiece
That I examined for so long,
Or that the dandelions wear
An identical yellow dress.

There'd be a familiar look
About possum and kangaroo,
The stamp of their recent forebears
I knew well. And the birds would give
The password of six years ago.

And human faces would recall
The names and details that fit.
I'd know this gesture or that walk,
The blaze or blankness in an eye
And the old grievance staring out.

And I daresay I'd recognize
The very bricks of walls that stand
Precisely where I saw them last,
And have a memory jump up
From every inch of the ground.

So much would be the same, and yet
The place I lived in isn't there.
I took it with me when I left:
It fitted in a tiny bag
Of the mind, but took years to pack.

Cured

I remember you as Fool,
Capering in your mind
As in a bright motley,
Droll as any jester,
Your lunacy being
A license to speak true.

I discover you now
Slumped sanely in a chair,
Weary of riddling truths
Into a mad king's ear.

SHORT STORY

Linda Davis
The True Definition of Fat

ze-nith *n.* **1.** For twenty years Alyson attempted every diet fad imaginable with no success. Grapefruit, South Beach, Suzanne Somers, Hilton Head; the list of Alyson's failed diets read like the glossary to a B-movie star's unauthorized biography. If only it were half that glamorous. Finally, when she was forty-two, she dropped forty pounds in three months. Her cousin Rip, who was the same age as her, had died suddenly of brain cancer. At a service on the one-year anniversary of his death, Alyson's mother said "Alyson and Rip were like two peas in a pod," and "as thick as thieves." Her mother collected clichés the way some people collected coins. Alyson, in canary horizontal stripes (she was making up for all the fat fashion taboos she'd eschewed all those years), corrected her, saying how they hadn't been close since childhood. Her mother, a good Catholic (still) looked shocked; her eyebrows disappeared under a brush-fire perm. The mourners were being herded into a line to greet Rip's widow, Sara, and their young daughter, Jewel. Alyson tried to slip outside unnoticed but the canary was too loud. "Excuse me, I'm not feeling well." Alyson flew towards the door. "They were as thick as paste, those two," she heard her mother say as she stepped outside.

yen *n.* **1.** (Three years earlier) at work, Alyson blew out the four candles on her fortieth birthday cake. "Are you four years old? You look older, Ms. Alyson. Are you four years old? You look older, Ms. Alyson . . ." Danny repeated over and over again, what seemed like fifty times. Danny was an autistic man who lived at Voices, the assisted living home in New York City that Alyson co-managed. He was obsessed with two things: Alyson and his Webster's Dictionary. The residents at Voices had no choice about the enclosed lives they led, which didn't bother them in the least, since most of their lives were lived internally. One resident fidgeted with the string of his party hat. "What did you wish?" he asked. Alyson lied, "I wished I was four again." What she really wished was the same thing she'd been wishing for twenty years: to be thin. After work, at her third floor Upper East Side walk-up, Rip had left a message. "Happy birthday, Ally wally." He never forgot. "Please call me back this time. Please." She pictured Rip in his swanky Beacon Hill office: the slicked back hair, blood red suspenders on a virginal white dress shirt. Alyson ate from her birthday cake box while standing up. This was what her life had become: standing while eating, not returning phone calls.

xerophagy *adj.* **1.** Alyson tried to lose weight. Every day. Diet words inhabited her brain, insipid as old lovers: Zone, Atkins, Grapefruit, Protein, Pilates, Water, Digestive Enzymes, colonics, fasting and self-invented diets: the All-You-Can-Chew Gum Diet, the Eat-Before-You-Go-To-A-Party Diet and the Toothpaste Diet. "I speak diet. I'm a diet scholar." Alyson chuckled over cocktails with Charles, a man she met through a computer dating service. Charles laughed at all of her jokes, but later, online, he felt compelled to be candid about his feelings publicly. He wrote, "Great personality, but not attracted to her." Alyson hated that his rejection made her eat a pint of Chunky Monkey. Her skin, it seemed, was the only thing about her that was thin. The heavier she got, the thinner her skin. "Webster's says you are pulchritudinous—that means beautiful." Danny had said this three days prior, his eyes not meeting hers. If only she had remembered that before eating.

wide *adj.* **1.** By thirty-nine, Alyson weighed the most she ever had: one hundred and sixty-nine pounds. As a 5'2" former ballerina, the weight was significant. At her yearly physical, she blocked her eyes when she stood on the digital scale. A crepe thin nurse with oversized freckles that resembled henna tattoos shouted, "169!" like some crazed carnival barker. In the examination room, undressed, Alyson noticed with horror that her chest had officially lost the race it had been in with her stomach. The doctor referred her to a nutritionist, a man from New Zealand who wore beads around his neck and padded around his ionized office in silk Chinese slippers. He put Alyson on a strict diet of raw food and supplements for a month. Three weeks into the regime, Alyson told him, "I feel like a civil war is being waged in my stomach, with casualties on both sides." Her stomach was distended like a water balloon. The nutritionist concluded she was going through early menopause, and there was nothing he could do to help her. "Both armies are raising their little white flags." At reception, Alyson asked if she could get a discount for that, the metaphor-stealing thing. The assistant looked at her with a face as blank as a snow drift.

vol·um·in·ous *adj.* **1.** "Life threw you a curveball." Her mother was visiting for the weekend. "You could have been a professional ballerina. I blame myself." Alyson reassured her mother, but deep down there was a part of her that expected, with each visit, that her mother would magically fix her life. Lately, their time together felt like a single woman's club; they talked about dates, drank white wine spritzers, said things like, "All the good ones are taken." After two drinks, her mother got teary. "Maybe you're right. Rip turned out alright and I raised him. Look how successful he is. Shrink to the stars. Did I tell you he's going to be on TV next month? Public access, but still. You should call and congratulate him." Alyson wished she could lose a pound for every time her mom told her to call Rip. Her mother adored her cousin and frequently used him as a self-esteem Band-Aid. Alyson popped open a can of mixed nuts, separated out the Brazils (her feeble attempt at dieting for the day), and shoveled the rest in her mouth. Everyone has their own version of Band-Aid, she thought.

un·bal·an·ced *adj.* **1.** Alyson had an idea. For one month, she would make herself sick with food. She slid dry pancakes that a previous IHOP customer had left behind into her purse and ate them at home later; she consumed a bottle of chewable vitamin C in three days; she had a salt and sugar derby, alternating between popcorn and nuts one hour and pie and cookies the next; she rose at two

> **Diet words inhabited her brain, insipid as old lovers: Zone, Atkins, Grapefruit, Protein, Pilates, Water, digestive enzymes, colonics, fasting, and self-invented diets: the All-You-Can-Chew Gum Diet, the Eat-Before-You-Go-To-A-Party Diet and the Toothpaste Diet.**

in the morning and ate bowls of cereal. By the end of the month, she felt healthier, more invigorated than she had in years. It lasted a day. Then, she got sick; heaved for three days straight. It was thrilling. She imagined all the calories leaving, like unwanted dinner guests. Danny regressed while she was out sick. Danny had a heartbreaking story; he'd lost his entire family: mother, father and sister, in a car crash, as if being born autistic wasn't enough bad luck for one lifetime. After reading his case file when she was first hired, Alyson ate an entire bag of roasted and salted almonds. All of the hurt in the world was a great reason to eat more, she thought. She was the first person Danny opened up to. He'd stopped speaking, spent hours watching his fingers twitch through crossed eyes. He even stopped reading his beloved dictionary. Coincidentally, a representative from the state health board was visiting that week and put in a recommendation to have Danny moved to a more intense program. The ensuing battle worked nicely as an excuse for Alyson to return to her regular eating habits.

thick *adj.* **2.** Alyson's mother surprised her with a ticket to see her childhood idol, Sylvie Guillem, perform in Ashton's *Ondine* at Lincoln Center. It was also a thinly veiled attempt at reconciling her with Rip—who flew down from Boston for the weekend with Sara. Alyson hadn't been to the ballet in twenty years. Ballet plus Rip equaled her past. As she watched Guillem float across the street, she remembered the year when Rip first got his license, how he always came early to pick her up at the Ballerina Academy. He would sit, feet up on a metal chair, and watch attentively. All of the ballerinas wanted to date him because he was cute, friendly, and frankly, interested. Alyson was so proud of him, she lied and told them he was her brother. Back in the packed Lincoln Center Theater, tears poured from Alyson's eyes like sweat on an August day in Manhattan. "Scraped cornea," she explained, squinting and blinking upwards, before she excused herself and left early, stopping and buying candy coated peanuts from a street vendor on her way home.

siz-a-ble *adj.* **2.** "You're my best friend, you have to be a bridesmaid," Crystal said. The thought of wearing the same hideous cardboard dress as five other women, all of whom wore single digit sizes, sounded like social suicide. Alyson could already see the photos, where she would look like both a sixth and seventh bridesmaid. The reception was at Crystal's wealthy sister's beach home in Southampton. The sister had a full-time staff and toddlers that drove electric cars over manicured lawns. Alyson nicknamed the sister, "The French Revolution," because of the way she'd seen her treat the help. Alyson decided to sit with her mother at a corner table, instead of at the head table. One of those bands they dragged out for weddings was singing "Endless Love." The singer wore a pale pink tux and winked at Alyson as she crossed the dance floor. When she sat down, the bridesmaid dress gathered around her like a tribe. She ignored the shrimp cocktail, played hard to get with the creamed soup but ravaged her salad and the salad served to the empty seat beside her. She also drank champagne. Lots. Everyone looked thin to her, or maybe she hadn't had enough to drink? This was America for Christ's sake. Even the teddy bear ice sculptures were looking awfully svelte. Then this bit of wisdom from her mother: "If you play your cards right, you could be married soon too." She nodded towards the singer. Alyson got up. "I feel like I have a full house now, Mom. Work and all. Let's leave before he starts singing the Captain and Tennille."

room-y *adj.* **1.** Alyson began to think that all her years of hiding were the real problem behind her weight struggles. She decided to switch to skimpy clothes that put her fat on display, like chicken thighs in the refrigerated case at the supermarket: skintight jeans and a camisole. Maybe if everyone knows how disgustingly fat I am, it will take my appetite away. She planned her "revealing debut" for the evening of Crystal's bachelorette party. In the packed elevator of the French Revolution's Upper West Side apartment, en route to the penthouse, a young girl stared at Alyson's waist for fifteen floors before whispering to her mother, "That lady is fat, Mommy." Alyson stayed on the elevator, took it back down. She didn't want to go home and eat, so she went to work. When she slipped the nurse coat over her bared body, she felt as if she were coming up for air. Alyson watched "America's Funniest Home Videos" with the residents. Danny told her she was "de rigueur—that means mandatory" to his happiness.

quan-ti-ty *n.* **1.** "Weight is an equation," a three-hundred-dollar-per-hour Park Avenue nutritionist told Alyson. "Intake minus exercise equals weight." "If that's the case," Alyson told Crystal over pancakes at IHOP, "my body is flunking math. I starved myself for a week, jogged daily, and nothing." Ophelia, the waitress who usually waited on their table, ignored them. "What's up with her?" Crystal asked. Alyson replied, "She's angry because we never come here anymore." Failing math or not, Alyson knew that the time she and Crystal spent together had shrunk from a squared number to a fraction ever since Crystal had met her boyfriend. "You can't quantify friendship," was Crystal's refrain. She was looking more and more like her sister; wearing hip, hip huggers and she'd barely touched her blueberry waffles.

preg·nant *adj.* **1.** "Sara had a girl!" Alyson's mother called her at work to tell her the news. Alyson felt her heart fall. "Rip is as happy as a clam!" Alyson played with her stomach. She was alone at the front desk at work. The flesh and fat had very little feeling which made it easy to believe that it wasn't part of her. There was the round bowl she could make when she gathered all the fat together in a circle in the middle and, of course, the love handles she fondled on either side of her waist. The most impressive shape of all was the one where she formed a small shelf upon which she rested her cereal bowl. She considered naming her shelf, like men named their penises. Maybe "Suzie," or "Cathy," something adorable. "Sara looks well," her mother droned on. A *People* magazine headline in the reception area screamed, "The bare belly is in!" Alyson flipped through the pages and stared at the exposed stomachs of the Jennifers, Kates and Nicoles. She convinced herself that all these girls smoked. "I gotta get back to work, Mom." Alyson left work early. Women everywhere on the streets were wearing bare midriffs. A conspiracy. There was only one place to go. At IHOP, Ophelia wasn't on duty. A new waitress who was so thin she had to wrap the strings of her apron around her waist twice asked her when she was due. A wave of sadness washed over Alyson, but she spoke quickly to hide it. "I actually just gave birth! I'll take a super stack with extra butter—for my milk. They say breastfeeding shrinks the waist. Here's hoping!"

ob·tru·sive *adj.* **2.** Women in Manhattan were thin and well-groomed European-types who lost weight eating baguettes and butter croissants. They got weekly pedicures, walked in stilettos whenever they were recycled back into fashion, accessorized themselves like Christmas trees. And they did it all with ease, without question. It made Alyson feel like beauty was a game that came with a set of instructions that her box was missing. Alyson stared at women everywhere she went. She considered homosexuality as if deciding between a matinee or evening performance. God, women were beautiful, she thought, even unattractive ones. One night, when Alyson was high on maple syrup, Ophelia from IHOP asked her to come home with her. She lived in a dreary fifth floor walk up in Queens. Cockroaches scattered like marbles when Ophelia turned on the light. She put on Janis Ian and walked over to kiss Alyson. Ophelia smelt like stale coffee and BO. Alyson imagined the hair she was sure to have under her arms; she could almost see her hopes and dreams walk out the door, catch a subway somewhere else. She apologized and told Ophelia she had to leave. "Your loss." Ophelia threw her coat at her. "I could have pleased you like no man ever has." Alyson picked up the dropped coat and thought, that's not saying much.

no‑ti‑cea‑ble *adj.* **2.** Rip and Sara arrived late to Christmas dinner. Alyson had hoped they wouldn't show. Sara was six months pregnant and wore a dark green wool knit skirt set and candy cane earrings. She looked more beautiful than ever. Alyson spent the day ticking off things she didn't like about Sara. The earrings were first on her list. She added: talks too much, has to be touching Rip every second, and goes to the bathroom often. So what if she bakes a perfect pie? When all was said and done, Rip would wake up and smell the coffee, and the truth would hurt. I'm turning into my mother, Alyson thought. "I started my own practice." Rip made the announcement at dinner. "Child psychology." Alyson coughed so hard, a kernel of corn flew out of her mouth and across the table where it landed on Sara's raised fork. Sara, who often changed the subject, ate the bite and pointed to her belly. "You're next, Alyson. How cool would it be if we had kids close in age? They could grow up together—like you and Rip." Curiously, this was one occasion when Alyson lost her appetite. It wasn't until after dinner when they played charades that Alyson began to feel remotely comfortable.

meat‑y *adj.* **1.** Though she told people that she took her job at Voices because she wanted to do something "worthwhile," Alyson really worked there for selfish reasons—to improve her self-esteem by being around people worse off than her. They weren't. She felt like the Grinch when he finds out that the people in Who-ville loved Christmas even when they got no toys. Simple things pleased the residents immensely. She met Danny Sherrill, an autistic young man of indeterminate age, who began to speak, reciting definitions, when she gave him a Webster's Dictionary. She told her mother about Danny. "Call Rip," she suggested. "He'll be able to help you. He just had an article published." Alyson asked her if it was related to autism. "No, but still. It's all the same, right?"

large *adj.* **1.** Crystal and Alyson took a New England road trip. It was fall and the trees littered autumnal rainbows on the ground. They stayed at B&Bs and explored coastal towns with glass-blowing shops. Crystal bought glass-blown teddy bears in different sizes. In Massachusetts, they surprised Alyson's mother. "I'm fit to be tied!" She crossed herself. They spent the evening looking at old photos, newspaper articles, and other bits of Alyson's ballet memorabilia. Framed pictures were everywhere. Alyson saw Rip, her father and mother together, and the different, thinner version of herself, watchful, beckoning. Hundreds of eyes staring at her, in concert: a symphony of stares. She tried not to look, but they taunted her like a nagging cough. "I had no idea!" Crystal gaped when she saw a picture of Rip. "You have a brother?" Alyson's mother answered. "It's her first cousin, though he may as well be a brother. They were raised together after my sister passed. She thinks he's a sellout now, but . . ." Alyson interrupted her. "Is it time to go, Crys?" Alyson's mother looked like she might cry, so they stayed the night. She made them sleep in her bed, while she slept on the sofa in the living room. Alyson would have insisted that her mother keep her own bed, but she knew she wouldn't have slept a minute surrounded by those photographs.

kit-chen *n.* **1.** Weddings: Were they ever enjoyable? Rip married Sara, a young woman whom more than one person said had resembled Alyson. "When she was younger," they added. Alyson knew they meant when she was thinner. The wedding was in a windowless downstairs ballroom of an ocean-side hotel. Alyson's father brought his new wife, a slim woman with mousy brown hair and a few facial moles that Alyson wanted to scrape off. Alyson didn't want to go to the wedding, but her mother had put her foot down. Both feet, and her knees, too. She preyed on her. Alyson brought a date to hide behind, though he could only hide a small portion of her because he was so slight. John was the maintenance man in her building on 83rd and York. He was so skinny, he leaned backwards when he walked, like a thin-stemmed flower. He drank eight cups of coffee a day and his tobacco-stained hands trembled when he reached for the cup. John made her feel like she was still beautiful. She gossiped to him about other men, as if he were a girlfriend. Often, he tried to kiss her. She laughed, said that her mouth was saved for eating. Though she joked about food, deep down she knew the joke was on her. Food was her lover; the way she dreamt about meals ahead of time, inhaled them with reckless abandon, and felt guilty later. Alyson stopped dating John after she met his mother, an Irish immigrant who had knitted a sweater for her that took a month to make.

jum-bo *adj.* **1.** Everyone, it seemed, had an opinion about Alyson's weight, as if her looks were public property. She saw how much they wanted her to be the way she used to be, so she gorged on bags of nuts until she felt like a beached whale, over-salted and marooned on the couch. Yet another floss-less night, sleeping in her clothes.

imm-ense *adj.* **1.** At twenty-six, Alyson weighed one hundred and fifty-nine pounds. People gave her "hint gifts" at holidays: diet books, running shoes and the "ab-detonator." Alyson re-gifted them the following year to her thinnest friends.

huge *adj.* **2.** Alyson's best meals were the ones she snuck from people's homes or the pantry at the art gallery where she'd been working for two years. The more she hid, the more visible she became. She felt like a well-situated billboard.

gross *adj.* **1.** While her weight continued to climb, men still climbed into bed with her. It was a veritable hiker's convention. The tent-like blouses she wore worked! Sex to her was a motel with a permanent "Vacancy" sign on the window. She went to BU to visit her old roommate and ran into her ex, Eddie Colfax, who told her he had written her a letter and asked if she'd come to his off-campus apartment to get it. "Let's go." She led him out the door by his two-toned school scarf. In the letter, he apologized for breaking up with her because she wouldn't have sex. She pulled on his belt buckle. Eddie looked puzzled, but not that puzzled. Afterwards, he told her she had an "eighteenth-century body." She told him he had twentieth-century manners and left quickly.

fat *adj.* **1.** "Human tongs." This was her father's nickname for her when she was young. Alyson was always the thinnest girl in the room; the girl whose thin arm was needed to pull things out of tight spots that other people's arms wouldn't fit into. She loved when her father called her that. It was possibly the most he ever needed her. He couldn't relate to her ballet accomplishments, and now that he and her mother were separated, he'd been swallowed up into the dating vortex. It had been a while since she'd seen her cousin Rip, though everywhere she went, she thought she saw him in a crowd. She knew a part of her missed the old days—playing ping-pong with him through both sides of *Abbey Road*, him helping her with her physics homework, her helping him with the finer points of *Bleak House*—but was surprised to find herself too proud to admit it. She'd assumed that she'd lost her pride when the weight she'd gained nearly surpassed her total body weight in junior high school. Her mother remained the only constant from her former life. "We all have our trials and tribulations; you'll bounce back. I'm glad you have Rip." She didn't want to burst her mother's bubble, so she grew her own—by eating more.

el-e-phant-ine *adj.* **2.** When she quit ballet and other parts of her life, Alyson had to earn money. She worked at a fish restaurant in Times Square but quit because she couldn't tolerate the tortured screams of the lobsters. She switched to an East Village vegetarian restaurant where the woman owner had long gray hair and wore socks under Birkenstocks. She got caught eating a customer's leftover tofu pumpkin pie and didn't return to work out of embarrassment. Alyson felt awful, because she liked the owner. Alyson met a woman in her building named Crystal. She didn't like her at first: too thin and she had this thing about teddy bears. And yet, there she was, wearing a Squeeze tee shirt and carrying a VHS of *The Lady Vanishes*. They spent an entire day together, longer than Alyson had spent with anyone in months. Crystal talked about her awful narcissistic sister. Alyson bit into a bran muffin, swallowed her memories of Rip. "I'm an only child," she said, mouth half-full. Crystal out-ate her, cementing their friendship.

dis·tend·ed *adj.* **1.** Alyson quit ballet when her new dance instructor, a widower in his fifties who had grandkids in Staten Island, developed a hernia from lifting her. Fifteen years of pliés gone. It didn't seem fair. Alyson told the instructor that there should be some sort of accrued interest for all the years she'd put into dance—a municipal bond, a 401K, something. "Life stinks and then you die," he said, clutching his lower waist. Alyson thought about introducing him to her mother. Without exercise, she gained more weight. Dress sizes passed her by like subway stops: 6, 8, 10, 12. Next stop, size 14. Without dance, Alyson's social life dried up as fast as a disposable contact lens. The only time she wasn't alone was when she walked down the corridors of Manhattan, staring at the sea of faces that surrounded her. Loneliness didn't preclude her from hiding. When Rip came to town, he telephoned. "Let's get together. It'll be fun. My number is . . ." Alyson deleted the message without listening, ate two cannolis and called a psychiatric doctor in the morning. "Just because you're related doesn't mean you have to act like you are," he said. Alyson didn't blink.

col·o·ssal *adj.* At Boston University, Alyson lost focus, even though she took up espresso. She drank huge quantities of beer, hoping it would cause her to miscarry. It didn't. She sat in large auditoriums and stared at her wrists, her shoes. Every professor sounded like the teacher in Charlie Brown. She had no interest in geology, physics, even French. When she failed all classes but Mural Making, she dropped out. "I got an offer I couldn't refuse from a New York dance troupe." Alyson enthusiastically lied to everyone who asked. She went to the Planned Parenthood on 33rd Street in Manhattan. Alone. No one even knew. She was surprised how hungry she was that night. She had thought her new-found love of food was due to the pregnancy. As much as she ate, she never felt satiated. Her appetite was like the horizon. She never got to the end.

big *adj.* **1.** That Christmas, Alyson consumed approximately 10,000 calories of food: 10 healthy handfuls of roasted and salted almonds (800 calories), 4 pieces of walnut-raisin bread with butter (600 calories); 2 ½ glasses of champagne (550 calories); 10 slices of assorted cheeses with crackers (900 calories); corn, sweet potatoes and spinach gratin (2,000 calories); salad (250 calories); 2 glasses of cabernet (900 calories); veggie lasagna (900 calories); slice of cornbread (300 calories); 2 ½ slices of pecan pie with whipped cream (2,600 calories); 10 Christmas cookies (1,000 calories); coffee with cream and sugar (200 calories). She avoided making eye contact with Rip throughout the meal. The few times she managed to sneak glances at him—when he was talking to someone—he looked ridiculous. Everything seemed to be pointing down on him: hair, eyes, mouth, shoulders and clothes. The things about him that she had once found pleasant: his solemnity, his intelligent-looking brown eyes, his boyish dark brown curls, now looked comically grotesque. Rip barely touched his food. It bothered Alyson, though she didn't know why. Spineless, spineless, spineless, she chanted in her head. He tried to have a glib conversation with her about music. How had she ever mistaken him for interesting? Alyson abruptly excused herself, grabbed a fistful of almonds, (80 calories) and went home.

ab-normal *adj.* **2.** Three weeks after lacrosse captain Eddie Colfax broke up with her for not sleeping with him, Alyson visited her cousin Rip at Northwestern. Rip lived with three other students in the quintessential college boys' home: four cars in the driveway, two of which had the hoods up, and a dead front lawn, even though it was the end of Chicago's rainy season. Inside, the carpeting was ripped. Three-day-old pasta-caked dishes sat in the sink. The home's dreariness was magnified by the multitude of mirrors on sliding closet doors that ran the length of the bedrooms and along one whole wall of the living room. Alyson and Rip were in a great mood—they'd been to a Rockpile concert. She expected to get the futon to herself, that Rip would spend the night on the brown corduroy living room sofa. But he climbed in with her, as if they'd planned it all along or at least on the drive home. Alyson didn't want to embarrass Rip. They'd been raised together. He was her best friend. Had she done something that invited this sort of attention? She trusted him more than herself. Maybe he was in love with her. Why should the fact that they were related matter to one's heart? He started by trying to undress her, than forced himself on her again and again. She feigned sleep every time. At 6:10, with the stereo on low (Rip's stereo was never off) and dime-store blinds flirting with the first light, Rip entered her from behind. Though his first touch had woken her up, Alyson lay still. All she could think of was the same thing that was never far from her mind when she thought about Rip: how sorry she felt for him because he'd been orphaned at age ten. He finished and started snoring—nearly within the same breath. She snuck into the bathroom, looked down and saw a dictionary. She looked up incest. "Sexual relations between persons so closely related that marriage is illegal or forbidden." Within thirty minutes, Alyson was on a Greyhound Bus headed towards Boston, clutching Webster's Dictionary to her chest, a gnawing emptiness eating away at her.

SHORT STORY

Rand B. Lee
Girl, Breastless, Dancing

When I was twelve years old, I went to my father and said, "I think I need a psychiatrist. Would you send me to one?"

He looked dubious. My father was a fat man and a writer, whom my mother called a Good Provider, but he had grown up in the Depression, the son of a factory worker, and spending money frightened him. "Why do you think you need a psychiatrist?" he asked.

"Because I'm twelve years old and I still sleep with stuffed animals," I said. This was not the real reason, although I thought it was at the time. Both my parents went to a psychiatrist—the same doctor, separately and together—and although they had a sense of humor about it (my mother was always saying things like, "Let's explore this," and shouting, "Doctor Freud!" whenever one of us made an inadvertent double entendre), it was clear to me that they took mental health—theirs and that of their children—very seriously.

There were four progeny still at home then. My oldest siblings—three half-sisters and one full sister—were off on their own in New Hampshire, New York, and Washington, D.C. My oldest brother, Tony, a tall, handsome, guitar-playing, milk-guzzling amateur folk singer, had turned eighteen that January and was headed for the Air Force Academy in Colorado the coming fall. When he wasn't working, he was out on dates, so I didn't see him much. That left me at home with Mom and Dad; a great many dogs, cats, and pet birds; my Marine Corps obsessed, terrifying, BB gun-toting brother Manfred, three years my senior; and my tale-tattling little nuisance of a brother Jeffrey, three years my junior.

I shared a room with Jeffrey. Jeffrey played piano, and liked to dress up as Elliot Ness from *The Untouchables*. Elliot slept on one side of the room, I slept on the other, and we had an imaginary line down the middle to separate his side from mine. At one time, several years before, our brother Manfred had shared the room with us, and he had lulled us to sleep with stories featuring a girl named Janie who always ended up being swept out of telephone booths by tidal waves of *pinkle* and *movie*, which were our nursery words for urine and feces. But since he had entered adolescence Manfred slept in his own room down the hall, in which he drew endless pictures of military aircraft, World War II soldiers, and Nazi swastikas, this last to horrify our father, who was Jewish and after whom my brother was named.

I was the only one of us who still slept with stuffed animals. I had done so since I was a very little boy, but instead of their number decreasing as I got older, it had increased to the point where, at twelve, I could only fall asleep at night if I were surrounded by them on all sides. Jeffrey had a stuffed animal, a Winnie-the-Pooh doll that was cousin to my Piglet doll, but he did not sleep with his doll any more. Our Pooh and Piglet were the real things, patterned after the original illustrations in the A. A. Milne books, not the dumbed-down cartoon characters of the later Disney films, and I fell asleep so many times with Piglet's upturned snout in my mouth that it turned a permanent dark grey. The only stuffed animal I had ever seen our brother Manfred play with was a little naked-looking pink ratpigpuppylike creature that he drew red, bloodlike marks on and shot over and over with his BB gun. He also had a black goldfish in a tank whom he had named Pigiron, after a Marine in a war movie.

I was clearly the most disturbed of us three. When I complained to my father that I was being bullied by Danny Went, the fifth grade star athlete, Dad told me to fight him. "I don't want to," I said. "You must," he replied, looking sadly wise. Then he told me a story about when he was a young man of twenty or so, and he had asked a professional boxer to knock him out, because (Dad was still Emanuel Lepofsky at that time, not the Manfred B. Lee he later became) had wanted to be a writer even then, and he had felt it was important for him to have lots of Life Experiences, including being knocked out. "Are you sure, Manny?" the boxer had asked. "Yes," Dad had replied. The next thing my father knew, the boxer was holding him by the arms saying, "Manny! Snap out of it!" When the boxer had struck him, my father explained, my future father had gone into a scarlet fighting rage, and it had been all the boxer could do to restrain him from doing them both serious harm. The inference was that, were I pushed hard enough, the same wild manly creature would emerge in me to counter the taunts of Danny Went. So Dad set out to teach me to fight.

We had one session, and it lasted five minutes. "Hit me," my father said. "Go on! Hit me as hard as you can!" I panicked and fled the room, though not before I saw the disgusted look on his face. Some time later I overheard my parents talking, my father expressing concern about my stuffed animals. So when I went to him and asked for a psychiatrist, I used my bed companions as my coup de grace. Dad said, "I'll see what I can do," or something similar; and several weeks later he (or my mother, I don't remember which; perhaps both) bundled me into the Buick and drove me to see Katharine Hawley Martin.

When I complained to my father that I was being bullied by Danny Went, the fifth grade star athlete, Dad told me to fight him. "I don't want to," I said. "You must," he replied, looking sadly wise.

Dr. Martin, as I was instructed to call her, worked out of her little house in a town about half an hour by car from our place. She was a child psychologist, and it was bright and cheerful in Dr. Martin's house. I think she had a cat, but her house was not filled with Chesapeake Bay retrievers, as ours was; nor was there a toucan named Mister Kipling shouting "Kip-kip-ka-KIP" from his flight cage eighteen hours a day. Mister Kipling was in love with my mother. When my mother went into his flight cage to change his food and water, Mister Kipling would sit on his perch and run her hair through his beak over and over, uttering low moans. All animals adored my mother. Our neighbors would bring her sick birds that they had found, and she would nurse them back to health. She got so famous that the local paper did an article on her. At one point or another during my childhood she had, in addition to Mister Kipling, several cows (the mom-cow, Faleen, and her daughter-cow, Molly); an Indian pony named Patsy; a coopfull of chickens, who stared at me with their beady little eyes and pecked my hands when I tried to gather their eggs; a long-tailed, black and white magpie named Billy who used to call the dogs and laugh at them when they came running; a wild garter snake that used to crawl into Mother's lap and fall asleep there when she was weeding in the garden; some parakeets; a few canaries; and a mated pair of lovebirds, whom Mother always described as "vicious."

There were also some sheep, including a ram who butted Mother halfway across the yard one morning, but they belonged to my brother Manfred, who despite his bloodthirstiness had our mother's way with creatures and, before graduating to slaughtering all the wild birds in our woods with his BB gun ("It was either that," he told me years later, "or Dad and Mom,") had made a small name for himself in the local 4-H club.

Dr. Martin was white-haired and nicely dressed, with a calm, observant, pleasant manner. I spent an hour with her once a week for several months that summer. I don't remember much of what went on in those sessions, except that she had me draw pictures, and work on a very complicated model of a battleship. It seems to me that she very seldom spoke. Once, when she asked me to draw a picture for her, I drew a picture of a little girl dancing in a swirl of autumn leaves. Dr. Martin looked thoughtfully at the picture, then asked, in her kind, intelligent, ladylike voice, "Can you tell me what's wrong with this picture?"

I looked at my drawing. I thought it was pretty good. She pointed to the little girl's chest and said, "She has no breasts." She said this very solemnly. I had been raised never to talk back to adults, so in response to her tone I adopted a thoughtful, serious expression. But privately I was bewildered. I had set out quite deliberately to draw a prepubescent girl, not a grownup girl like my four older sisters, or a grownup woman like my mother, who unless she was getting dressed up to drag Dad to a dinner party hid her big breasts beneath old sweatshirts. She smoked Camel cigarettes, and made up words like "boozy-boo" for "boulevard," and when she noticed you had left your fly-zipper down by mistake she would always say, "Are you open for business or pleasure?" Mother had been a professional actress and writer, in radio, mostly; she always played bad girls and divorcées on radio because she had a sexy alto voice, and in the Thirties and Forties all the good girls were sopranos. When she went out to restaurants, she ordered Manhattan cocktails; Jeffrey and I used to vie with one another for the maraschino cherry, so she would order extra cherries on a little plate just to keep peace between us and to keep herself from getting too drunk.

At the end of the summer, Dr. Martin had my parents in for our last session. She made me wait on a seat in her hallway while she talked with my mother and father behind the closed door to her private study. Eventually she opened the door, and with a smile said, "You may come in now, Randy." I walked into her study and sat down in the seat she showed me. It was a nice room with white walls, windows, and lots of books, just like the rooms in our house. My parents were sitting on chairs across the room. My father had on a tie and sports jacket, and my mother was wearing a coat over her dress. It was 1963. My father was leaning slightly forward, an intent look on his face. My mother had on a soft, encouraging expression. I had absolutely no idea what was going on.

Dr. Martin said, "Randy, do you think you could say some swear words for us? Don't be afraid; you won't get into any trouble. Just say whatever words come into your head." We all sat there. Three pairs of adult eyes looked straight at me. Nobody said anything. I did not know what to do. All my life I had been taught it was bad to swear; that only grown-ups swore, and that children who did it were bad, like Roger Nelson at school, who smelled funny and had a dirty neck and a transparent little moustache on his upper lip; or like my brother Manfred, who shot his gun off in the woods and liked to jump out of nowhere to make me scream and touch me and groan, "Yuck! Grease!", and wipe his hand on his shirt (because touching my fat little body was obviously the most disgusting thing any person could ever be called upon to do).

We sat there in silence, and my parents and Dr. Katharine Hawley Martin looked at me; and I wanted to shrink down, down, down inside my clothing until there was nothing of me left for them to look at. But a practical part of me knew that if I did not do what they wanted, we would sit there like that forever. So I said, "Damn. Shit. Fuck." Or maybe it was, "Shit. Fuck. Cunt." Anyhow, I said the three worst words I could think of, and I said them in a complete robot monotone, trying not to hear myself saying them, feeling them dirty my lips as they came out of me and fell onto the floor into the middle of the silence. I remember this very well.

Instantly the three of them relaxed, and an almost festive air of triumph replaced the tension in the room, an air of Rubicons crossed and peaks o'ertopped and Gordian knots sliced in two. Everybody smiled at me (my mother with tears of joy in her eyes). I had passed my test: I had expressed Healthy Hostility, the repression of which had (apparently) been the cause of many of my problems, though not all (my sexual repression, which my father kindly explained to me later had been symbolized by my drawing of the prepubescent girl, had presumably accounted for the rest). Dad's money had not been misspent after all.

I never saw Dr. Martin again, though I think I may have written her a letter once, which she answered on her own stationery. And not long afterwards, sure enough I stopped sleeping with stuffed animals.

My brother Manfred eventually joined the Marines and went to Vietnam, where he was made a sergeant and led a platoon, and from which he returned a decorated veteran who slept with a hunting knife under his pillow and once threatened our mother with it, the knife I mean not the pillow, though he never sought to frighten me again and even talked our father into sending me to an expensive private high school because the local public high school was so violent my brother didn't want me to suffer it. I eventually discovered masturbation and airbrushed male bodybuilding magazines, which I bought with my meager allowance and hid in my room, pretending I was accumulating them out of a need for weight training guidance.

I wish, now, that I had kept on sleeping with Piglet and the others until I was really ready to stop. I wish, now, that in the study that day I had said no, no I will not utter those bad, awful, repugnant words, because they were ugly and harsh and I loved words (and still do), and if saying bad words was what grownup meant I wished to remain a child, even if the closest image to the kind of child I felt myself to be was that of a breastless, dickless little girl dancing in a swirl of autumn leaves.

POETRY

Bruce Cohen
A Rare Condition

After being poked & blood tested by the specialist who spoke Hmmm
In several dialects including an obscure amputee sign language I eavesdropped
On her conferring with beleaguered foreign colleagues by the soda machine,
Whispering vowel-heavy polysyllabic antiseptic gibberish; apparently,
She'd never examined anyone with opposing thoughts in one skull before.
In the section of the country where I grew up everyone called it soda. Here they say pop.
I had my whole life an inkling my internal arguments were in constant conflict—
Choosing up sides in schoolyard games, my soul always the last pathetic pick.
Not that I wasn't prepared for bad news: I'm a big boy. But I anticipated something
More along the lines of tumors that grow overnight like Chia Pets, arteries clogged
With apple-smoked congealed bacon fat. Even as a child adults scolded me—
Get with the program, be of one mind. But I never knew which head to place
My thinking cap on. After my Siamese twin brains were separated I starting yapping
Out both sides of my mouth & was instructed to avoid other patients. I, I, I (the
Medication makes me stutter) commenced to see the world through the eyes
Of a seeing-eye dog, but after the transplant who is the real master? Naturally,
After rehab, I landed a gig as a professional dog walker whose poodles sport little
Doggy sweaters that match their owners', like those dog-humans who wear their silly
Brains outside their heads. I vacationed in every examination room east of myself
& sat naked for weekly eternities on icy stainless steel tables sketching the diagrams
Of the color-coded digestive system, or taking a peek at previous patients' charts.
Staring at the medical scale, I could be the carnival guy who professes to guess

Your actual weight within two pounds & awards you stuffed cartoony-colored animals
If I'm wrong. Hearing the radiator clank I could be chained to a radiator composing
Fortune cookie wisdom. Waiting for the new doctor I could be the faceless
Who squidgy-cleans your windshield when you stop for a red light. (You did stop
At the red light didn't you, even though it was 2 a.m. & maybe you had a little too
Much to drink)? My shirt size is so evolving I buy irregulars. I am the dull thought
Of any man who's been laid off for a decade but leaves the house each morning
With an unstoppable grin as though nothing's wrong & pushes his pen so deeply
Into the racing forms at the track the sheet rips. His wife isn't with the program;
She's only cultivated one brain; so they have no children. Walking home, I am
Confused by the emaciated girl in the picture window who looks more like a mannequin
Than the mannequin she undresses. Oh, I can still talk to myself. My reflection
Is almost always in the mirror, shellacked with radioactive radio waves rationed
In the most advantageous ratio of life & living. I am my own disease & the cure.

Art Therapy

I make illusionist efforts to bend the cereal spoon
With my mind, ignite birds at the bird feeder by self-effacing, flirtatious
Blinking—since we agree I am Picasso I have these morning rituals—
It seems I have a password for every thing but my own mind—
It's a strange world Cheri. Car dealerships & banks counter
Intuitively close on Sundays & spirit sales are Blue-Law banned.
I rent black & white American films—women in poodle skirts

& pony tails avoiding erratic traffic, deceptive puddles,
& manhole covers. An excessive amount of bouncing goes
On in America, some of which occurs on bedsprings!
Abandoned mattresses sprout edible mushrooms in the woods behind
My zone, in the woods behind my zone a decade of discarded
Holiday tree skeletons stutter & decompose like unpracticed speeches.

Furthermore, too many passwords mushroom in my brain.
In order to get through the days I convince myself I am Picasso.
I am also a special guest-appearance of Dali in reruns
Of To Tell The Truth, sporting a suit two sizes too small,
Top button unbuttoned—strategic chest hairs sprouting,
Mustache overly waxed, bug eyes bulging! Windows
Are the most receptive inanimate see-through beings though

Oxygen molecules hitchhike into my lungs. Before I consume
My Cocoa Puffs, dotted with seasonal fruit—fruit, that is, in season,
I double my studio, take over the entire outside—the Cosmos.
I get more done every day when I address myself as Pablo—
For I am Picasso. At my best I am nothing but a fleshy machine
Gun libido able to impregnate inanimate objects. See how even

Dead holiday trees process oxygen & exhale. It's the first warm
Day in America & girls are sticking their bare feet out car windows,
Unleashing their pale winter cleavage on the shotgun side.
As Lao Tzu, the famous Taoist mechanic said,
If the car breaks down, hitchhike. On days like this, one will
Not have very long to wait. It is not now approaching at all the end
Of the world when we can assume anyone's identity we like.

Divine Wow:

Select one isolated cloud.
Spy it your entire life, like a personal impersonator.
The fish in the diner's aquarium blink twice for yes.

God sends cryptic messages, only to me, on these stained menus
After the 24-hour diner closes.
During my meal I express to my imaginary waitress the free water tastes

Like it's smuggled from an aquarium; I detect a hint of algae.
I concede doughnuts are three-dimensional, but why
Are waitresses smuggling new bacteria out of this world in their tips?

What if God were common lint?
I'll leave the car running on the approach to the bridge.
No lousy tipper, as the wind kicks up I peel off C-notes & Sawbucks & Fins

& lonely George Washingtons & let them migrate off the bridge.
I did not fathom the full extent of myself until I reached the very top of the bridge.
A disorderly V of geese broke rank in complex denominations—

All prime numbers. One feather less than prime.
Select one fish from the aquarium & wink. The river below is a replica
Of an aquarium whose H2O is vaguely three-dimensional,

Where I can smuggle exotic fish out of this glass world.
Cumulous clouds are God's spies. My life has been lived badly already—
By a stunt man, an extra. I am my own twin—the problem & solution.

I have seen this movie already. Both the original & the remake.
Who among us is not an abstract number composed of a whispering
Linear math wind? Who is not a regular guy slumping in a diner slurping coffee?

I wanted only to have a repartee of driver's licenses representing the dozens of disparate
States all with capital letters, lots of aliases,
Blow up sex dolls & hitchhikers buried along the Interstates,

Like a sequestered jury brushing its collective teeth, sharing one toothbrush.
Illogical to think there is one God, still, or still no God.
In the evening I scrape together change from sofa cushions & glove compartments

In the humdrum. Or is it conundrum?
God's a stunt man, a stand-in, who takes my place when I'm living in my elsewhere—
A little hung over from innuendos & the brittle silence after,

Coming to grips with coffee aromas diligently regressing back
Into their beans of embryonic origin, will I forget & simply drive away
Or simply drive away?

POETRY

Gillian Parrish
tilth

This was supposed to be about a field.

Whenever I see 'supposed'
I see milk-white ceramic hands.

The field would've favored production: rows
of marl and pleated green. A harrow and 'we
sprinkle in the seeds.' I suspect

you are suspicious. The backstory gussied up.
I suspect ease and 'this time' and my motives.
The field to be called The End

of Trying. Told my messed up arm the deal (how softly
the turnstiles), 'Then we weed and protect it.'

Misgivings, their tines all flapped away.

might come to rest

'in dog-skin
          slept'
  & white mouthful
  of lilies'   (it was a story
i loved as a child)

  tell it,   midnight
      and what can be true
          of a body   'strewn across the plain'
in bloom   *in bloom*   in blood-red moss
    and the clear water   'for the terrible cup'

    for the tongue
believes it must be difficult
    back of the teeth   "blooded"
'the things we want become like mad dogs barking'
half-fed   *so that no one else*

  'this monster is quite honest'
fistfuls of rice   in the roots of the pine
    my tourniquet ~~my heart~~ *my crown of envy*—
(her owl face her face of flowers)
 and the dancers just walk on their knees

 'for three years she sees nothing'
       fistfuls of rain-dark hair
   studied ~~grudge~~
         the ghost river
'for upon the charnel ground is built the palace'
  though she would deal hard for the dead

what is this spell upon me
i said something about the ~~dreams~~ rains
and i must go inside,
said the young woman softly
    in dog-skin slept
as if asleep

'what you need,' said the fox,
what you hide what you find
   ~~cruel~~ cool as a wish   a cup
of partless water   passed through the dark
  become it   (your child face
your face of jade) 'this fathoms-deep
body'

there would be many hesitations
   (far and far)   there would be dross
  scribbled girlish my dogheart
but to ford the black river—
        rue. and a kiss
   'there is no spell upon you'
begin to ask what fills your mouth

'how I never wanted to be this woman'
   law of the small   the green
        stems
'so you must make it,' said the fox, to
   the isle of the dead
and the well there   (as if there)
   ~~one day~~ on a day you will bring rain'

but did we plan our plans—and did we linger
over ~~love and meat and~~ doubtful things
(half-curst be all wanderers)   three lifetimes
fled floods   in your own turning   *oh the*
      birds   I followed west—
'cut away piece by piece'
  even then I was free

'and how should I regard my dreaming?'
my sow face my face of famine my face
  of faraway my face of ought
my boy face my face of laurel of lily of dog's eye
of no-more-yearning of pearl
           the ground

pushing up
through me
(secrets I learned from saints)
ford the river by trapped light   by half-light blest
by loosed skins by tendril   *crossed*
to the green isle   made
of myself   a well

SHORT STORY

Lawrence Cady
Help Me, Christina

Things had come full circle once again, and he was home after having driven half the night from somewhere—he couldn't remember just where—some distance away. And once inside his room downstairs, with his door unlocked, his broken-leaning lamp switched on, he could think once again, lying limp and helpless on his gently sloping mattress like the girl in the picture up on the wall—"Christina's World"—Mr. Andrew Wyeth's fine, fine depiction—the pretty farmhouse just out of reach. It was as if he were her, lying prone and helpless in that vast rural countryside clipped from a magazine and taped up there long ago.

He'd waited quite a while this time, he thought, as if to compliment himself. He'd been good about it, waiting whole weeks before having to take care of things, before letting it overtake him once again from the brain on down. It had started as it always had: that hollow, sinking sense of something wrong, something needing to be fixed, put right. And then, of course, Christina and all the other pretty, pleasing farmland pictures he'd put up on the wall going blank and oddly dark; pieces of meaningless paper where sometimes one or another young man's sweet, weeping face might appear, or even his own face as a young man, his father's shadowy form making itself known, too. All those vast golden countrysides and milky-blue skies would be gone, blotted out with faces, too many faces, but only until he'd taken care of things and come full circle, Christina and the countryside pictures on the wall alive and cheery once again.

He hadn't asked to be born here, to be stuck in this city, doing the things he knew he did—But why did he do them?—Why?—over and over and over again. He was thirty-five years old now. One day he checked. He got his head back long enough to go upstairs where he kept some things in a closet and thought it out. He was thirty-five goddamn years old.

Was it the city itself, the nature of the city, drawing him in, sucking him back in to the easy way out, the easy way to ease the bad thinking, the craving that had to be attended to? "It must be," he would sometimes say to himself, and have some soup with his door open and unlocked. It must be because things always had to be taken care of, sooner or later. And if he waited too long, if he fought it like a trooper, he would be out of himself, his insides dissolving, fading to black, Christina and the countryside photographs on the wall glittery dark, his father's face popping up every-goddamn-place: in the water stains on the ceiling, at the bottom of an empty soup can, sometimes in the corner behind the furnace or up the stairs when the door was closed and locked tight.

It was in the streets, among the scattered windblown scraps of paper and debris, where he found the disillusioned young men. They were everywhere, like little rain-soaked rats, sons of rats, and don't fool yourself, they are vermin, vermin offspring, all heaped on top of one another in this city like one big pile of shit. All caged in, locked in together, where they can't help but slip through the cracks from the top down, the streets their last refuge, their last resort.

How many times had he dreamed as a child—and as an adult, he guessed—of the countryside, of clean, untarnished folks who smiled at you and said, "Howdy, my friend," and let you be? Just let you be. How many times had he pleaded with his mother, when she was still around, "Let's go. Let's just pack up and go. Where? To the flip side, for Christ's sake. Where they treat you kindly, where there's never any trouble and the folks are untarnished from head to toe." How many times, over the years, had he driven alone out over the bridge, into the wooded foothills, and parked along the side of the road just to breathe, just to get the city out of him so he didn't have to fight it anymore, didn't have to turn angry, astonished, the bad thinking rising like smoke from within? How many times had he sat on his mattress in his concrete room, the door at the top of the stairs open a crack—only a crack!—and watched for hours, even days, while pretty, kindly Christina crawled up the hillside toward the farmhouse and the denim-clad field-hands in the other pictures maneuvered their tractors and wagons around barns, silos, and meandering herds of cattle?

That smiling man there, right there, Christina! Standing beside the stacked-up bales of hay. He'll talk to you, he'll say hello, he'll wink, nod, say, "Howdy, neighbor," and let you be. Just let you be.

How many times had he awakened down there, where he kept his mattress and blanket off to the side, behind the shadowy bed-sheet curtain, remembering only a glimpse of his father's stern, terrifying face, the sound of the boy's disgusting-pleasing whimperings and muffled crying out, not a barn or silo in sight?

How many times?

He wasn't sure.

Those precious days after things had been taken care of he would go to the corner store to stock up, wary, though, keeping an eye out. The city lurking around him, assholes peeping out their windows and doors to check up on him. Little vermin skateboarder creeps sliding by, the little assholes, little pecker-heads. But with the need pushed down to his toes—at least for a time—he walked gladly to the store, picked up Campbell's soups, some bread and pieces of candy and paid the man and came back. Those days after having taken care of things, he could even leave the door open and let the daylight spill down into his basement room for a time. He could sit and whistle or listen to the little radio he plugged into the light socket piece: a station played songs he remembered, or thought he remembered.

How many times had he dreamed as a child—and as an adult, he guessed—of the countryside, of clean, untarnished folks who smiled at you and said, "Howdy, my friend."

It used to be, years ago, that those times after things had been taken care of were not very happy times. Back then, he would become angry and confused, pitted against himself from the inside out. "What am I doing?" he'd say. "My God, I must be crazy. I'm fucking crazy." But after—how many years?—ten, twelve maybe?—it seemed there was no escaping it and it was his lot in life to be who he was and that was that.

Maybe it's that someone has to do these things, he often thought, and I'm the one to do them?

*

Moving about the shadows now, staying well outside the serrated wedge of light dropping down the steps, he remembered how it used to trouble him, and he laughed. At himself, of course. He couldn't laugh about the hurting and the silencing that simply had to be done, that, really, was more God's will than his, for Christ's sake. That was serious business. Damn serious. He could laugh about himself, though, because it was as if it wasn't him doing these things, it wasn't his brain, his arms, his powerful hands and fingers going through the motions. It was a switched-on machine, a switched-on robot brain inside his brain, and when it was time, when the urge came on him like the need to breathe, then it was, All right, here we go.

He put it out of his head, Christina and the countryside photographs up on the walls glowing in the bright, fragrant daylight he'd let in. The rows of corn, the abandoned farmhouse, the tractors and harvesters (John Deere, Caterpillar, Ingersoll-Rand) in the wheat fields over there, on the far wall, roaming the hills like giant green bugs: alive and real, sweet like salt-water taffy down at the wharf.

Sometimes these scenes of pretty, untarnished life would strike him suddenly and at the worst possible times, as if they were calling out to him, as if they were a part of him, a part of who he was or at least who he thought sometimes he should be. Going over the bridge in his car, sweaty and electrified—the tarnished vermin youth in the car beside him, the filthy little rodent, already complaining, already crying out: "Hey, mister, where are we going? What are you doing?"—he would see silos and farmhouses, and Christina, too—Help me, Christina! Can't you help me?—in among the iron workings of the bridge towers or out over the bay or golden-green foothills beyond. And always—the need, the hunger sharp like a dagger within—his fucking father in there, too, that bleak, weather-worn face watching him, studying him, knowing all there was to know about him.

But that would subside, the confusion, the seeing of those things at those times, and then he and the frightened young man would be out in the foothills in no time, where he would park the car and a wash of love and hate would allow him easily to handle the little vermin down the access road above the outer towns, where no one would see, no one would hear, because they were his, once he got them this far out, though they were usually struggling by then, kicking, scratching and striking out. Jesus, with the power in him, the wide-open wanting and craving inside him, they would easily succumb, take a tumble or two over some boulders or down a hillside, and then he was on them, tooth and nail, as they say, little tarnished son's of bitches. They would succumb.

*

It has only been days and the basement door is shut tight and locked. No daylight now. None. Are there farm fields up on the wall? Fuck no. Even if he switched the light on, could he see them up there—Christina, the farmhouse, the nice guy leaning up against the bales of hay? Fuck no. And, uh-oh, there's his father again, watching from over there, behind the snarl of silvery furnace piping. He's over there, but don't look. Oh shit, he's there.

He fixes his eyes, as though dumbfounded, on the little crack of light under the door—his father be damned!—and inside the blood is surging, the mind racing. It's only been days and he's full circle. Jeeeesus, that's not very long. But when it strikes, when that bottomless inner opening he thinks now comes from that brain-within-a-brain makes itself known, he's got to take care of things. He's got to make his move.

He gets what he needs for the night. His pieces of rope and tape, a little money for gas, a straw and the carton of chocolate milk he likes to drink while driving through the city's forgotten neighborhoods. When he gets to his car around the block, he puts the things under the seat and starts the engine. After he's some blocks away, he sips at his carton of milk and begins his search. They're all over town, if you look for them, slinking up and down a major boulevard or through the park or out along the bay. But there's always just the right one, the one whose boyish face strikes him suddenly, whose form and movements of the arms, legs, and hips have a look of youth, tarnished vermin youth.

He wheels around a corner in the lowly west part of town and glides by the parked cars and near-empty sidewalk. He goes slowly, edging down low in his seat, Christina and the barns and silos threatening to appear—Help me Christina! help me!—but powerless now. Weak and forgotten. His palms begin to sweat, his breath comes on fast and jittery, and his insides open up like the jaws of an animal.

Then, up the block, in the pale yellow glow of the street lamp. It's him, right there. Soiled black leather jacket, faded jeans, a daring little swagger. Alone in the night, walking, moving along quickly, foolishly, but nowhere to go.

He slows, keeps pace with the walking boy. He rolls down the window, puts up a smile.

"Hey, buddy . . ."

POETRY

Robert Nazarene
On the Whereabouts of a Mouse Studying to Be a Rat

A fatal crash in your father's Chrysler, a garbage
Scow filled above the brim with lies told just prior
To your solemn oath: I swear to God! Ash Wednesday's
Cross of ashes adorning the foreheads of those who
Believed someday you'd change your . . . You!
You, for God's sake! At the moment of impact
You are cart wheeled out like a circus performer.
Which is what you were. The string of beer tins
Tied to your back bumper settles down quiet
As a mouse. Mice and brakes say: Squeak, squeak
You've just mastered another language besides
Bullshit. No one comes to your rescue. Even fewer
Come to your unceremonious burial. This is what
Is known as: hitting bottom. Bullseye. A garbage
Truck drives up and dumps another load of you
Over you. A sign on the truck says: "Yesterday's
Meals on Wheels." The rats couldn't agree more.
Wheels. What comes around goes around.
Your trailer park calls and leaves a message
On your voiceless mail: Their trash is missing.

Joi de Vivre

Our man's carriage is about to throw
A wheel. His house is ablaze

And he is trapped inside. His
Jailers have come to take him

To the gallows. He shrugs.
He crawls along the bottom

Of the sea for days, embarrassing
The whales and dolphins. Three

Bullets pass through his heart.
A rattlesnake raises its head

To strike. (He is the earth beneath
Gettysburg, Iwo Jima, Da Nang.)

He disputes the horizon as his
Parachute fails to open.

He attributes everything to alien
Beings. He sleeps in the desert

Beneath the noonday sun.
He pulls his blanket up over

His head. He is a wise man, a
A joyous man, fearless. He holds

The keys to a plentiful life. He lives
As if he were already dead.

SHORT STORY

Chris Gavaler
The Marriage of the Strawman and the Patchwork Girl

FOR L. FRANK BAUM

Jack's father is a very busy and important girl. She wasn't always a girl, but she is one now, and though she is very busy and important, she is not so very busy and important that she can't take time to carve Jack a new head when his old one starts to rot, which it has today. There are white spots up and down his right cheek, and the eye above it is drooping. His left eye has kept its shape, but its edges are dark and lined with crust. There's also a soft spot in back, which Jack can't see but can feel with the fingertips of either hand. He smells bad, too. His friends don't say so, and perhaps they haven't noticed yet, but Jack knows that sharp bright scent peppering the air. He's spoiling again.

    Jack has suspected it, but this morning as he lies on his back staring at the rounded wall of his little house in the thinning darkness, he is almost certain. His head rots more often than he would like, but his head is a pumpkin and that's what pumpkins do. Sometimes Jack wishes that he had a head made of something other than an empty pumpkin. Jack knows people whose heads are made of such things as tin and copper and bone and rubber. He knows people whose heads are filled with cotton and straw and meat and gears. Meat rots, too, but not when it is inside a person's body, or is a person's body, when meat is what a person is made of, which many persons are. Jack knows all kinds of meat people. His father, for example, is made entirely of meat, every inch of her.

    Jack didn't sleep again last night. He doesn't know how to, but when the sun tips beneath the Shifting Mountains and the color drains from his fields and he has nothing but the dark to stare at, he likes to lower his body across the floor of his little house and imagine how pleasant it might be to not be awake. He doesn't know where the thoughts of meat people go when they sleep, somewhere especially not here, he thinks, a place that Jack is almost certain he has never been. After not sleeping, he usually uses up his morning and afternoon and evening snapping pumpkin seeds with his wooden fingers at a metal pail across his floor, *tink*, *tink*, *tink*, but today Jack begins the terrible and unpleasant process of standing up as soon as the sun climbs the bottom pane of his window. The problem is his wooden joints, which give way when bent very far in either direction. Jack is built for standing, not for standing up. A sensible pumpkin-headed man would almost certainly not lie down at the end of each day and struggle up at the beginning of the next, but Jack suspects that he is not a sensible pumpkin-headed man and doubts very much that one exists.

His head rots more often than he would like, but his head is a pumpkin and that's what pumpkins do.

As he fingers the squishy spot on the back of his head, he thinks how happy his father will be to see him today. Jack's father is always happy to see Jack. After inching up the curve of the wall, he braces his spindly hands and flings his wooden hips forward. Usually his pegs jerk upright, but if his balance is off, as it is this morning, or if one of the old sole-worn shoes his father gave him should step on a patch of slick seeds, as one of the shoes is doing now, there is no knowing what shape his spinning joints will make as they flap for balance. That Jacks finds himself standing afterwards surprises him. He knows that he is standing because he can see the back of his spotted vest and his arms slowing to a gentle swing. He can also see the pointed spike of his neck branch poking above his collar. One of his spindly fingers reaches up to touch it before flopping down again. Jack's head is on the floor, rocking softly against the heel of his father's old shoe.

Sometimes Jack wishes that his father built him better, and his father wishes so, too. She made him with no eye for the future, she said. Jack doesn't care about the eye—two are plenty—but clumsy joints and rotting heads are a nuisance. He doesn't blame her though. His father was only a rough and rugged boy then and not the very busy and important girl she is now. That is why Jack sometimes lets his head go a little longer than perhaps he ought to. He doesn't want to be a nuisance.

After feeling for damage—there's a crack along one side of the pumpkin, but not terribly deep—Jack tries to settle the head back onto his neck, but the hole at the base is too wide and soft at the edges to grip the spike. Jack has to ram the point through a new spot a few inches to the left. This means his face is lopsided, and so the world is lopsided, for a moment, until Jack gets used to the angle. It's quite inspiring, thinks Jack, the things a body gets used to when a body has to get used to such things.

"Quite inspiring," says Jack, and then he says, "The Strawman and the Patchwork Girl are getting married."

This is news to Jack and he's surprised to hear it, especially from himself. He has no idea why he says and thinks half the things that he says and thinks. Thoughts are just the spill of leftover seeds in his hollowed shell, and there are only so many ways seeds can jounce and jumble themselves—although when a head gets old, seeds can dry and split and grow tacky with rot, and then there's no knowing what queer thoughts a body might hear itself thinking. But the Strawman and the Patchwork Girl getting married is a wonderful thing to think, and so Jack's glad that he has. He would say it again, but he can't because now he's saying, "Time to get a head," which he nearly forgot.

Outside the air is clear and crisp with a faint damp chill lifting with the orange sun. Pleasant weather for picking, thinks Jack, as he totters down his front step and into his pumpkin patch. A green field, a yellow sun, a blue sky with soft bright clouds. The sky is like an egg shell, thinks Jack, an egg shell peppered with clouds. Jack is pleased with himself for thinking this, but then he starts thinking about what is inside of the egg and what is outside of the egg and what baby chickens are made of and whether they are baby chickens only when they're on the outside and would they be something else if they had to stay always on the inside, and then Jack gives his head a shake, and his seeds rattle into a quieter position.

Pumpkins are everywhere. Nothing frightens Jack more than the thought of not having a head when he might need one—though for what he might need one he can't imagine—and so Jack farms an endless crop of waiting heads on his tract of land, a short walk from his father's walled city. Surrounding Jack are enough heads for an army of pumpkin-headed men, though some of the pumpkin-headed men would not look entirely pleasant with heads still green or too large or grown lopsided in the rounded shade of their droopy leaves. Some of the pumpkins are so large that Jack could never lift them above his shoulders to ram onto his neck. The largest, resting on its side at the far edge of the third row, is the size of Jack's house and, in fact, will be Jack's house after his friend Nick Chopper comes to gut it with his tin axe. But Jack isn't thinking about new houses today. Jack is thinking about new heads.

Averaging pumpkins for best shape, color and firmness, he creaks down and plucks the first in arm's reach. It's a fine choice, a little green along its bottom grooves, but solid, smooth and shapely. Jacks shakes it once, the way a child rattles a wrapped present to imagine its insides, but the pumpkin makes no sound, and since the pumpkin on Jack's neck makes no new sounds either, Jack turns and begins loping in the direction of the low and orange sun and his father's walled city.

The road's not long, but Jack's gait is slow, especially with one or the other of his knees snapping backwards every few steps. Sometimes the pointed roof of a farmhouse rises from the distance, and soon a hedge of evergreen or yellow rose bushes borders the road, and then Jack turns and smiles his broad perpetual smile in the direction of a closed door. The pins in Jack's joints creak as he plods on. He's wondering when the Strawman and the Patchwork Girl's wedding day will be, tomorrow or the next day, and whether they will have a baby by then. He hopes so. Jack would love to see a baby, a new baby, even if it's not made of meat but is just a straw-stuffed ragdoll or a cotton-stuffed sack. Jack has seen babies before, the same ones over and over, babies that mew and wheeze and cackle but never turn into bodies that talk or think or rot. Whenever Jack sees one of these babies, his seeds quiver and rattle and jump and won't settle. Jack wonders what his seeds will do when he sees the Strawman and the Patchwork Girl's baby. Perhaps they will shake themselves into some especially different shape, a shape that Jack can't even begin to imagine yet.

The thought of the Strawman and the Patchwork Girl's baby carries him to within a mile of the city walls which glow a glassy green greener than the grassy green of the meadows surrounding it. There are red tents, too, a half dozen staked in a row outside the city gates, with their silk sides fluttering and their silk banners fluttering. This is how Jack knows that the Royal Sorceress is visiting his father today, too.

After greeting the guardian of the gate and winding his way through the blinding green shimmer of the city streets, Jack lopes into the courtyard of his father's palace and up the royal stairs, taking one royal stair at a time due to his clumsy gait and the pumpkin cradled against his wooden belly. The shadow of the pumpkin lurches one stair ahead of him.

Inside, a green-gowned servant returns Jack's broad and perpetual smile with a thin sharp smile and leads him to a sitting room. "You may wait here until your father is able to see you."

"Has she gone blind?" asks Jack.

"Please sit," says the green-gowned servant.

"Thanks," says Jack. "But I'm built for standing."

And so Jack stands with the pumpkin drooping in his arms, at first staring at the fine furnishings and pleasant paintings, and then the fine rugs and the pleasant palm leaves settled in the fine pots in the corners of the pleasant walls. There is a head, too. A large dirty elk's head tilting from a mount above the door leading to the royal hall. The elk's glass eyes stare at nothing as the tips of its great antlers hang over Jack.

"Good morning," says Jack.

"Good morning," says the elk's head.

Jack and the head know each other. They were created from the same batch of the Powder of Life when their father was still a rough and rugged boy. There was more of the elk then, and not just elk parts, but a pair of sofas, a broom tail, and a set of wings made of palm leaves. A clothesline held him together. Now the clothesline uses up its time outside holding articles of Jack's father's royal wardrobe and flinching whenever somebody pinches a clothespin on too tightly. The rest of the elk is scattered around the sitting room. After his adventure flying his father to or from somewhere probably very terrible and important, the elk asked to be taken apart again. Jack has never thought of asking to be taken apart. He's never imagined his branches unhinged, the cylinder of his bark torso unfastened, the stake of his neck never holding the weight of a fresh pumpkin again. It's never occurred to Jack that he could stop being Jack or what not being Jack might be like, and though it occurs to him now, it stops occurring to him because the elk is talking again.

"What d'you got there?" He tips an antler at the pumpkin in Jack's hands.

"Nothing," says Jack. "Just my new head."

"What's wrong with your old one?"

"It smells," says Jack.

"You should get it embalmed like mine."

"I would rather have a new one."

"I'd rather have a new head, too," says the elk. "But then I'd be somebody else. You here to see Dad?"

"Yes," says Jack, wondering what it would be like to be somebody else and remembering that his father used to be somebody else, that she'd had a whole other body once, and he wonders whether his father remembers what being that somebody else was like.

"She's in talking with the Sorceress."

"I knew that," says Jack. "But then I forgot."

"Not everybody has a head for remembering," says the elk. "Take mine for instance—it doesn't have any members at all."

Jack wonders what he should say to this, and then he wonders what he should think, and then he rattles the pumpkin in his hands like a present.

Jack knows all kinds of meat people. His father, for example, is made entirely of meat, every inch of her.

"Wanna know what they're talking about?" asks the elk. "They're talking about the Sorceress's Great Book of Records, and how big it's getting and what they should do about it." Jack knows that the Sorceress's magic book writes the exact history of everything that happens everywhere in the world exactly at the moment that it's happening, and not just inside the kingdom, but outside, too, in places where things are happening all the time every day.

"The outside," continues the Elk, "has gotten so big that the book keeps getting bigger and bigger so that the Sorceress's army spends every hour of every day stacking new pages into heaps inside every room of her castle, and now there's no room for anything else."

"Where's that again?" asks Jack. "The Outside?"

"Not sure really. Though I visited it once. Must have been before the Sorceress cast her spell over everything. To keep the outside out."

According to Jack's father, who has never been there, and to the Sorceress, who's never been there either but who sometimes reads whole sentences about it and repeats them to Jack's father, the Outside is terribly unimaginable. When a body's head rots, for example, the body can't just pluck a new one from a green and shady field and ask its father to hollow it out. And it's not just heads that rot either, it's whole bodies, everybody's bodies, one, two, maybe as many as three meat bodies rotting there all the time everyday.

"Wasn't much to visit," adds the elk. Its glass eyes are looking off, one eye in one direction and the other in another. "Though I wouldn't mind living there."

Jack is trying to wonder if he wouldn't mind living there too, when he hears his head say, "The Strawman and the Patchwork Girl are getting married."

"What?! How's that—well, I'll be! Are you sure? That's amazing! When's the day?"

"Tomorrow," says Jack. "Or the-day-after-tomorrow. I'm not sure. Maybe the-day-after-the-day-after-tomorrow. I'd have to check my—" Jack pauses as a lone seed rolls up and flattens itself against the back of his squishy skull. "Calendar."

Jack isn't sure exactly what a calendar is, but before he can ask, the doors to his father's royal hall open, and the Royal Sorceress and his father step through. The two are turned in conversation, with the Sorceress a step ahead, her ringlets of crimson hair coiling on her shoulders and slithering down the dark satin of her crimson dress. Jack has heard that the Sorceress is the oldest body in all the kingdom, from before the kingdom was the kingdom and was just any old place where people grew up and died and were born all the time everyday. Jack has heard that the Sorceress is hundreds and even thousands of years old, which almost certainly means that she was born before the-day-before-the-day-before-yesterday, but Jack would have to do the math. Jack doesn't need to do the math to be sure that the Sorceress doesn't look terribly old. Though the tip of her glistening crown juts a foot above the tip of Jack's father's glistening crown, and though the front of the Sorceress's dress is much larger and rounder than the much smaller and flatter front of Jack's father's dress, the flesh of the Sorceress's milky face and the milky skin of Jack's father's face share the same bright and unbroken smoothness. They are both milky and bright unbroken girls. They are both made of meat, too, every inch of them.

"Well, hello, Jack," says Jack's father, smiling at him, and then the Sorceress turns to the pumpkin-headed man, too. It's difficult not to smile at Jack because the smile that his father carves is always so large and so round that anybody who looks at it must feel like smiling, too, unless the body is the Royal Sorceress'.

"Well, if it isn't Jack Pumpkinhead," says the Sorceress.

"Well, it is," says Jack, and then he turns his smiling head toward his father. "Are you happy to see me, Father?"

"Of course I am, Jack. I'm always happy to see you."

"Are you *very* happy to see me?" asks Jack.

Jack's father's bright unbroken face continues to smile at Jack, without changing, without the very slightest of changes at all. "I'm always happy to see you, Jack."

Jack's seeds, but not his smile, quiver. Jack, Jack thinks, must be happy to see his father, too, because Jack and his father are always happy to see each other—even if he might have hoped that maybe, just this once, perhaps they might have been very happy instead.

His father was there the day that Jack first became not dead. That was a long time ago, perhaps a very long time ago now, and so not earlier today. Before that Jack was dead, or his parts were, the wooden ones. His head was only just plucked. Jack's father was a boy then, a rough and rugged boy who hoed and husked and dug in gopher holes and napped between rows of cornstalks. Jack's father did not wear satin slippers then and gauzy silky robes did not float about her like a cloud. He was an orphan, a slave of a terrible witch who changed him so that no one would know that he was the daughter of a dead king and rightful girl Ruler of the kingdom. Luckily, the Royal Sorceress said she found him and turned him back into a girl, whose waves of silken golden hair now fall across the front of her flat and satin dress.

As Jack's father says goodbye to the Sorceress, the Sorceress promises to return the following day, after trying to burn the book as Jack's father has asked her to. "But I doubt it will work," the Sorceress says. "The pages are magical. Throwing them into the Deadly Desert probably won't work either. And if we do destroy the book, how will I monitor how the Outside is growing? It's not the book that's the problem; it's the Outside. There's too much of it, and somehow, sooner or later, something's going to get in, unless we act."

The girl Ruler nods and smiles. "Until tomorrow then," she says. After the Sorceress has gone, and the *tink, tink, tink* of the soles of the Sorceress's sharp and crimson shoes have gone, too, Jack's father smiles at Jack again. "So," she asks, "is that your new head?"

Jack holds up his pumpkin. "Would you mind carving it? I know you're very busy and important."

"Of course I don't mind, Jack. Come in."

Jack follows his father into her large and grand throne room, and when he lifts either of his feet, the ruined sole reflects in the glassy floor, and when one of the ruined soles clacks against the floor, its echo flutters against the high high ceiling like a lost bird. Jack's father's dainty and satin slippers make no noise at all, as the cloud of her dress washes across its glassy reflection.

While Jack waits at the foot of the circle of steps rising to the green throne, the girl Ruler finds a pocket knife in a dirty brown satchel tucked behind her royal chair. She clicks the rusted blade open and runs her thumb across the blunted edge. Then she presses the tip into her flesh and looks at the soft dent.

"I'm thinking triangle eyes this time, Jack. What do you think?"

Jack looks at the pumpkin he's set at the foot of the steps. He suspects but can't know for certain that his old eyes are triangles, too. That, he thought, is just the shape the world comes in.

The girl plops down on the bottom step, hikes her gown up, and rolls Jack's new head between her white knees. Her fingers tighten around the handle of the knife. "Don't worry," she says. "This won't hurt a bit."

Jack doesn't like this part and stiffens when the knife stabs into the lid of the shell. The jagged cutting is no better, and he feels light-headed when his father yanks the crown up by its torn stem. The nest of stringy guts tear and stretch and tear. Worse is the handfuls of insides his father scoops and plops in a wet pile, and the orange scent, and the scraping of the white flesh with the dull blade. Jack knows better than to watch any of this, but his eyes don't know a thing. Jack's eyes watch and watch and watch.

"Did you hear?" asks Jack. Bright seeds cling and drip in the tangle of gut strings puddling beside the upturned lid. "The Strawman and the Patchwork Girl are getting married."

The girl Ruler leans back with the knife staked into what will be Jack's new left eye and flicks spots of pumpkin juice from her hands onto the steps beside her. "Oh, Jack," she says. "You're so silly." She turns the head and begins sawing at a new angle.

"But," says Jack. His eyes are watching the girl's arm working beneath the ghost of her sleeve. "But I heard that the Strawman proposed."

"Did he?" mumbles the girl. She rattles the blade free, and the first triangle eye plunks into the hollowed shell. Jack doesn't really think that he heard that the Strawman proposed—whatever that is—but he would like to think that he thought so, and he would if only he could shake his seeds into the right shape.

"And the Patchwork Girl said yes."

"Well, I'm sure that would be very exciting." Jack suspects that his father is not particularly listening. He watches the way the bones in her arms move, how the elbows shift inside the soft meat. Her legs are bare under her gown. Jack's legs are bare under his clothes, too, but his legs don't look like his father's legs. He wonders what color her bones are, whether bark-brown or the gray of polished wood. His father's meat parts are nice, too, solid, smooth and shapely, with no signs of rot at all.

"And, and everyone is talking about it."

The second eye pops through. It's the nose that gives her trouble, the way the blade keeps sticking so she has to work it in and out of the same spot. She leans back again and shakes her hand, clenches the fingers, shakes them out again, then switches to her left hand as her knees tighten around the head. Jack tries to remember the last time there was a wedding in the kingdom. He thinks that he might remember that there hasn't been a wedding since he stopped being not dead, but he's not sure. Jack hopes his new head will be a better head for remembering.

"We can have a banquet with jeweled dishes and crystal goblets and make toasts and eat peach pies, and the old Wizard can do magic tricks and juggle his piglets, and we can dance and clap, and the Strawman can do his sword-swallowing trick."

"That sounds like a wonderful idea, Jack."

"We can have it outside of the city on the grass so everyone can come and watch and cheer and wave."

"Yes, Jack."

"It will be like one of your royal birthday celebrations. We haven't had one of those in a long long long time, have we?"

The girl Ruler doesn't answer. Her face is bent close to the pumpkin's half-face as she struggles to pull the knife free where she's rammed all of the blade and part of the handle into the unripe flesh. She makes tiny breathy grunts through her nose. It's a pretty nose, small and girlish and so, suspects Jacks, probably not the nose she had when she was a rough and rugged boy. Changing a body must be just like changing a head, thinks Jack, only more so. Thanks to the Sorceress Jack's father only had to change his body once. Now he will always be a soft and gowny girl with exactly the same body and head and thoughts forever. Jack wonders if Outside people ever get to change their bodies. The Sorceress says those people wake each morning with a new body exactly one day different than the body they had just the day before. The Sorceress's book is crammed with Outside people who wake up with new bodies all the time every day, who wake sometimes with new bodies for the first time ever, or bodies that are rotted and squishy and too terrible ever to wake again. People like that are cramming the rooms of the Sorceress's castle with pages and pages of their changing and squishy lives at this very and terrible moment. Jack hopes that some of those people will come to the wedding.

The pumpkin lurches from his father's knees when the knife tears loose. The nose is done. It's just the mouth now. Soon Jack's new head will be on his neck and Jack will be on his way home again to the little pumpkin house in the pumpkin field not a short walk from his father's walled city. His father stabs the knife high into Jack's new cheek and begins sawing the bottom crescent of a broad and perpetual smile.

"Do you think," Jack asks, "that the Patchwork Girl will move into the Strawman's corncob house, or will they build something new? I hope they build something new. Like a baby. Can you build a baby from straw and patches? I bet you could, if you had two bodies, and your bodies were made of straw and patches the way the Strawman and the Patchwork Girl are made of straw and patches. I bet they could make loads and loads of new babies."

"They're not getting married, Jack." The girl Ruler rests an elbow on her bare and juice-spattered knee and says, "No one is getting married."

Jack stands, watching the worn soles of his father's old shoes shuffle against the soles of their reflections on the icy floor. He doesn't know what to think. It is always very hard to know what always to think. Always thinking is so terribly always. Nothing frightens Jack more than always. Nothing frightens Jack more than nothing, because everything is only all of the parts of nothing wound up tightly and twined together with a clothesline and peppered with the Powder of Life. Jack is frightened that he could stand here in his father's royal hall thinking about this sort of always and nothing forever. Luckily, carving his new mouth takes no time at all.

"What do you think?" Jack's father asks.

Jack's new head grins at him from his father's lap. The smile that his father has carved into his new face is so large and so round that when Jack looks at it he feels like smiling, too, which he already is.

"Looks just like me," says Jack.

Jack's father rolls the new head beside her before standing and holding Jack's spindly hands in her own. She sits him down onto the stair so she can angle the old head from his neck. The back of the pumpkin squishes against her fingers.

"Went a bit long this time, Jack."

The pumpkin tips free with a soft tug.

"Ouch," says Jack.

"Oh, don't be silly."

Jack's father settles the head beside Jack on the bottom stair before wiping her hands on her soiled gown. Orange spots dot her sleeves, with the largest and orangest stain between her legs. Tiny seeds cling to the tips of her hair. She picks up the new head, spins it in her hands until the face is facing her and lifts it above her head.

"Ready?" she asks.

"Ready," says the head on the floor.

Jack braces his wooden body, and the girl Ruler rams the pumpkin onto the spike. The head, never having been a head before, is surprised. It stares at Jack's father, tries to blink, can't, and then stares some more. "Wouldn't have seen that coming in a million years," it says.

Jack always hopes that his new head will say something new, but Jack's new thoughts are always the same as Jack's old thoughts, only more crisp and clear and not so terribly damp and squishy. It's much easier to have a head that thinks the way a head is supposed to think, and so, thinks Jack, he must almost certainly be very happy again. Jack would like to wonder if he could be thinking anything different about his new head, but his bright new seeds are rolling into a neat clean row at the base of his fresh shell. The new pumpkin holds his neck spike firmly. His father is smiling at him.

"What are you smiling at?" asks Jack.

"Nothing," says his father. His father is smiling at him exactly the way she is always smiling at him.

Jack's old head watches from its spot on the glassy floor. The new head towers from Jack's shoulders like a bright and unbroken sun. It's like a sunrise, thinks Jack's old head, and a sunrise is something that the old pumpkin has seen before, almost certainly more than three times, but now it wonders whether it was ever sometimes a different sun, or if it was the same sun, did it always have the same seeds inside.

The girl Ruler wipes her hands again, finds the old and worn pocket knife beside the heap of orange guts, and runs it up and down her sleeve before snapping the blade closed against the heel of her thumb. She looks at the old pumpkin on the stair before dropping the knife into her old satchel.

"I was thinking," she says.

"I don't recommend it," says Jack's new head.

"About what you should do with your old head." Jack looks down, surprised to find his face looking up at him as though from an old and crusted mirror. "Maybe this time," continues his father, "you should take a trip to the Deadly Desert and roll it into the sands. That way it would turn to sand, too, and not be such a nuisance. It would be like it never existed."

"I wouldn't like that," says the head on the stair. "I'm almost certain I wouldn't like that at all."

"Shush," says the girl, "I wasn't speaking to you."

"The Desert?" asks Jack. He thinks his father may have suggested this once before, possibly many times before, but Jack can't be sure. He can't be sure of anything. He shakes his head and a memory arranges itself—new seeds, old memories, or at least Jack thinks they are old memories. Jack doesn't know how to remember otherwise, and remembering otherwise sounds like a terrible nuisance. That's why they have the Sorceress's book. The Sorceress keeps track of the past, and if the past isn't what it used to be, well, the future isn't much to speak of either. At least, thinks Jack, he has the present. There's no time like the present, thinks Jack.

"Yes," says his father. "The Desert. What do you think?"

Jack knows that the desert surrounds the kingdom and that its sands are magical and deadly and as endless as the sands of an hour clock that never runs empty. The Sorceress made the desert when she sealed them in. It keeps the Outside from getting Inside. It also keeps the Inside from getting Outside, but Jack doesn't know how to think something like that. Instead, Jack thinks how if a body were to wander into the sands, or if an old pumpkin were to be rolled into the sands, the body or the old pumpkin would blow away in a thousand pin-pricks as though it had never been alive, or at least not dead. Jack suspects that not being alive and not having existed are not exactly the same thing, though what the difference might be is a nuisance to try to think about when your seeds are clear and crisp and lined up as tall and unbroken as the Sorceress' and his father's tall and glistening crowns.

"Take the Sawhorse," says his father. "He can carry you. Or better, leave the head here, and I will ask the Hungry Tiger to take it for you."

"I don't want to go with the Hungry Tiger," says Jack's old head.

"Shush," says Jack as he picks the head up and cradles it in his wooden arms. It's damp and dented against the bark beneath his sleeves, but he doesn't mind. It's a fine head, perhaps the finest head Jack has ever had, with the exception of this new one. He knows that his father only wants to spare him the nuisance of burying it again, but Jack likes to keep track of his old heads. They may not be any good as heads anymore, but they almost make him think of something, a something that his seeds are no longer trying to form.

"I'll think about it," says Jack.

"Don't think too much," says his father. She sighs to herself, before tucking the dirty brown satchel behind her green throne and saying she must go and clean up now. "Look at me," she sighs, spreading the folds of her ruined dress. "I've made such a mess of things." The orange stains widen and close in her hands as though breathing, as though holding in something breathing inside of her, something that might have wanted to get out once but can't begin to now. The girl stands and stares at the stains moving between her gowny legs. "I've made such a mess of things," she sighs.

Her lips remain pursed, as though wishing to say or do something she can't imagine, something that Jack and his new head can't imagine either. Instead Jack thinks what a beautiful girl his father is, so milky and bright and always. He thinks how terribly lucky he and the kingdom are that the Sorceress found them such a beautiful girl Ruler. A rough and rugged boy Ruler would be something almost certainly less pleasant. A boy Ruler might soil his gown every day and not just on days that Jack's head is spoiling. If Jack's father were a boy Ruler his palace might be messier than the Sorceress's palace with all of its rooms and hallways crammed with loads and loads of her Great and messy Book. How so terribly lucky it is that the Sorceress made Jack's father into a girl Ruler before sealing the Outside out. A boy Ruler would be such a nuisance.

Jack's father is still standing, eyes wandering, her thoughts like the thoughts of a sleeping body's. She sighs again, and then the girl Ruler smiles a girlish smile at Jack, not a Sorceress's smile, which is something very different. Jack's father's smile is a childish smile. Jack's father's smile will always be a child's smile. After Jack says goodbye, too, Jack listens for the sound of her dainty and satin slippers as she and her gown float beyond the edge of the royal archway. Jack wonders when he'll see his father next and thinks how happy she'll be to see him then.

Leaving the royal palace, Jack gets royally lost in a maze of hallways. New heads are good for a great many things, and getting lost is one of them. When Jack is done wandering halls, he finds himself outside again, tottering down the royal stairs to the blinding green street below. He wanders to the city wall where the guardian of the gate returns his smile, before tilting his head at the ruined head staining Jack's shirt.

"And what have we here?"

"Just an old pumpkin," says the head.

Aside from brown dents torn in the grass, there is no sign of the Sorceress's army and their red tents and fluttering banners in front of his father's walled city. Lone trees spread their shadows across the road as Jack plods home. The sun is tipping over the Shifting Mountains and because it is round and orange, Jack can't help but to think that it looks like a pumpkin. It could be nice to have a head that thought the sun looked like something other than a pumpkin, but Jack doesn't know that, and neither does his new head. He shuffles between rows of pumpkins toward his pumpkin house, where he does not stop. The tract of land that he farms is tiny, but the fields behind it are broad and deep. The soles of his father's old shoes flop against the loose dirt.

"Where we headed?" asks the head.

"I think you know," says Jack.

Soon Jack comes before a small mound flattened by the shadow of a headstone. Jack can't read and neither can either of his heads, but they all know what the dents and grooves filling the headstone's face spell: *Here Lies the Mortal Part of*

JACK PUMPKINHEAD *Which Spoiled April 9th.* The headstone to the left of the first headstone is the same, except that its face reads *October 2nd.* The third says *January 24th.* The next has no date, nor does the next after it, nor the next after that, nor any of the others. It was his father who used to carve the dates, but then it got to be such a nuisance.

Jack passes between two rows of his private graveyard toward a stack of tin headstones made by Nick Chopper on a press in his tin castle. Jack doesn't mind that his stones aren't made of stone anymore, or that their faces are almost wordless. He can't read them anyway, except for his name, J-A-K, which he asked Nick to carve on the bright new batch. Nick gave Jack a bright sharp shovel, too, which Jack finds across a dark spot of earth at the end of the last row. He sets the old head softly to one side and begins to scatter bark-brown dirt. The head can't help but stare.

"I'm really sorry about this," says Jack.

"It's not your fault," says the head. "Or at least I've never been one to judge."

"I could put it off until tomorrow."

"Or the day after."

"But you smell so terrible."

"The buzzing is getting to me anyway."

"Those are flies."

"I know."

It takes Jack no time at all to dig the tiny new hole. Jack always thinks it will take longer, with his clumsy joints and his spindly fingers, but he's always wrong. Nick Chopper makes the grave markers with tin points at their bottoms. One plunk and they're standing. Jack's done before he knows it. He steps back, and the head at his foot grins up lopsided, its back squished flat.

"I'll never forget you," says Jack.

"Give my regards to the bride and groom."

"Is somebody getting married?" asks Jack.

"No," says the head. "But it's a nice thought, don't you think?"

The pins in Jack's hips creak as he bends and nudges the head onto its roundest edge and rolls it across the dirt. He settles it on the lip of the hole, and though he would like to guide it slowly, it slips from his fingers, tumbles the few inches, banks against the opposite edge, and flops to a stop on one eye. The other dark crust-lined eye stares at the worn toe of one of Jack's father's old shoes.

"I'll miss you," says Jack.

"You know where to find me."

Jack knows that his old head will be in the hole, but his new head begins to wonder where the old head's sleeping thoughts will go and whether someday its own sleeping thoughts will go there too, go to some terribly Outside place where Jack definitely has never gone and never will. At least, thinks Jack, his heads can go there, and if his heads aren't exactly him, then perhaps he's not exactly himself either. Someday, when his new head starts to rot, he might try wondering who he is if he's not himself, but Jack can't think about that right now. He can't think about much of anything.

"So long," says Jack.

After the old pumpkin says nothing, Jack waits for what may not be such a large and grand moment, then shakes a shovel of dirt across the pumpkin's face. As he works, Jack knows that his own smile is as broad and perpetual as ever, but his eyes feel more empty, the space in his hollowed shell more hollow. At least the old pumpkin will have something to fill its head now.

There's no sun when he finishes, but the strip of moon grins and sets the strips of tin markers shimmering. Jack clacks the shovel across the next empty space and stares out across the kingdom's only graveyard. The markers tilt and droop along the spreading hills, the furthest as thin as a soft round pin-prick. Jack has heard that there are hundreds of graves, perhaps thousands of graves, but nobody knows for certain. There are, he thinks, almost certainly more than three.

POETRY

Yonatan Maisel
Self-Esteem, by-Proxy: On How Your Downfall Quells My Angst

You high and mighty bastards, oh, how I loathe thee,

and the world at thy Midas-like fingertips!

Your God-given speed, dexterity driving golf ball with 3-iron,

and ability to propel a fastball;

Your devastating good looks, and that damned Versace handbag of yours.

The blood-red Ferrari you drive, and your rich daddy.

Now, blissful fate, the great Zen-like equalizer, strikes an impetuous blow.

Sinking, you have fallen;

Spiraling dizzily downward, attaining new depths.

Oh how I delight in thee, heavenly-ordained reversal of fortune.

You, yes you, arrogant egotistical jock,

with season-ending ligament tear!

You, unbridled serial-womanizer, who now,

shamefacedly, suffers from erectile-dysfunction,

You, greedy, pension-swindling multi-millionaire CEO,

bereft now of your chauffeured stretch limo and penthouses,

on your way to do time at the "big-house!"

You, murderous mafia don, dispatcher of evil,

lying in a pool of blood with lead slug now in brain!

And you, smug, leggy supermodel with unquenchable coke habit,

which rots your teeth and prematurely ages your skin.

I gleefully revel in your failure!

I cheer your impromptu unscripted demise,

for it evokes within me such shameless triumph;

So passionately and heatedly tickles my innards.

Yes, it's cathartic, therapeutic;

It gratifies, tempers my angst-filled soul.

A source of perverse self-esteem for me,

born of your tantric nosedive.

You are no different from us now, ordinary miserable wretches.

I thank you most kindly,

express my gratitude to thee,

for with your all-too-heartening downfall,

with your enchanting fallibility,

you raise me, by-proxy,

to delectable new heights.

SHORT STORY

Ersi Sotiropoulos
An Almost Guinea Fowl

Translated from Greek
by Karen Emmerich

FOR KAY

Telis came home that afternoon in high spirits. The crisp air had relieved his headache. The atmosphere in the small apartment was pleasant, if a bit stuffy. Everything was orderly and peaceful. It was perfectly quiet, Maro must have taken the baby for a walk. He opened the balcony door and stepped outside to admire his plants. He had arranged the pots in the best way possible on the narrow balcony. Of course it was a northern exposure, and the adjacent buildings cut down on the light, and since the apartment was on the fourth floor the wind was often strong. But thanks to his calculations, before long they would have a little jungle out there.

He leaned over the railing and looked down. The traffic on the avenue was dense and chaotic. He went back inside and closed the door. It was April now, and though the days had grown perceptibly longer and the trees along the street were bright green, with heavy, lustrous leaves, this week had brought a sudden stretch of bad weather. As he walked past the mirror in the hall he smiled. The cold spell allowed him to wear a sweater under his jacket, which made his tie sit better. For a young lawyer these things mattered.

He went into the kitchen to get a beer.

Babe, I bought you a very special guinea fowl. I won't be late. I LOVE YOU, read the note on the table.

They had gotten into the habit of leaving one another notes in the early days of their relationship, or rather after they had silently agreed that things were getting serious. Maro had started calling him "babe" after the baby was born. At first it amused him, but then it started to get annoying. "But don't you see, it's because the baby hasn't changed *anything* between us," she would say.

"A very special guinea fowl," he said to himself as he opened the fridge. That meant it had cost more than they could afford.

He was drinking a beer in front of the open fridge door when the idea took shape. The telephone rang. Without hurrying, he went into the hall, carrying the can of beer.

Babe, I bought you a very special guinea fowl. I won't be late. I LOVE YOU.

"Christos, I was just thinking about you," he said. "I was about to call."

". . ."

"Maro bought a guinea fowl, she got it from a hunter."

". . ."

"Free range, it's been doing somersaults in the hills and dells."

". . ."

"You two should come for dinner. We can watch the match, too."

He winked at Maro, who had just gotten home and was pushing the door open with the stroller.

"Great, around eight-thirty," he said and replaced the receiver. "Christos and Jeanette are coming for dinner," he said, unbuckling the baby.

"He's fussy today," she said a while later.

They were getting the baby ready for his afternoon nap. He laid him down in the crib while she put the powders and creams back in the cupboard with the diapers. He often thought that this was their best moment as a family. The two of them with the baby. A parenthesis of peace and autonomy.

"There's something I should tell you," Maro began, hesitating. "It's not a guinea fowl."

Telis looked at her incredulously. "You're joking."

"I'm serious, it's not a guinea fowl."

Her expression said that offense was the best defense.

"What kind of game are you playing?" he asked, his voice rising a notch.

He went back into the kitchen. He opened the fridge and took out the bird. Its skin was yellowish and pimply. He kneaded it with both hands, then sniffed it.

"It's a chicken, a plain old chicken," he heard her say behind him.

"Why did you tell me it was a guinea fowl?" he asked, trying to keep calm.

"To make you happy, like that time with the frog's legs."

"What do you mean?"

"I just cut the wings in half. I dipped them in batter and fried them."

Telis was silent for a minute. Maro looked at him and he thought he saw the shadow of a small triumph in her eyes.

"You'd better find a guinea fowl by this evening."

He grabbed her wrist and twisted until the skin was red, the knuckles white.

"Let me go!"

"This is the first time we're having them over since the baby was born."

Telis walked the baby around the apartment until six. Finally, around six-thirty, he managed to put him down. He opened a beer, made a sandwich and sat down in front of the television. At seven Maro came back weighed down with grocery bags and went straight into the kitchen. Telis drained his beer and followed her in. Four birds lay in a row on the table.

"Duck, goose, turkey, pheasant . . . I couldn't find a guinea fowl," Maro said, on the verge of tears.

They all look more or less alike, Telis thought. Only the turkey still had its head. A plucked skull with glassy little eyes.

"There's this, too," Maro said, pointing to a shrink-wrapped package. "Rabbit, already butchered. I paid with the money from the store," she added, as if answering a question. For a few years she had been part owner of a small bookstore. After the baby was born she'd sold her share.

"Which should we choose?" Telis wondered.

He put an arm around her shoulders and they bent together over the table.

"Which should we choose?"

"They look so defenseless," Maro said after a while, drawing her index finger along the turkey's back. As she leaned over the table to look at the birds her ass showed round and tight under the thin fabric.

"Shhh . . ." Telis whispered. "They're vultures . . . come on, follow me . . ."

He took her hand and led her into the bedroom. He pulled down her panties and entered her from behind, gently and almost indifferently, as if he had something else on his mind. Then he gave a few hard thrusts, waiting to hear her breathing grow short, to deepen and change. He pulled out, then started to move in and out quickly and rhythmically, maintaining the greatest possible distance between them, so that the tip of his prick sank into her for a fraction of a second before slipping back out again.

"The baby's birth changed him a lot," Maro said as she made a salad.

"That's how it goes," Jeanette replied, blowing smoke.

They were sitting in the kitchen, to keep an eye on the guinea fowl roasting in the oven. The whistles and shouts from the match mingled with the noise of the exhaust fan over the stove.

"He's become very possessive. I have no time to myself anymore."

"The problem with men," Jeanette said, "is that they can't tell their ego from their superego."

Maro set her knife down in the strainer with the lettuce leaves.

"And you know what happens if you have a superego as big as an Olympic stadium and an ego as small as a punching bag . . ."

She filled her glass with wine and drank it down.

"I have the feeling I'm going to start smoking again," Maro said, reaching for Jeanette's cigarettes.

"We lost by three points," Telis said.

He was clearing all the books and things off the desk so they could set the table. Maro stood there waiting for him, holding the plates and silverware.

"Who wants wine and who wants beer?" Jeanette asked.

"You've had enough already," Christos said.

"Could you cut the bread, please?" Maro asked.

"How about I bring in the wild bird?" Jeanette giggled, then did a pirouette and ran into the kitchen.

"I don't believe it," Christos said.

"Come on, let the women have their fun," said Telis.

The desk was clear and he spread the checked tablecloth, smoothing the creases with his palm.

"The baby's crying," said Maro. "Can you take the plates?"

*

"A guinea goose with gooseberries," Jeanette said and stood up from the table.

"They were prunes," Maro said.

"I was joking," Jeanette sighed, sinking into the couch. "Who's going to pour me some wine?"

"Wonderful, delicious, pure ambrosia," Christos said, stretching in his chair.

"You ate it all, you cannibals," Telis laughed. "What are you doing, smoking?"

"Just for tonight," Maro said.

"I want wine," Jeanette said again.

The two men carried the dirty plates into the kitchen. Maro took the bottle of wine and sat next to Jeanette on the couch.

"Something's happening to me. I have a little ball with feathers in my stomach," Jeanette murmured.

"You want me to help you to the bathroom?" Maro asked.

"No, pour me some wine."

They sat there silently for a while, their heads resting on the back of the couch.

It must have been after midnight. The hum of the avenue had died down, the building was quiet. Every once in a while they would hear the elevator wheezing as it headed for other floors. The heat had gone off hours ago and the apartment was starting to get cold.

"I only like cooking for friends, like the two of you," Maro said. "Otherwise it's such a bore."

She glanced over to see if Telis was listening.

"I only like cooking for Christos," Jeanette interjected with a little laugh, the tone of her voice tender and ironic.

Christos coughed to clear his throat.

"My father and I used to go hunting sometimes. When he was alive, I mean."

He had sat back down in the chair. His elbows were resting on the table and he was looking down at them, his head in his hands.

"We would shoot woodcocks, wild ducks, occasionally a rabbit. I don't remember any guinea fowl."

"You know how I feel?" Jeanette said excitedly. "Like that time we smoked pot on vacation on Santorini."

"I think the baby's crying again," Telis said, looking at Maro.

"Do you want us to leave?" Jeanette asked, half rising from the couch.

"It's still early, we haven't had dessert," Telis said.

"My father was a great hunter," Christos said, as if he were talking to himself. "and a fisherman, too. In the summer he would set trotlines and—"

"Your father was a jerk," Jeanette interrupted, throwing a leg over the arm of the couch.

"The baby's crying, don't you hear?" Telis asked.

Maro lit another cigarette from Jeanette's pack and blew the smoke between her fingers.

"I think it's your turn," she said, her voice flat.

"What did my father ever do to you?" Christos asked.

"He made you really boring," Jeanette replied. Then her voice grew more animated. "Guys, I feel like I'm high."

"You're drunk, that's all," said Christos.

"What are we celebrating today?" Jeanette asked Maro.

"What are we celebrating?" Telis repeated, coming into the living room. "My lovely little wife wanted to cook me something exotic and . . ."

He looked at Maro, waiting for her to finish his sentence.

"Why don't we play a game?" she suggested.

"Cards," said Christos.

"Biriba," said Telis.

"Truth or dare," said Jeanette.

"Truth or dare," echoed Maro.

"Dare?" Jeanette said, pleased. "Okay, take off your pants and your underwear—that is, if you're wearing underwear," she said, laughing, "and walk around the table three times saying—"

"Forget it," Telis cut her off.

"Come on," Maro egged him on.

Telis licked his lips and looked at each of them in turn. Then he started to unbutton his pants.

"Say 'I was a good boy today, ma'am,' and run around the table."

"Happy?" Telis asked.

He was down to his underwear and socks.

"Are you kidding?" Jeanette said.

"Then I'll take truth," Telis said half-heartedly.

"Guys, should we accept?"

"That's cheating!" Maro shouted.

"Just this once, it's fine," Christos said.

"But you have to stay in your underwear," Jeanette said, "and tell me quickly, the truth, have you ever cheated on Maro?"

"Never."

"The truth!"

"Never . . . while we were married."

"Who was she?" Maro asked.

"He only has to answer one question," Christos said.

"Who was she? Tell me who she was."

"I feel that little ball in my stomach again, it's like it has feathers . . . or corners, sharp ones . . ."

"If it has corners, it's not a ball."

"You don't understand."

"I'm dead tired. Let's go."

But he didn't get up.

They were alone in the living room. Telis and Maro had gone into the baby's room.

"I'm sure it's a ball. Do you think I have cancer?"

"Tell me, do you know anything about Telis?"

"Yes."

"Well?"

"What, are you stupid?"

"I want you to tell me who she was," Maro repeated.

She was leaning over the baby's crib, changing his diaper.

"They'll hear us," Telis whispered.

His cheeks were burning. The room was lit only by a nightlight and he hoped she couldn't see his expression.

"If you don't tell me, I'll tell them it wasn't a guinea fowl."

Telis laughed nervously. He was still in his underwear and felt ridiculous.

"Tell them," he said listlessly. "Tell them, if it'll make you feel better."

Maro started to cry, little sobs that kept getting louder. Her tears fell on the baby, who woke up and wriggled around in the crib. She picked him up and pressed his forehead to her wet cheeks. He was warm and very soft, almost spineless, and every so often his little body would give an irritated jerk as if shot through by an electric current. Suddenly he let out a loud shriek and hit her face hard with his head.

"I'm going back," Telis said.

She stood there in the half darkness, with her back against the door and the baby in her arms. They were both crying, pressed up against each other, and the sound of their breathing, fitful and erratic, pierced the milky light of the room.

Christos and Jeanette were holding hands on the couch. They had brought the dessert in from the kitchen, eaten, and left their dirty plates on the floor.

"Come and see my plants," Telis said as he entered the living room.

He'd put on a new pair of pants and was buckling his belt as he walked toward the balcony door. He wasn't sure whether they'd heard the fight and the plants seemed like the best distraction.

"I couldn't possibly move," Christos said.

Jeanette stood up and Christos lay down on the couch.

Out on the balcony it was biting cold. Telis stepped aside to make room for Jeanette.

"This summer we'll have gardenias," he said, bending over a flowerpot where a little shoot was peeking out.

Jeanette looked up at the leaden sky and stretched, about to take a deep breath. But she stopped midway and he heard her exhale impatiently.

"Are you going to tell her?" she asked.

"Are you crazy?"

He turned toward her jerkily and stumbled. They were so close that the scent of her body lotion hit the roof of his mouth and he felt as if he were swallowing wheat and honey.

"Do you want me to tell her?" she asked, squinting her eyes as if searching for some distant star.

Her voice was colorless and strained.

Telis took a quick look into the apartment. Christos was sleeping on the couch, his mouth hanging open. The apartment was a mess. Someone had knocked over the stroller in the middle of the hall.

"Come on, be serious," he said and grabbed her hand.

In the few centimeters that separated them, he felt that her body was a familiar yet threatening thing, and if he came any closer, if he touched her body with his, he would collapse altogether.

"Come on," he said again, "you'll get cold," and pushed her gently inside.

*

The next morning the sky had cleared and it was still cold. Telis got up early, feeling as if hadn't slept at all. He had fallen asleep on the couch without a blanket and had shooting pains in his back. The ashtrays were full, the wine had gone sour in the glasses and stank. A war zone, he thought, looking around. For some reason, instead of depressing him, the previous night had lifted his spirits. He began to clean, mentally dividing the apartment into three zones: kitchen, hall, living room. Hope, desire, disappointment. He started with the living room and worked his way in. Hope, desire. He washed the dishes, dried them with a clean cloth and put them away. He felt that the previous night had taught him something, and, as he methodically cleaned, he tried to figure out what it was. The message was there inside him, but it kept slipping away. Fragments of thoughts sat in his mind without moving through it, without leaving traces. But his mood remained light, natural, pervading his movements, as he brought order to the chaos around him.

At around seven-thirty the hot water started to come up through the pipes, passing into the radiators with restrained momentum and a hollow purring noise. Telis paced as he drank his coffee. Should he be feeling guilty about this little inspection? The house was now neat and sparkling clean, just as he had found it the previous afternoon.

The baby gurgled in his crib.

Babe, he wrote, *it wasn't anything serious, I love you.* He hugged the baby to him and kept writing. *A near-betrayal, believe me. We're going out for a walk. Is it worth throwing everything away over an almost guinea fowl?*

"An almost guinea fowl . . ." Maro read.

She had woken up with a headache. The kitchen smelled like bleach.

She walked barefoot to the fridge and opened it. The birds were all lined up on the second and third shelves. Only the rabbit was gone. She closed the door and sat down in the chair in front of the note, but didn't reread it. It was freezing. She looked at her bare feet on the tiles, which were still wet. On her pale toes, the round nails with their red polish shone like ten glossy little beaks.

I'm on alert, she thought. She tore up the note and went back to bed.

SHORT STORY

Kyle McManus
Other People's Boredom

Down on the street there's some kid kicking a ball against a wall. Just some kid. Looks poor, in a tatty tracksuit, spotty, fat on cheap crap. Andrew has been watching him. Andrew watches a lot. He has a flat on the second floor of a square building surrounded by other square buildings.

 He stands at the window, wearing his dressing gown, drinking tea. It's four PM. The sky's grey and everything's quiet. Muted. He watches the kid kick the ball against a street light. Too hard. It comes back and smacks his face. He falls flat on his back. Andrew chuckles. He can appreciate that sort of thing. It's funny. The kid looks like he could use some sleep anyway.

 He looks away from the street. The buildings nearby all look dead. There is one, though. One window with curtains open. There's a woman sitting on a chair. Plump. Long black hair. Wearing a dressing gown, too. She's watching TV, some historical epic. All Sundays are good for.

 He sips the tea. It's long since gone cold, but he doesn't care. Mo used to go nuts over that. 'How can you drink it cold?' she'd say. He'd shrug and slurp it down. She'd shudder and throw a cushion at him. Always the same cushion. Always the same couch, too. Brown and uncomfortable, flattened by their swollen behinds. These thoughts make him sad. He liked that couch. Probably. He spent enough time on it.

 The woman gets up, walks out of sight. She looks young, thirty maybe. He keeps watching. Nothing else to do. She comes back with a small black box on a plate. She sits and peels something off the top of it. She jabs a fork inside, then lifts a lump of something to her mouth. Microwave meal. He's been living off them since he came here. Never cooked, even with all these chefs hijacking TV. Too hard. All ends up looking the same anyway.

He watches her eat. She plays with it a lot. Maybe she's got no appetite. Maybe she wants to lose weight. She puts the plate down then stares at the TV. Andrew looks down onto the street. The kid is getting to his feet, shaking his head. He picks up the ball, runs away. The woman picks her nose, wipes her finger on the chair. He watches for a bit longer, then stops. Other people's boredom is just boring.

Monday. Tony phones, hopes Andrew will enjoy his week off. Andrew is sure he will. Seven days away from collecting fat bin bags. Seven days away from people asking how he is after the divorce. Hard to answer when he doesn't know.

He watches the woman eat her breakfast. Looks like cereal. She has her hair up today. She watches some program with two people sitting on a stage, arguing.

When he looks back in, she's wearing a tight tee shirt and shorts. She's jumping up and down, waving her arms. Copying some woman on the TV. Her shorts look too small. Her buttocks wobble all over the place. So do her breasts. She should wear a sports bra, Andrew thinks. Strange watching a woman exercise. Mo never did. She used to get taxis everywhere. No wonder they were always broke. She said she like travelling in style.

The woman drops. Press-ups, with knees. Andrew watches where she places her hands. Her arms are spread too wide. She slips and ends up on her stomach. Andrew doesn't laugh. Not that he feels sorry for her. He just doesn't find it funny. She gets up, switches the TV off. She stands still, probably catching her breath. She walks out of the room. Andrew watches TV for a while, but she doesn't come back.

Tuesday. Andrew gets a letter from his daughter in Essex. She's lived there for ten years. When they told her about the divorce, she visited for a day. Didn't try to talk them out of it. Had probably been expecting it. In the letter, she said she hoped he was all right. He was, but he decided not to write back, like she asked. Never was any good at expressing himself. Found words tricky. Always a bad speller.

He put the letter on the coffee table. Would read it again. Maybe later. He always left reading mail to Mo. She was a good reader. Fat paperbacks, mainly. Romance ones. His idea of hell. What's the point? They always end with a wedding. She used to do crosswords too. In bed. Worked out well for him because he'd gone right off sex. With her. Still liked a bit of XXX TV when she was at her bingo Wednesdays.

She knew all about it. Used to encourage it, too. Said she couldn't be bothered with it anymore. Said it was a young person's game.

Tomorrow was Wednesday. Did Mo still go to bingo?

Andrew goes to the window. The tea is cold. No problem. Has less flavor hot. The woman's been out. Now she comes back into her living room. With a man. They're both dressed up, probably been out. It's late evening now. They sit on the couch. He puts his arm round her. She turns and looks out the window. Andrew worries she'll see him, then remembers. His lights are off. He's invisible.

> **He's not ashamed. He's not stalking her. Just curious. Wants to see what she does outside the flat.**

The man's nuzzling her neck. She puts her hand on his head and pushes his closer to her. He massages her breasts. She pulls his head up. They kiss. Andrew hasn't seen anyone kiss in real life for ages. He feels himself rise to the occasion. He finishes the cold brown swill. Puts his hands in his pockets. The woman is topless now. Her bra's huge, even from this distance. Bets she's wearing a padded one. All a big con.

They leave the room, hand in hand.

Andrew makes himself another drink.

Wednesday. Andrew sits on the couch, prodding his belly. Definitely getting fatter. At least Mo kept him trim. Now he eats what he wants, when he wants, all synthetic. Five a day? Half of one a day, maybe. Likes a few peas with his microchips. Exercises while working, walks street after street. Maybe eats too much, not burning it off. Even getting boobs.

He picks up his cup of tea. Wonders what it's been sitting on. Picks up the letter. A big brown ring in the centre, a kiss after chocolate. He screws it up and throws it away. No use keeping it now.

Mo always said he needed to be more sentimental. Said he drifted through life. Said he needed to make more effort. But he liked drifting. Said people would wish to be like him. Just going along, no worries. He didn't like getting bogged down by stuff. These days, everyone's got a problem. A gripe, whether global warming or human rights. He can't change these things. What good would it be to panic?

He goes over to the window. Woman and man, watching TV. Both in dressing gowns. Eating cereal. Andrew peeks round the curtain. Doesn't want to get spotted. No idea what they might do.

The woman puts her bowl down. She stands and goes to the TV. Off it goes. He pauses, bowl in hand, spoonful of cereal halfway to his mouth. She turns and starts shouting, hands waving. Andrew can't hear, but her mouth's open wide and she's pacing. The man's frozen, watching her go nuts. Andrew feels sorry for the guy. Mo used to fly off on one. It'd come from out of nowhere. That vanished before the divorce, too. Virtually no communication at all. Not that it bothered him. Always hated women's need to talk. Wanting to discuss feelings all the time. His daughter's probably like that now.

Andrew reaches back to the table, grabs the cup. Sips while the woman slaps the man's head. His bowl drops. Milk everywhere. They both look down, then she carries on. Probably blames him for dropping it. Must've smacked himself over the head. He stands and shouts. She smacks him again. He shakes his head, walks out. She sits on the floor and puts her hands over her face.

Two minutes later, he's on the street. Wearing his smart clothes. Gets into a car. Drives away. Andrew sips his tea, watches her sit there. Her hands stay over her face. Andrew checks his watch. Mo's probably getting ready to go to bingo.

Thursday. He's been watching her for a while now. She's done another workout, had a bowl of cereal. Mo sent him a text message before. She had sex last night. Some forty-eight year old stud, she says. Best one yet, she says. Andrew replies saying 'masturbated last night. Best one yet,' he says. Gets no reply. Tells himself he's won that round.

He's angry, though. Very. Wants to believe she's lying. Knows she's probably not. "Young person's game," his arse.

She's wearing a coat, putting on some trainers. He wants to know where she's going. Wants to know if she's going to see that man. He puts on his trainers. A few seconds after she leaves, he leaves. He's walking behind her. Trying to be stealthy. Imagining he's a spy.

They go through the loud estate. Kids on bikes. They go through the back alleys. Plastic bags and graffiti. He's starting to think they're going to the supermarket. He sees he's right. They get to the trolley bay. She gets one, he doesn't. They go round the magazines and the newspapers. She buys a paper, he buys the same one.

They end up in the cereal aisle. She buys a few boxes of crunchy squares. Then she buys a pile of microwaveable meals. He buys the same.

She turns and looks right at him. He looks down before her eyes can meet his. He wonders why. He's not ashamed. He's not stalking her. Just curious. Wants to see what she does outside the flat.

She buys a lot of stuff. He stays as far behind her as he can without losing sight of her. She goes to the checkout. He lets an old lady go between them. The girl scans her items. She pays, then leaves. The old woman is taking too long. The woman's almost out the door. He thinks. Leave the stuff or lose her? He pushes past the oldie. Gets a few feet behind the woman. Hopes she doesn't know he's there.

They go back through the alley. A couple of kids climbing over someone's wall. They go back through the estate. Nobody about. Sky of charcoal. She turns. He crouches down behind a bin. Wasps fly out. She carries on. He jumps up, swatting. She goes into her building, he goes into his.

Mo used to love the weekly shop. Bought fruit, bags of chocolate. Days later, empty bags, rotten fruit. He'd just follow her round, grunting. Didn't care what she made, as long as he could eat it. He wonders what she's doing now, seeing that forty-eight year old, maybe.

He puts his shopping away. Checks his voice messages. Tony, again. Asks if he wants a pint later.

He goes to the window. The woman's in her chair. Coat's still on. She's eating a chocolate bar. Her shoulders are going up and down. Laughing. Crying. He can't tell. He makes a drink. Lifts his top, squeezes the gut. Huge. Almost as big as Mo's. Funny how she could feed him good stuff but not herself. Fat, plain. Bad clothes. Wonders how he stayed with her so long.

Sips drink, watches the woman. She stands, takes off her coat. Looks at the window, walks over. She looks down at the street, then up. At him. She isn't surprised. Isn't anything, just looks at him. He waves, slowly. Doesn't smile. Isn't sure what she'll do.

She closes the curtains.

SHORT STORY

Jeff Hart
The Amazing Dreamer Stays Awake

Today Flob-O uses a piece of thread and some paper clips to hang himself from the tiny ceiling fan of his mini cubicle. He kills himself while I am in the break room getting my third cup of coffee. Marcy and Craig are there and they comment on how bright and lively my new tie is and I tell them that it was a gift from my girlfriend and Craig jabs me in the ribs with his elbow telling me what a dog I am and I humor him by barking and this just has Marcy cracking up until Phil walks in and then, wiping tears from her eyes, Marcy heads back to her desk joshing us about our boys club and next thing I know we're talking about last night's game and Phil is showing me some new pictures that he snapped of his kids Brett, Bobby and Brenda with the new digital camera he was able to afford thanks to the Hopecon Non-Denominational Holiday bonus and so really this turns into quite the bull session and by the time I return to my cubicle to finally knuckle down on some of these expense reports, Flob-O's little body is already swinging, his eyes all bugged out sort of comically, his bowels emptying all over the carpet.

    I get down on my knees over Flob-O's cubicle and try to lift him out of his noose, but he has tied some darn good knots. His body has the consistency of marshmallow, like one of those puffy neon Easter candies, the rabbits and the chicks, the ones that are always deep-discounted well into May. Flob-O feels just like that, only rapidly cooling, the frantic hilarious life already gone from his gelatinous body.

    I bite through the thread with my teeth and Flob-O drops to the floor, bouncing with a wet bloomp noise. I use my fingers to administer CPR, pushing into his soft flesh where I assume Flob-O's heart would be but before I get very far, he starts to evaporate. Flob-O turns into a dark blue smoke that smells a lot like cotton candy laced with sulfur. His cubicle starts to fall apart too, crashing in on itself, melting back into the gray Hopecon carpet until the only things left are Flob-O's two googly-eyes, floating a few inches off the carpet, staring at me and then they blink and are gone.

I sit down at my desk and turn my attention to today's expense reports. Between the long coffee break and Flob-O's suicide, I've lost all my morning momentum. Basically, I'm behind the eight-ball and it's not even lunch time. I put Flob-O out of my head. He wasn't Hopecon material anyway.

Pretty soon I'm going to need another cup of coffee. I haven't been sleeping well lately.

After work, the Pygmy Rockers are waiting. When I step outside, the entire shriveled retinue breaks off from anxiously thrumming their guitars with their shrunken hands to glare at me. I haven't seen these guys in weeks. **They've been giving me the tiny cold shoulder since I missed their battle-of-the-bands with Alligator Death Squad. Apparently, Adolph Alligator swallowed a few of the Pygmies, most of the rhythm section, and they blame my absence for the carnage.** As if I could've done something if I hadn't been at home trying to figure out how to animate a bar graph on PowerPoint.

"We thought you'd like to know," squeaks the lead-singer, "that Rhinopotamus is dead." His wide Pygmy eyes blink back tears.

"Oh," I respond, glancing over my shoulder. "What happened?" I move slowly, cautiously, not wanting to agitate the Pygmies, but also wanting to get down the block, away from the prying eyes of my co-workers.

"What's the matter, Dave? Afraid some of those suits will see you associating with Pygmies? Don't they like punk rock at Hopecon?"

I almost laugh, imagining some of my colleagues from Hopecon at a Pygmies show. How out of place and awkward they would be, buffeted about the moshing pit, sweating through their Sears suits, afraid for their lives. It was always the threat of violence that made the Pygmies live shows so thrilling, and I can just picture Phil or Mr. Drueger taking a spear to the throat during the second encore's ritual sacrifice. Of course, then the Pygmies would be the ones out of place. They'd be in our world, filing claims and typing out statements, assigning liability. Shitting red tape, as Phil likes to say.

"That's not it at all," I say, shaking my head as I usher them further away from my office. Behind me, Craig and Phil are talking about happy hour. "Come on, let's go talk in this dark alley."

Pygmy-Harpsichordist begins screaming in Pygmy at Lead-Singer-Pygmy, looking outraged and bloodthirsty. Many of the other Pygmies nod in agreement and Tambourine-Pygmy even pulls one of the ornamental skulls off his thong and smashes it on the sidewalk.

"We don't want to talk!" shrieks Lead-Singer-Pygmy, tremors of anger shaking his frail, nearly naked body.

I notice that some of the Band have begun brandishing their poison dart blow-guns and are fixing me with that just-give-us-a-reason look.

"So what do you want?" I ask as I make a subtle glance at my watch, giving off one of Dan Dawkins' fourteen physical indications that my time is valuable as laid out in his book 'Fourteen Ways to Indicate that your Time is Valuable Without Resorting to Words'.

"We want you to help us move his body."

I trail a few feet behind the Pygmy Rockers at all times as they scurry through the rush hour foot traffic, leading me toward Rhinopotamus. This is just the kind of stuff that would hurt my reputation at the office. I think back to the time that Roger caught Intern Jenny kissing another young lady at a club, how quickly that spread all over the office, all the hilarious 867-5309 but gay song parodies that people CC'd me on. Being seen with the Pygmies would be much worse, especially now, at a time when I really need to look good, what with the institutional accounts manager position opening up, the sort of promotion a guy like me could really sink his teeth into. I visualize myself as a guy with a pay raise—he's a happier, wealthier Dave. He's a guy I'd like to have a drink with. We'd belly up to the bar and I'd pick his brain about how to get ahead. Unfortunately, fantasy promoted Davis is clueless. He just shrugs and tells me hard work, and then he tries to change the subject. He can't help me get past Mr. Drueger. It's been keeping me up at night, thinking about the interview, how Drueger will hit me with tough questions, and suddenly I'll break into a cold sweat and have to turn the light on, frantically flipping through the copy of *101 Killer Answers to Deadly Interview Questions* that I keep next to my bed. Even once I have the right answer and I'm running the phrasing through my head, visualizing my calm smile and wink placement, even then I still can't sleep, still can't slow my heart down and the only thing that relaxes me are soft-core fantasies of Astrogirl and I spending a sexy week on a Polynesian island thanks to my bonus money. Maybe then I get some sleep, have some dreams about work, or some dreams about not being able to fall asleep and I still wake up exhausted and nervous because maybe they weren't dreams at all. Tonight, I'm sure, visions of Mr. Drueger bumping into me consorting with Pygmies will keep me up well after Leno's monologue.

"Here," says Lead-Singer Pygmy as we reach Rhinopotamus' bloated, smelly body. He collapsed while the Pygmies were trying to parallel park him. A few of the band members still sit astride him, digging their tiny heels into his sides with forlorn futility.

"He definitely is dead," I say.

"No shit, Dave."

I'm thinking about my dry-cleaning bill as I put my shoulder into Rhinopotamus' side, trying to push him onto the sidewalk. He doesn't budge and after a few minutes of this, me pushing while the Pygmies tug at Rhino's ears and tail, we give up.

"You know," I pant, "it looks like Rhino could've used a visit to the vet. Maybe if you guys had real jobs," I trail off, the Pygmies all glaring at me, too appalled and hurt to even shake a spear. Lead-Singer Pygmy combs a hand through his dreadlocks and shakes his head. I had no idea their tiny faces were capable of expressing such disgust.

"Go home," he sighs. "You fucking sell-out."

So I do. Before I've gone far a poison dart whistles by my ear. When I turn around to admonish the Pygmies, they, along with Rhinopotamus, are gone.

I arrive home to find Astrogirl setting out cartons of Chinese food. She smiles when I enter, warm and a little rueful, her teeth perfectly straight and shiny.

"I hope you don't mind," she waves a hand over the food. "Busy day."

"Of course not," I tell her, and we kiss. Astrogirl is still in her Astrosuit, purple and gold latex hugging every inch of her lithe form. There is the familiar feeling of her soft body pressed against mine, the smell of her platinum blonde hair, her pina colada shampoo over the vaguest hint of sweat, a good, sexy, active smell. I run my hands over her hips, massaging the spot on her side that I know is sore from a day of carrying around the Raygun that now hangs by the door.

"So tell me about your day," I say as I pull out a chair for her.

"Oh you know," she shrugs carelessly, so unrepentantly airy and girlish, despite her near invulnerability and super strength. My beautiful cosmos-hopping avenger. "There was a breakout on the Saturn containment station. No biggie. What about you?"

"Getting closer to that promotion." I tell her about the word that came down from the District Manager; that he liked my proposal for overhauling the HR department, that he'd been ribbing Mr. Drueger about how much paperwork I'd saved him, and how I seemed like exactly the kind of level-headed self-starter they needed to head up Institutional Accounts. I omit the details about Flob-O's suicide and my run-in with the Pygmies.

"Promotion or no promotion," she says, "my love for you is unconditional."

After dinner I unzip Astrogirl's Astrosuit and her nudity pours across me like sunlight. Every inch of her is smooth and toned, tanned, pert and nubile, her areolas in perfect proportion to her nipples. She laughs playfully as she unbuckles my belt and leads me by the front of my pants into the bedroom. We make slow, languid love, which crescendos with a simultaneous orgasm. Then we collapse against each other, her hair fanning over my face as her head fits neatly against my chest. Her breathing slows and she is asleep. I stay awake.

Our bedroom window is open a crack. A cool breeze blows through, goosing our curtains and letting in the moonlight. The pale blue light falls across Astrogirl's back and that's when I notice it, there, on her shoulder.

A constellation of acne.

Maybe my lungs are collapsed. Maybe I have a brain tumor. Maybe my eyelids have turned transparent.

I try to match the shallow rhythm of Astrogirl's breathing, but it just isn't happening. Something is wrong in me. WebMD diagnosed my condition as sleep apnea with ninety percent certainty. But I'm not overweight and I don't think my tonsils have grown back—I had them out when I was a kid and it was ice cream and movies with mom for a week. And anyway, maybe I wasn't even totally honest with the computer. Do I fall asleep and then wake up? Or do I never fall asleep at all? How am I supposed to tell?

Of course, the next question I should be asking here is obvious. What is sleep? At least that's what Dan Dawkins tells us to ask in his best-selling book *Can I Sell This? Twenty-Six Rhetorical Questions, and Answers.* I know this is a totally way out metaphor, but what if I was trying to sell sleep to myself? What is the defining characteristic of sleep? What is the hot button? The steak sauce? The big rubdown?

Dreams. Bad or good, wet or dry, lucid or the opposite of lucid—dreams are the saleable quality. They're the bubbles in the Coca-Cola. Dreams are how you know that you are sleeping or have slept. But me, I can't tell the difference anymore between my dreams and the shadows writhing on my ceiling, slowly bleeding into daylight. Am I dreaming about shadows and ceilings? Or am I just not dreaming at all and, therefore, not sleeping?

And golly, am I tired of having to ask myself these questions. What would Craig, Marcy, and Phil think? I bet they'd have a real good laugh at poor tired Dave the philosopher and then Phil would launch right into his spot-on Confucius-says routine, but if they only knew just how much this was nagging at me—the not sleeping, or the maybe sleeping—and how exhausted I feel and how much coffee I have to drink just to stay up and how much productivity that costs me in trips to the bathroom alone even though caffeine also suppresses the appetite and so most days I can just work right through lunch. Pretty soon they'll be talking about Dave the insomniac and everybody knows that you can't spell insomniac without maniac. Next thing I know I'm getting called into Mr. Drueger's office to talk about my home life and maybe I should talk to someone. Good luck keeping that from spreading all over the office, especially with big mouth Tina handling the psychiatrist bills at the benefits desk. Might as well kiss that promotion good-bye.

Now I really can't breathe.

I tiptoe out of the bedroom and downstairs into the kitchen where I fix myself a glass of warm milk even though it never puts me to sleep and tastes pretty gross to boot. At first, staring out the kitchen window, I don't even notice him. His skeleton face hovers out there—grinning at me with all his teeth, the two howling abysses that serve as his eyes flickering bemusedly in my direction. His billowing cloak of unearthly material culled from the nether regions of the shadowzone dances in the wind, the Bonesword slung over his shoulder glinting lethally in the moonlight. When I do finally pick him out of the darkness it is too late; Skull King the Crusader is already phasing into my kitchen.

"Hey buddy," he says as he settles his armored bulk before the breakfast nook. "Tough day?"

"Yeah," I say, feigning a yawn. "I was just about to turn in."

The Bonesword glows an unholy azure as it detects my lie. Skull King the Crusader fixes me with an impatient look.

"Come on, Dave," he says. "Don't bullshit with me."

He pats the spot next to him at the nook, his gauntlet loudly clanging against the marble.

"Hey, hey," I start. "You'll scratch it."

"Sorry."

I sit down next to him and let me tell you, I am feeling really inadequate. I find it hard to believe that I once did battle with Skull King the Crusader over the mouth of an active volcano or, for that matter, at the nexus of time. Hard to believe that we once formed an uneasy alliance to fight off the invading Ron-Demons. And a lot of good any of that did either of us anyway. Interdimensional Combat didn't even make Dan Dawkins' top 100 Resume Busters. Heck, suddenly I'm not feeling so darn inadequate. I mean, me, I've moved on. And here's Skull King the Crusader still acting all theatrical, still up prowling at all hours of the night. He doesn't know what real work is.

"So," I say, "to what do I owe the pleasure?"

I bet he can sense it—the cool, brusque aloofness in my voice, the kind of tone I can imagine myself using with a subordinate. I bet Skull King the Crusader can sense it and he realizes that carrying around an enchanted broadsword is no way to get ahead because he seems to deflate a little right there in my kitchen.

"I've been thinking," he begins slowly, "about the trees."

"What trees?"

"If a tree falls in the forest and no one is around to hear it, does it make a sound?"

I snort.

"Of course."

"You can't possibly know that."

"Look," I tell him. "You could set up a camera or a microphone or something. And then when you ran back the tape—"

"Okay. Okay, you're right. But what if a tree fell in the forest and no one was around to hear it and there wasn't anything around to record it?"

"There are satellites—"

"God dammit, Dave," he pounds his gauntlet on the counter, rattling the fruit bowl. His hollow eyes spark with coldfire. "Just forget it, all right?"

"Just trying to play devil's advocate," I tell him while shrugging innocently and feeling guilty. Even though there's no shame in putting the tough questions to your colleagues, I realize that maybe this was one of those times where my deductive reasoning should have taken a backseat to my earnest listening skills. I mean, here's poor Skull King the Crusader trying to have a moment, really trying to work something out, and I'm inhibiting him. If only I wasn't so tired and out of it, maybe I'd have picked up on the need in my old nemesis' voice but that's gone now, he's already drawn himself back into his cloak of shadows, staring churlishly into the distance.

"So," I begin, "you're feeling like a tree. Like no one listens to you."

"I heard about Flob-O," he says. "And Rhino dead too. The Pygmies dropping like flies."

I don't know what to say. How does he know about Flob-O?

"How long do the rest of us have before we end up like them?"

"I don't know what you mean."

"We're the trees, Dave."

"Huh?"

"If a tree falls and nobody thinks about it, does the forest stop existing?"

"Have you been drinking?"

"You're killing us."

"Look, it's getting sorta late here."

"What about Astrogirl?"

"What about her?"

Skull King the Crusader is glaring at me now and the Bonesword is glowing madly, so bright that outside the neighbor's dog starts to howl, so bright that it hurts to keep my eyes open.

Dan Dawkins says that the cubicle is a womb and that after the three "try-mesters" we'll all be birthed into prosperity.

Dan Dawkins says that a practical man never stifles his creativity, but that a creative man always stifles his practicality.

Dan Dawkins hates the term "grind."

Dan Dawkins says that realists never have to give up on their dreams.

Dan Dawkins is the author of twelve books and the CEO of the hugely successful DotCom.Com. He is widely credited with inventing such concepts as Hawaiian-Shirt Day and Take Your Daughter to Work Day. He lives in Seattle with his wife and two children.

*

My eyes snap open when Craig loudly clears his throat and, startled, I nearly spill my second cup of now lukewarm coffee all over my lap. He's leaning at the entrance of my cubicle, smirking.

"Resting your eyes, captain?" he asks.

"No," I snap, annoyed at my uncertainty. Was I? Did I blink or doze off?

He shakes his head, laughing.

"Christ," he says. "I don't know if I'd make it through the day here without a catnap. But, shit man, don't do it out here. Drueger spots you and you're toast. I usually catch a few with my buddy John."

"John?"

"Yeah, John. All the coffee you drink, I'd think you'd have met."

I stare at him.

"I sleep on the toilet," he says.

"Oh." I nod. "That's clever."

Craig squints at the stack of expense reports that I had been working on. Then he squints harder and next thing I know he's leaning over my shoulder.

"Who's this little guy?"

It takes me a minute to focus on what he's talking about, on the curls and loops and bubbles that I've drawn all over my expense reports. Though I don't remember doing it, there he is, Flob-O, in all his corpulent gelatinous glory. He capers stupidly across the top of the page, dancing and jiving and then, suddenly plummeting off an unseen cliff only to bounce safely on his expansive rear, rebounding off the footer and landing safely in Column C where he wipes off a single bead of sweat and then resumes his dancing. I never thought I'd see Flob-O again, not after his suicide and subsequent evaporation, but here he is, drawn by my hand, ruining my work.

"I had no idea you could draw," Craig is saying.

"I didn't—I mean, I must've done it when I was sleeping. I guess."

"Wow. You sleep-draw?"

I shrug.

"Well, he's pretty funny."

"That's Flob-O," I say, sounding maybe a little incredulous. "You don't remember? He used to work here."

"I think I'd remember if we had like some fucking gumdrop man working here, weirdo."

He looks over the drawings for a moment longer as I feel increasingly uncomfortable, wondering if Craig will report me or just start telling people that I draw in my sleep which, you know, I'm not even sure if I really do or not. But then Craig sighs and pats me on the back.

"You should've been a cartoonist," he says.

I shake my head. "I've got to redo these," I reply, crumpling up the reports.

"You know, I used to play a little guitar."

"I didn't know that," I tell him.

"Yep," he says, and then we're quiet.

"I got the promotion," I say as I close the door behind me, beaming at Astrogirl. Leaning against the counter while eating potato chips out of the bag, she is still dressed in the baggy cardigan sweater and khaki pants that she wore to work today. Her nametag says 'Carrie'.

"That's awesome," and she rushes over to kiss me. Her mouth tastes like salt and vinegar.

That night we celebrate with a box of wine in front of the television, laughing like crazy at that Charlie Sheen show, you know the one. I try to remember this great line about men and their lawnmowers, but I can't get the phrasing down and anyway, I'm sure Phil will have it locked and loaded for tomorrow, cracking people up in the break room. He's so great at stuff like that.

Carrie can't stop talking about how with my promotion we can move into a bigger apartment and she even drops some hints about me being able to realistically save for an engagement ring. Finally make an honest woman out of her—wink wink.

After the local news we retire to the bedroom for some promotion sex, but it's late and neither one of us can stop yawning. We're just yawning right into each others faces while I hump her until that dissolves into exhausted sighing laughter. So I roll off her and we say goodnight.

And then I'm at Hopecon, in the human resources department, filling out the forms for their highly competitive and super flexible retirement plan. There's a guy from HR interviewing me, asking me health questions, except that it's not any of the usual people I've dealt with down in HR—it's Skull King the Crusader. His salmon colored Izod polo and wrinkle-free slacks strain at the seams, pulled as they are over his suit of armor. Skull King runs me through all the basic questions on the LF-10 form and I answer mechanically, trying to figure out just what the heck he's doing here, crammed into that dorky outfit, the Bonesword's deadly glow reflecting dully off the soul-sucking taupe of this non-threatening, windowless, pointless little box of an office. What is he doing here, Skull King, larger than life and stuck in this little pen, filling out forms like some automaton? Why him? I wish it wasn't so.

"Well, Dave, we're almost set here. Just one last thing. We here at Hopecon, we realize that this might not have been your first choice. So, in no more than thirty words, what did you really want to do with your life?"

"What?" I say, this question throwing me. I lean across the desk. "That's not really on the form."

"Sure it is," Skull King replies, but he shields the form with his body. "It's in the Ambition and Wasted Potential section."

"Let me see."

He shields the form with a spiked obsidian gauntlet.

"Just think about it, okay Dave?" There is a note of alarm in Skull King the Crusader's voice. "But hurry up."

I try to remember, thinking back to college. Before that. I try to remember what I used to tell people when they asked what I wanted to be when I grew up. I try to remember what I'm good at, but the memories are murky, faded, and then it's too late because the ceiling of the office rips open and blinding light fills the room. In the distance, the sound of trumpets.

"You don't have to answer him," a booming voice calls down. Dan Dawkins descends from the ceiling, the heavenly light radiating from his body. He is wearing a sports coat and jeans. His hair is slicked back, his beard is perfect. He looks just like the picture on his book jacket.

Dan Dawkins grabs me by the shoulders. "There are childhood aspirations and grown up perspirations, Dave. Part of growing up is learning how to sweat."

"That's from your book," I mumble.

He shakes me. "Don't you answer his question, Dave! The hungry are always successful, but are the successful always hungry?"

Skull King shoots to his feet, shattering the desk with one mighty blow of his gauntlet.

"What does that mean?" asks Skull King. "What does that even mean? Speak like a person you fucking hack fraud."

"It's from my book," growls Dawkins. "*Are You a Winner: Or Is Your Wallet Getting Thinner?* Best-seller."

"You've accomplished nothing," Skull King bellows, his fury shaking the walls of the office. "Your books are ghost written by fortune cookies."

I feel very cold and that's when I realize it's because Dan Dawkins created a vacuum into space when he blew that hole in the ceiling. My breath mists in front of me and I can feel myself being pulled into the abyss. The sweat on my forehead freezes my eyebrows.

"Negativity is a cancer," Dawkins shouts as he teleports behind Skull King. "And proactivity is a skilled surgeon."

Maybe it is the business casual attire that slows down Skull King, because he doesn't even bother to turn when Dawkins snatches the Bonesword from its scabbard. Or maybe he is too busy staring at me, trying to impart some last bit of wisdom. But whatever lesson he has for me, I don't grasp it. It takes too long to learn, it doesn't rhyme, it isn't easy to memorize and, frankly, I'm too concerned with the vacuum of space.

Dan Dawkins lops off Skull King's head. Bone fragments and coldfire hiss against my face and ears. As Skull King decomposes into the carpet at an accelerated rate, Dan Dawkins hurls the Bonesword into space. All the while, he stares at me.

"The only capital punishment I know," he says, "is the lack of a progressive benefits package." Then, he glances at his watch.

I awake with a start. I must have been twitching like crazy, or moaning, because Carrie is propped up on her elbow next to me, her fingers working through the sweaty knots in my hair.

"What's wrong?" she whispers.

"A nightmare," I pant, my mouth dry.

"Oh baby," she nuzzles her face into my neck. "Forget it. They're only dreams."

POETRY

Karina Borowicz
"Mystery Piano Found Deep in Cape Cod Woods"

—THE CAPE COD TIMES, NOVEMBER 24, 2008

I didn't want to bother anyone.
Wanted to make music in the middle
of nowhere. Why is nowhere so hard to find?
And why are they taking away my piano?
The birds listened, the nuthatches paused
in their furtive wood-picking for my *Come Rain
or Come Shine*. As time went by
it wasn't so hard to imagine people
like that, faces tilted, eyes unlocking
their grip on things, people hearing the sounds
I made and liking it, people wanting
those pale notes, and every black note of me.

Long Time

Back in the old country when I was sitting
on the edge of it all I had a vision
brilliant flying shards of glass all colors
even ones we didn't know yet
and that *yet* was the key to everything
and everyone was part of it falling into place
falling falling even then on the darkened bus
that was headed to the capitol with the accordion and static
on the radio and the sky's soft palm
protecting our heads we've been falling
for such a long time now

Neon

The gas is a furnace of life

a sizzling assembly line of wings
and hair-like legs

I must have been put together like that
in a sudden burning string of letters

SHORT STORY

Robert Repino
We Have the Answer to the Apocalypse

The world was going to end at 11:36 that night. It would be very anticlimactic; the universe, due to some comical flaw in its construction, was simply going to collapse on itself at the speed of light. An international team of scientists had calculated it down to the minute a few months earlier so that everyone would have time to prepare. And people did their best to get ready, in all the sentimental ways that they thought were unique but really weren't: writing letters, going on pilgrimages, making peace with estranged kin, sleeping with exes.

But Wilma, the failed actress who was now the youngest bus driver in her school district—not to mention the only woman—refused to take part in any of these activities. While taking her middle-school passengers to the last classes of their unfairly shortened lives, she told herself that she didn't need to do all of those things because she had lived every day as if it had been her last, with plenty of disappointment but no regrets. It was only after she dropped off the kids that she admitted that she was fooling herself, and that now it was too late to make things right. When the world ended that night, somewhere in the middle of Jay Leno's monologue, she would be alone, and she deserved it.

And so the world got ready without her. The government mandated that the television stations only showed things that made people happy or sentimental. So *M*A*S*H**, *I Love Lucy* and *The Simpsons* came back to the airwaves those last few days, twenty-four seven. The folks at ESPN considered replaying Super Bowl III, the game in which Joe Namath guaranteed victory, but the government vetoed it on the grounds that Baltimore fans wouldn't like it.

Meanwhile, preparing for the end became a huge industry. Books, videos and movies appeared, all of which Wilma assumed were being peddled by the same assholes who had sold Y2K kits a few years earlier. Oprah, of course, had a special episode about coping with The End. Tee shirts asked, "Where will you be?" Churches claimed that God's kingdom was at hand, brothels advertised their product openly, and both earned record profits. There was the eventual backlash against all the hype, and many people declared that they would simply carry on as if nothing was going to happen. Either way, people seemed to be very accepting of the situation. The President declared the relative calm to be a sign that the human race, despite its failings, had truly achieved enlightenment as its end approached, and that we should all be proud.

This cheerful march toward Armageddon was made all the more ironic for Wilma because, right before it was announced, when she was at her most miserable over her breakup with her fiancé, Gary, she had read what seemed at the time to be the most depressing newspaper article ever. A stray, late season hurricane—coincidentally named Wilma—traveled up the coast and soaked the Northeast. In the aftermath, it was reported that a local cemetery had been flooded so badly that the coffins had floated out of the muck and had collected in a ghoulish mountain of corpses. The bewildered groundskeeper, a little Asian guy whose leathery hand held a nearly dead cigarette, had said it looked to him like the end of the world. It was so sad to Wilma. She couldn't stop imagining her own corpse emerging from the mud, with the hair and fingernails still inexplicably growing. There would be no one to put her body back into the ground, no one to arrange the flowers. It was as if news like this had sought her out to remind her that humiliations would follow her even into the afterlife. But then the real apocalypse was unveiled the next day, and Wilma wondered if anyone would care enough to help the poor man put his Humpty Dumpty back together again. She supposed that people had more important things to do now that the clock was ticking.

While everyone left behind the groundskeepers and bus drivers of the world to seek their destinies, Wilma concluded that people accepted The End because, deep down, it was what they had been hoping for all along, not for true love or picket fences or a 401K. People now realized that they had always been imprisoned in their lives, no matter what degrees they earned or money they made, and now they could finally rest. Wilma had come to this conclusion long before she took the bus driver job, long before she hastily shaved her head and quit her theatre program, long before Gary began fucking Susan.

www.blogland.com
Username: wilmakillsmiranda
Wilma's interests:
<u>General</u>: Television
<u>Books</u>: N/A
<u>Movies</u>: I used to eat sushi and watch movies with my roommate at Temple. We would splice the word sushi into the titles of the movies, so there was *Sushiblanca*, *Sushifellas*, *The Sushishank Redemption*. We used to think that this was original, but it probably wasn't.
<u>Television</u>: All day, every waking minute. Reality shows that my smart friends are embarrassed to admit they watch; sitting in my shorts on a hot afternoon and watching *Poltergeist II: The Other Sushi* in español, not feeling ashamed of it, because things are on their way out anyway, as I've known long before The End went prime time.

Wilma's Details:
<u>Status</u>: Single (thanks, Gary)
<u>Here for</u>: Nothing
<u>Hometown</u>: Baltimore, MD
<u>Occupation</u>: School bus driver
Wilma's Schools:
Temple University
Philadelphia, PA
Degree: M.A., Theatre
Graduated?: Dropped out, graduated—same thing!
<u>Latest Blog Entry</u>: May 19, 2:37 PM
If you're reading this, you should have something better to do on the Last Day. Haven't you heard the question: "Where will you be?" Looks like you're sitting on your ass. Then again, so am I. Welcome to the end of the world.

 I have nothing better to do either, as I just worked my last day, dropping the kids off at school. Some of them have been told by their parents that they're going to wake up tomorrow and that all of this hysteria will pass. The rest of them are smart enough to know that going to school is a waste of time, that this silliness about continuing with normalcy as if things were normal is bullshit concocted by the government to keep people from rioting or fucking in the streets. None of the kids said goodbye to me today, but they never have, so I didn't sweat it.

For some idiotic reason, my pit-stained boss asked me to return the bus after work. He wanted to have some kind of office party, but I don't see the point, and he's probably sipping coffee and eating stale doughnuts by himself right now. He never liked me anyway—he knew that I took the job because I dropped out of college. He was under the mistaken impression that I still held out hope of going back to school and being an actress. Little did he know that that dream was long gone, and that I'd be stuck in this job until the Apocalypse.

So I went back to the apartment and watched TV for a little bit, but that wasn't working out. All the stations are playing that schmaltzy crap when I'm in the mood for soul-crushing reality shows—or *Gilligan's Island*. I figured that since I had a vehicle for the day, I might as well drive around. But, with nowhere new to go, I ended up parked behind the school. There's a spot in the parking lot where I can steal wireless with my laptop, my last remaining item from my parents' house. Good thing I'm a woman, because a man who hung out here would probably get arrested.

But now I don't know what I'm up to for the rest of the day. If you're reading this, send me a photo. We can pretend that we'll go on a date, and then get married, if we only had the time.

If not, I might have to drive the bus over a cliff.

I'm serious.

I have the cliff picked out and everything. Just try me.

<u>0 comments</u>

Tired of typing, Wilma started up the bus and drove aimlessly. She figured that no one was going to place a comment on her blog, not even the pervert who had written several times about eating sardines off of her nipples. Even he was busy today.

She passed by two church revivals, a traffic jam of abandoned cars, a woman having sex with (or getting raped by) two men in the back of a pickup, and a cop smoking a cigarette and chatting with two teenagers as they looted Playstations from an electronics store. Apparently, not everyone had embraced the idea of carrying on as if there would still be a tomorrow.

No matter how much she tried to fight it, she couldn't help but wonder what Gary and Susan were up to. Susan, a transplant from the West Coast, was probably trying to talk him into splurging on some fancy restaurant or something. Perhaps

Gary was trying to muster the courage to ditch her, and play a final game of basketball with his little brother in his parents' driveway. That scenario made Wilma smile, as she first met Gary in an intramural game at Temple, in which she elbowed him in his stubbled chin by accident. They had been the only two sporty students in the theatre department and, once they started dating, they often made fun of their awkward colleagues. None of those nerds could run the pick-and-roll. Susan was just a joke then, a shallow bimbo with a trust fund, someone that Gary and Wilma giggled about in bed. Susan could only name one of the members of the men's basketball team, and that was only because, in her words, he had "nice eyes." Gary seemed to enjoy Wilma's viciousness in judging other people—even though, later, he told her that that was what drove him away.

This cheerful march toward Armageddon was made all the more ironic for Wilma because, right before it was announced, she was at her most miserable over her breakup with her fiancé, Gary.

The "roommate" with whom Wilma watched movies like *Gone with the Sushi* was in fact Gary. He had come up with the spliced titles. Watching TV was merely a diversion back then. She had other things to do—a life, one would say. But when Susan appeared at the auditions for *The Tempest*, wearing her low-cut black shirt that screamed "Fuck off, I'm getting the part of Miranda," Wilma could see what was coming next, almost like moves in a chess game. Susan got the part of Miranda, Gary was Fernando, and Wilma was one of the faceless extras, doomed to watch from the shadows all the shared glances and awkward fumbling of hands between the two leads. Susan's laughter angered Wilma the most. It was a semi-concealed snicker as she scrunched her freckled nose. Even worse, Gary couldn't hide the fact that he enjoyed hearing it.

The director, a guy named Bob who had interviewed Wilma when she first applied to the program, let Wilma know that he noticed the drama; he had seen it among the students virtually every semester since he took over the theatre department fifteen years before. He was a silly man with soft little hands that he clapped when making a point, and he had been Wilma's father figure since her arrival, letting her baby-sit his two sons every now and then. His favorite line when things were going wrong was, "No big whoop—it's not the end of the world."

Guys had always left her for the prettier ones, and she wanted to just accept that. So, when Gary told her that they had to talk, Wilma already knew what was coming. She even offered to leave the apartment, provided that Susan would take over her half of the lease. Gary seemed to resent her generosity, which Wilma in turn found irresistible. It felt even better to leave the voice-mail messages from Gary unanswered when he called to ask why she had dropped out of the program.

Even though she couldn't face Bob, leaving school made sense now that she had accepted that she was never really that good at the only thing she was ever good at. When news of The End came around, just a few weeks after Wilma had found a job driving the bus, it felt like a vindication of her decision to drop off the face of the earth. Watching the news that night, she saw images of people crying in the streets, hugging each other, cowering in the face of the future, while the cheerful news anchors spoke as if things would work out, right after this commercial break. Gary and Susan wouldn't get to enjoy each other's company for very long. Wilma took pleasure in thinking like that, until she remembered that there was a time when she never would have.

www.blogland.com
<u>Latest Blog Entry</u>: May 19, 5:22 p.m.
As I type this at the local library, where I parked the school bus after getting bored with driving around, I am tempted to tell you that you are living vicariously through the wrong person! Go search the people who graduated from your high school, or who like your favorite sports team, or who enjoy using butt plugs or something. Or, better yet, get out of the house and find something useful to do. And when you find it, let me know—I need some ideas, fast. T-minus six hours :-(

I have no one wondering where I am. No friends. I got drunk at the last party held by my classmates and puked all over the shower curtain while Gary and Susan made out on a pile of coats and purses. Meanwhile, my parents are in Baltimore. I left a goodbye on their voicemail—too tacky? Well, probably, but I think I did them a favor. I spared them the tedium of lecturing me again about the waste of a career I've chosen. I also spared myself the temptation of telling them that I now drive a school bus. So everyone's happy, I think.

My only victory of the day, which occurred just a few moments ago, was my decision to not pursue Gary tonight. I still indulged in fantasies of finding him and then refusing to accept his apology for leaving me. (There is still a part of me that's holding out hope that he's reading my blog right now, however. Hey, I'm a weak human being. Give me a break.)

The librarian—and she looks every bit the part—just told everyone in the computer room that the library closes in twenty minutes, so we should wrap up. I asked why—not to be a smartass, I just didn't see the point in kicking us out when there wasn't going to be a tomorrow. Hell, we could re-create *Fahrenheit 451* in here and it wouldn't matter (Don't worry, I didn't say that out loud). She looked like she didn't understand the question, so I asked it again. Then she ran out of the room crying.

The other folks in the room glared at me like I was the biggest asshole in the world, and who I am to tell them they're wrong? There's a fat guy in a tracksuit who's still looking at me over his shoulder. What? Turn around, fatass. Okay, he finally did.

I guess I've been expecting my life to be like this for so long that I ended up wanting it to be this way. Some people are just good at wrecking things, at separating themselves from everyone else. My life is one self-fulfilling prophecy after another. Why can't I be so damn self-aware when I do something good? I know (believe?) that I've done something worthwhile in this life—why can't I sit back and reflect on that, and how it defines who I am and all that, instead of wallowing in moments like making the librarian cry?

. . . Okay, that's it—I know a quarry out on Route 1, right outside the city. I could bust through the gate, ramp this fucker right into the crater. Maybe there'll be an explosion, Hollywood-style. Bye bye, Wilma.

Only you can stop me.

<u>0 comments</u>

Wilma sat shaking at the keyboard for a while, past closing time. It turned out that the librarian who had given her twenty minutes fell into the "let's-pretend-everything-is-going-to-be-okay" camp, whereas the other librarians did not. So Wilma was free to sit in the wooden grade-school chair and relive all of her mistakes for as long as she wanted.

And after she moved past Gary, and giving up on the theatre program, and severing her ties with her family because they never seemed to approve of anything, she moved on to the future—or what was left of it. Driving the bus into the quarry was starting to sound good. She hadn't contemplated suicide since she was fourteen. Back then, it was just a fantasized escape from high school, something she hoped was normal. Now it was something real. Thanks to all the tee shirts asking where she would be at The End, death had become a tangible thing, a boring given; it was no scarier than talking about next Wednesday.

Maybe suicide would be her only concrete triumph in this sea of failure. If only there was a way to make Gary and Susan know about it. They shouldn't be able to escape feeling guilty just because the world was coming to an end. But still—wouldn't it hurt to be in a crashing bus? And what if she didn't die right away? What if she only broke her back and then spent the rest of the day sitting in the bottom of the quarry, imagining Gary and Susan until the end of time? Maybe she could just connect a hose from the tailpipe to the driver window, seal up the bus, and go to sleep. Was there a hose around here? The library had a little garden in front, so there had to be a hose somewhere.

She was breathless, both horrified and exhilarated at the thought of doing herself in before 11:36. Standing up, she realized that she wasn't ready to go through with it yet, so she sat down again. Instead of relaxing her, it only brought more frustration. She had never been offered such a clear-cut choice in her life, and she was still failing to decide. Pathetic. She punched the table, making the keyboard chatter and the monitor shake. No one in the library said anything to her.

Shaking her head, staring at nothing in particular, she caught sight of a small change on her computer screen. It was the change she had trained herself to look for ever since she started this stupid, self-indulgent blog, but which almost never came.

Under her latest entry, there was a link waiting to be opened: <u>1 comment</u>.

Clutching the mouse with her sweaty hand, Wilma moved the arrow over the words and clicked. A new window opened to reveal this: "The end is the beginning is the end is the beginning is the end is the beginning. **Hey, <u>Wilma</u>. Don't go out before The End. We have the answer to the Apocalypse.**"

There was an address out in the suburbs underneath, then that phrase "the end is the beginning is the end" repeated indefinitely for as far as she was willing to scroll down.

Wilma didn't like the way her name appeared to be simply plugged in there, like some form letter. But this was what she had been asking for. The idea of dying alone in the bottom of the quarry popped in her head one more time, and then she pushed it away.

The streets were crazier now that the sun was beginning to set. There were no cops anywhere, and the store where she had seen kids looting video games was now on fire. A brigade of streaking college students—co-ed, mind you—ran along the side of the bus for a few blocks, slapping the door and screaming in voices that were either threatening or celebratory. Wilma couldn't tell. An old man wearing what must have been his soldier's uniform in World War II or Korea walked down the street in front of some overturned cars and shot a rifle into the air. Wilma watched as he got into a shouting match with some kids wearing black bandanas over their faces. She looked away, but what came into her view now was a vendor's hot dog stand, flipped over so that the wieners were spilt on the ground. A pair of feet stuck out from behind the stand, and two guys wearing football jerseys reached inside to pick out some soft pretzels. They caught Wilma staring at them and shrugged their shoulders, as if to say, What are you gonna do about it? Then Wilma heard gunshots and screaming coming from the direction of the old man. She floored the gas pedal. Funny how protective she was just minutes after considering driving off a cliff.

Soon she left behind the fires and the makeshift roadblocks, one of which she had to plow through with the bus. The address was about a mile into Delaware County, not too far from the quarry, on a street that ran along the stone wall of a cemetery. It took Wilma a few passes before she realized that the address was in the graveyard itself.

She pulled the bus into the gate. There was darkness at first, but soon more fires became visible, illuminating the trees and making the tombstones glow. There were people here and there: a couple holding hands, a man barbecuing in front of a mausoleum, a pair of kilted men playing bagpipes in front of a grave that read, "McCullough." One of them waved to Wilma as she drove by.

She felt as if she had been here before, even though she knew that was impossible.

The road led to a main thoroughfare, lined on either side by torches and marked in a giant pink arrow, drawn in chalk, wider than her bus. People were everywhere now, wandering among fields of old tombstones, many with the names worn away. There were small ones for dead babies, tall obelisks for important men, statues of angels with broken noses, rows of generic stones for poor families that just said "Mother" or "Brother." They were all chipped and cracked, and had turned green over the course of a hundred or more Pennsylvania winters. It was a godforsaken part of the cemetery, with dead trees leaning toward the brown grass.

Wilma cut the engine and watched as the people walked among the headstones with clipboards, recording the names. A construction truck with a giant digging arm scooped up dirt in front of the crooked tombstones. Soon after that, a group of five people carried a mud-caked casket over to a hole and gently lowered it in. The truck then pushed the soil over it, and the "pallbearers" placed flowers on the mound.

Wilma could see the scene being repeated all around. There were flowers in every direction, their bright colors seeming to glow amidst the desiccated grass. People took the flowers from the back of a dump truck that was brimming with daisies and roses and other blossoms; the local florists had probably thrown them out after Mother's Day. The people rested the flowers, a few at a time, at each freshly filled grave. They were so delicate about it, and even seemed to be praying or whispering something to each of the dead people as they passed.

Wilma opened the door and heard music. As she stepped out of the bus, she saw that a makeshift band was playing something she had heard before—it took her a moment to realize it was the end of "Crazy Little Thing Called Love." Following the applause, the band began playing some rap song—"Baby Got Back"—before breaking down in laughter and trying something more manageable by the Beatles. There was laughter everywhere, in fact. The tall shadows cast against the faded tombstones were not threatening, but instead danced in the orange light, calling to her.

And then her eyes caught sight of what at first looked like a pile of concrete slabs. But they were coffins, she realized, the same ones that had been dislodged during Hurricane Wilma. Just like the photo from the newspaper a few months before, the caskets had gathered at the tree line beyond the tombstones. The evergreens had stopped them from sliding completely away. People were carrying the coffins back to the graveyard for reburial.

A man stepped toward her, a short Asian guy of indeterminate age, wearing a black tee shirt and jeans with holes at the knees. His bare feet were stained green by the grass and a cigarette wiggled in his lips. He smiled as he approached, and his glasses reflected the torches and small fires nearby.

Wilma wasn't surprised when he said her name.

www.blogland.com
Latest Blog Entry: May 19, 10:42 p.m.
The end is the beginning is the end is the beginning is the end. I still haven't figured out what that means, but I guess it sounds cool.

Liu, the stranger (yet not a stranger—more about that later) who invited me here, put me right to work. He's been at the cemetery for years, and was given an insurmountable task that, he now realizes, he was never expected to finish: creating a map of the old section of the graveyard, complete with a catalog of names of the dead, some of which cannot be found except by matching up the burial plots with ancient records. Then the hurricane destroyed everything, making his job even more complex.

When The End was announced, Liu started recruiting people from the Internet to help. And people came. Liu knew just who to look for: those who had no one to see tonight, those who felt they had a debt to pay to people who no longer wanted them around, those who could not answer the tee shirt's question, "Where will you be?" The bodies at the cemetery comprised the only family Liu had known for a long time, so there was no question about his plans for the last day.

These dead folks that we are helping are just grateful, he tells us. They're grateful with no baggage attached. No Gary/Susan bullshit here. This is the only purely good act we could hope for. Sure, a few people turned right around when they found out why Liu had brought them here. For good reason, I guess. But there are some good reasons to stay as well, which is what I did.

I guess, in all this time, I've been lamenting the fact that no one cared about me, and had forgotten how good it felt to care for others, even if they're strangers . . . and dead. Oh, god, that sounds like a Hallmark card—except for the dead strangers part—but I can't bring myself to delete it, so just pretend you didn't see it if you're too cool for crap like that.

No matter. Now, with our work done, this graveyard is a garden, and the dead are at rest again, and so are we. The menacing trees are feeding the bonfires, and flowers are covering the dry grass. We sit among the flames, recline against the stems and petals, watch the smoke rise against a backdrop of stars. I get the feeling that most of us haven't seen anything so beautiful in a long time, or if we had, we didn't know it, or didn't care.

Somehow, I'm still getting a signal out here, and I'm hoping that my computer's battery lasts until The End. Liu says it will. I've already figured out that he's the pervert who's been posting comments on my blog over the last few months, and he tells me that, yes, it was him. Oh, well—his fascination with "the pissed off actress-turned bus driver" is what brought me here, so I can't complain. He also says that I shouldn't have shaved my head, because the photo in my blog profile is much nicer. I tell him I'll have to let it grow back then. Oh, wait, we might not have time for that. He laughs at this.

I can't say that it's all perfect. Gary and Susan crept into my head a few times while I was cataloging names and placing flowers, and there was even a little sadness when we were finished, and we knew that there was so little time left. There has never been enough time. But I feel good at the moment, so good that I only have two things left to ask for: first, that those people who are stuck at home can read this and, at least for a moment, not feel alone anymore. And second, that we all keep this feeling for at least the next hour. That way, as the fires die down and the flowers grow cool to the touch, we'll still be wishing at the last moment that there will be a tomorrow.

<u>519 comments</u>

SHORT STORY

Faye Reddecliff
The River

In the harsh mid-day light, heat shimmered above the asphalt road. It filled the small store crowding out the air. The two women were on opposite sides of the worn wooden counter.

"It's a hot one, Lily. I don't remember it ever being so hot." Dorothy Burnell, on the customer's side of the counter, produced a handkerchief from underneath her belt and wiped her forehead. Perspiration made a dark v-shaped stain at the neck of her housedress and small half-moons under her arms.

Lillian, the store owner, longed to return to the cooler back room but Mrs. Burnell seemed inclined to stay and, with the new store five miles down the road, it wouldn't do to offend a customer. Lillian finished bagging groceries and slid the bag towards the other woman. "Share a Popsicle with me, Mrs. Burnell? On the house."

"Don't mind if I do." Giving up all pretense of picking up the groceries, she settled one ample hip against the wooden counter.

Lillian reached a sweat-glistened arm into the ice chest; the cold raised goosebumps. The chest needed cleaning but she liked the mounded ice—pure white, peaceful. Then too, everything needed doing but, in spite of endless days, she could not bring herself to do anything.

"Is death different?" she asked Jack. Since her husband's death, she'd begun talking with him or really some new image she had of him. Conversations that never would have taken place when Jack lived, about how she felt or, more often, about her lack of feeling. It was a new, different Jack who considered her words, who was with her as old Jack never was. Dying allowed her to make him up.

Now, new Jack had no answer but the old Jack appeared, to raise a condescending eyebrow and then leave her.

Mrs. Burnell stared at the Popsicle Lillian held. "Grape's my favorite if it's all the same."

Lillian exchanged the orange Popsicle for grape, broke off half and handed it to Mrs. Burnell.

"Listen, I meant to stop in and see you right after Jack died. I told Tom I've got to get over and see poor Lily Dobryn. Poor soul with no family to comfort her."

"It's all right." Lillian thought of the waxen face on the white satin cushion. The heat was dizzying; she gripped the counter to steady herself.

"No, really. I know how you feel. If something should happen to Tom, God only knows."

"It's all right!" The words came out overloud, surprising both women.

Mrs. Burnell stared, the Popsicle half-raised to her open mouth. "Yes. Well, I didn't mean to upset you."

"Sorry, I guess I'm tired."

Lillian still held the counter; Mrs. Burnell patted her hand. "No need to apologize."

While Mrs. Burnell finished her Popsicle, Lillian straightened groceries on the shelves—a perfect line of Oxydol boxes, next to them the narrower line of Rinso and on the shelf below, the colorful Jell-O packs. As a child, while her father bent over the counter "figurin" or collecting groceries for a customer, she'd take whatever she needed from the shelves and arrange them on the floor, a circular wall with herself in the center.

The high-pitched hum of Mrs. Burnell's voice ". . . all alone here. You should move into town."

From somewhere behind her, old Jack spoke. "She's right. Remarry, Lil, you're still young enough. Find a man."

"I like being alone." Did she? What was it? Emptiness filled with store opening, closing, silence. Although she'd never been alone before, she couldn't really feel it. Just after her father's death, she'd married Jack. He was as silent as her father had been. Certain things had to be done, bills paid, clothes washed, orders placed, certain things said. It was only now she asked why? What was it all for?

"It's not good for you. I've been meaning to have you over but you know with a husband and kids . . ." Mrs. Burnell went on.

A diesel motor roared on the upgrade. The four o'clock Greyhound from Memphis drowned out the woman's voice. It slowed and stopped. Dropping off a package, thought Lillian.

"Someone's getting off." Mrs. Burnell had gone to look out the window.

From somewhere behind her, old Jack spoke. She's right. Remarry, Lil, you're still young enough. Find a man.

The brass bell above the screen door tinkled and a young soldier stepped inside. For a moment, he stood blinking in the dim light, his khaki uniform wrinkled and creased as if he'd slept in it. He dropped an army duffel bag to the floor and nodded at the two women. Then he walked slowly around the store, picking up and examining groceries as if he were in a museum—a bottle of catsup, strawberry preserves. Nodding to himself.

He was looking in the ice chest when Lillian spoke to him. "Looking for somethin' in particular?"

He jumped as if startled from a dream. "No." He looked at Lillian, eyes open, assessing, not guarded. "Jest looking." Then he continued to stare at her, as if he'd forgotten she was a live person, a person not to be stared at like a can, or bottle, but a person owed an explanation.

"Why do you keep starin'?"

"You're right pretty but you're too pale. Like not altogether here, ma'am."

Lillian blushed, pleased and stung at the same time.

"Mind your tongue, mister. We don't hold with that kind of talk." Mrs. Burnell spoke.

"Wait a minute." Ignoring Mrs. Burnell, he came up to the counter. Behind him, Mrs. Burnell gestured at Lillian with her eyes and head. "I would like a Royal Crown Cola." He spoke the words as he'd handled the groceries, as if each had special value.

"That will be . . ." Lillian gave the transaction as much weight as he did.

From a handful of change, he lay a row of coins on the counter, one by one, then took his time choosing a bottle from the cooler. Before opening it, he held the sweating glass against his forehead then touched it to each cheek.

"Anybody been looking for Raymond Lowell?"

"Nope."

"Who you expecting, boy?" Mrs. Burnell spoke to his back.

He took a long swallow from the bottle.

"Where are your folks coming from?" Lillian avoided Mrs. Burnell's eyes.

"Who said anything about folks coming?"

"Wellll . . ."

"Nobody's coming."

Lillian considered for a moment. "You did ask if anyone was looking for you."

"Just wanted to put my name out here. You know? Just put my name out." He looked at her hard, challenging her to dispute it.

"Whereabouts you from then?"

"Just down the hollow." He took another swallow. "Bout three miles out."

"Thought I knew everybody in the hollow. Don't know folks name of Lowell, don't know you."

"Don't know everybody then, do you."

"Guess not. But I sure don't know why not. This is the only store within ten miles." She remembered the new store. "Once was."

The boy shrugged. Then nodded and went outside to sit on the wooden bench and stare down the dusty road.

Mrs. Burnell leaned across the counter, "What do you make of that?"

"Nothin'."

"Maybe he deserted, run away, or worse."

"Why do you say that?"

"Read your paper. Happens all the time. He could be a murderer."

"Ha! A murderer." Lillian jerked her head in the direction of the small figure.

"Who is he then? What's he doing here? He's a smart aleck for starters and God knows what else. You best lock your door tonight." As she left, she looked back over her shoulder at Lillian, "Just you phone us if you need to." Then, looking at the boy, "and Tom'll be right over."

Lillian finished the afternoon unpacking cartons and filling shelves. Listening, watching for the new Jack, the Jack she could talk to, who would hear her, understand her. Finally, in the heat and tedium, she gave up the work and the search for new Jack; it was time to close the store.

When she went to lock the door, she saw that the soldier still sat staring at the trees across the road. Bent over, elbows on knees and head on hands, he looked too young to be a soldier, too small. She went outside to stand beside him.

"You know you been sitting here over an hour?"

"That right?" He shifted position to stare down the dusty road, stiff-shouldered, proud.

Lillian noticed that with his head bent forward the back of his neck looked thin and vulnerable. Scrawny, like a chicken's stretched out and running.

"I'm going to close the store and make some supper. You're welcome to come in for a bite."

Old Jack spoke: Don't be foolish, woman.

The boy said nothing.

"Suit yourself." She'd done all she could. Anyway, there *was* something odd about him. Was he waiting for his folks or wasn't he? If he wasn't, what was he doing here? Maybe giving him supper wasn't the best idea.

She padlocked the door and was walking away when he rapped on the window and gestured for her to open the door.

"I reckon I am hungry if you're still offering."

"I guess I'm still offerin', Raymond."

He had been swinging his duffel bag up and over his shoulder. At Lillian's use of his name, he dropped it back into the dust.

"Isn't that your name?"

"I reckon it is."

"If we're going to have supper together, shouldn't I call you by name?"

He considered. "All right. What's yours then?"

"Lillian."

"Lillian. That has nice sounds, like water."

"Lillian," she said again to feel the sounds in her mouth. "Actually no one has ever called me Lillian." She heard her father's voice, "Lily!" and Jack's, "Lil, hon." Her mother, dead since Lillian was two, chose the name. Perhaps bending over the crib, she'd whispered, "Lillian." Perhaps the word, the sounds from her mother's lips had touched her, washed over and through her: Lillian. "What would you like to eat?"

He didn't hesitate. "Fried chicken."

"I have chickens," she said, pleased. Chicken was Sunday dinner for as long as she could remember. First her father then Jack regularly killed and cleaned a chicken each week. Since Jack's death, she just fed them and gathered the eggs to eat and sell. "Can you kill a chicken?"

He considered. "Never have but I don't know why not."

She led him to the backyard. It was dusk. Together they watched the chickens in the fading light. Most were heading up the ramp into the coop for the night. A Rhode Island Red and a Barred Rock still pecked and scratched in the dust, oblivious of the two watchers.

This part, choosing the one to die, was Jack's. For her part, she'd fed the birds and cooked them and tried not to think. Sometimes a memory came unbidden: her father walked ahead of her, a dead chicken, Henny Penny, dangled from one hand; she, six years old, followed him her eyes on the trail of translucent red, dust-edged pearls. Seen through heat and tears, the drops of blood shimmered.

Raymond spoke without taking his eyes from the chickens, "What do you do? Hit them with something?"

"No. Wring the neck."

He stepped into the yard between the two remaining birds and the ramp. The Barred Rock ran off squawking but the Red stood frozen. Man and bird staring at each other.

The word *stop* rose and stuck in Lillian's throat, died.

Raymond crouched and lunged in one smooth movement. When he straightened, he held the rigid chicken with both hands. With one finger, he stroked the feathered neck. The hen relaxed, one beady eye fixed on Raymond. Lillian stared too, at Raymond. Nothing in his face changed but she knew when the bird was dead.

As she cut the cleaned chicken up, he walked around the small room, staring at things. "No photos."

"No, we don't. . . . I don't have a camera. No need for photos."

He slipped a worn wallet from his back pocket and as she stood frying chicken, he held out pictures for her to see. A thin blonde woman in a sleeveless dress squinted out of a much-creased photo. "Your wife?" she said, surprised to think of him married.

"Nah, I'm not married. I'll tell you. . . . I got these, all of them and more, from a woman selling things by the side of the road. In Illinois right outside Chicago. A fat old leather photo album filled with people."

She looked from the pictures to him but he stared only at the faded images he held.

"Can you figure that? Someone selling their pictures?"

"No." But she found it harder to imagine someone's buying them.

"You married?"

"No. He died."

"No pictures. Funny, huh. Me with pictures but no wife and you a husband but no pictures."

Lillian tried to think what it might mean.

He looked at the plate she sat in front of him. "This is nice." He turned the plate for a moment, admiring it from different angles and then began to eat. He examined each forkful and chewed slowly, silently . . . smiling, not at her, but at something only he could see. In the silence, she could hear the crickets.

Jack had eaten quickly, noisily chewing with small grunts of satisfaction. Usually, she turned on the radio to shut out the noises which made her feel lonely, excluded. Now, sitting across from the strange boy, she felt comfortable with the silence.

He pushed the plate away and leaned back in his chair, "That was a good supper, Lillian. I thank you." He stretched. "It feels good here. But I gotta be going. Got to catch a bus."

"What are you talking about?"

He stood up.

"What bus? The only bus tonight is the nine o'clock to Memphis."

"That's it."

"But you just came from there."

He shrugged again, his mouth tight.

"Do you just ride around?"

"When I'm on leave."

"But just riding around . . ."

"It's not bad. Chicago, New York. Big cities like that, I stay in the bus station. Get something to eat then catch the next bus. New York's got long benches like in a church. Small towns are best though. Pretty, like this."

Lillian looked around. Wondering what he'd call pretty. "Why don't you go home?"

"Ain't got one."

"Must be from somewhere."

"Everybody's from somewhere. That don't mean it's home." He spoke slowly, a teacher to a slow student.

"Don't you get lonely?"

"No. You can be alone and not lonely with strangers."

Something about that caught her. She realized she thought just the opposite—you could be lonely and not alone.

"It's like you're on your way somewhere—don't think too hard about the somewhere and people make it up for you. They see the table set and a family all smiles and hugs and hellos with a dog maybe, waiting for you."

"Oh." She didn't really understand. Looking at him, he didn't look at all like someone on his way home.

He continued the dream. "They'll put an arm around you. Say things like 'Bet your folks'll be glad to see you.' or 'Let me buy you a piece of pie, son. Not like what you'll get when you get home but maybe it'll hold you.'" He looked down at his plate. Then glanced up again. "It's as if it were real. As long as you don't ever get there." For a second, he met her eyes; the intensity shocked her. He looked quickly away. "What's this place like?"

What was it like? She tried to think, to understand what he would want to know. "I don't know. It's pretty quiet. Summer's hot like now, winter's cold."

"I like the trees."

"There are a lot of trees." Then, inspired. "Would you like to look around? There's a path in back. Goes down to the river. There'll be another bus."

"Ain't that the truth." He smiled and the smile caught her, relaxed her. She laughed.

"That's something I might like to do."

"Maybe you'd like to go for a swim, cool off."

She hadn't been to the river since Jack died and seldom went there while he lived. She had memories of it from when she was a child. The vine swinging out over the dark, swift flowing water, the boys daring her. The ache and pull on her arms as she clung to the vine. The fear and the longing to let go—to swing out and let herself drop into the cool dark below but she clung to the vine on the river bank.

"No swimsuit."

"You could skinny dip."

The boy blushed.

"No one would see you."

He said nothing.

"You could wear a pair of Jack's shorts. I've been meaning to get rid of them." Before he could answer, she was in the bedroom, digging through a drawer she hadn't opened since Jack's death. "Here. These should do."

He took the baggy shorts, holding them at arm's length as if uncertain what to do with them.

"Take them in the bedroom. Try them on."

Minutes later he came out. It was as if the uniform had been a shell, part hollow. The ribs of his chest showed, the narrow shoulders curved forward. Like Jack's chest, in the end, as he lay on the bed struggling for breath. The thinness and the struggle, the only sign of the disease inside. But this was a boy's chest not yet filled out. Jack's was a man's chest. A dying man's chest. The shorts hung loose hiding the boy's sex. Still he blushed as she looked at him.

"Aren't you going to get ready?" he asked.

She hadn't meant to go along. "The path goes right to the creek. You can go alone."

"Come on. I guess I'd like company." He waited. "Wouldn't you?"

She listened for Jack's voice, old or new, but nothing came. Outside it was growing dark, cloaking the familiar in vagueness and uncertainty. She felt a twinge of fear. "Just follow the path," she urged him.

"Come on! I ain't afraid and you live here. You belong here."

Without speaking, she opened the door to look out at the woods. She realized she had never been to the river in the dark. All the years she had lived here. She wanted to go with him, to see the woods and river through his eyes. "All right. I won't go swimming but I'll go along."

She led the way down the cool mysterious path cushioned with years of pine needles. Overhead, treetops created a domed ceiling, sieved with moonlight.

At the edge of the river, he whispered to her. His words coming from behind and above like the soughing of the wind in the trees. "Take off your shoes," he whispered. "Feel this river mud with your toes."

She understood and slipped her shoes off.

He came from behind her, touched her shoulder as he passed and took two quick steps into the river. "It's warm, nice. Come on in."

As she stood, wavering, the soft night entered her, filled her with serenity.

"You're missing something." He waded further out and then, with a little jump, slid into the river.

She felt abandoned. As though, he'd gone on to something better and left her. She strained to see him in the silver water, turning to wherever she heard splashing.

He called to her. "Come on in! We'll be night fish!"

"I don't have my suit."

"You can skinny dip!" he answered.

"That's okay for you . . ."

"It's too dark to see anything. It'll be okay."

The idea of stepping into the dark water, without clothes, appealed to her.

His voice floated over the water. "It's like silk, warm silk. Come on, Lillian . . ." Finishing her name under water so that it came out a soft gurgle.

"I'm afraid."

"Of what?"

"I don't know. Snakes maybe." Snakes moving just beneath the surface, hardly causing a ripple until the strike. And the darkness, the unknown. Nothing to enclose her. She shivered and hugged herself. Then shook herself.

"Don't worry about things you can't see and don't even know if they exist. You could be stuck forever."

The silent cancer moving invisibly until it was too late. Where was he, old Jack? Why wasn't he with her? "How deep is it?"

"It's not too deep," he called. "Anyway I'm a good swimmer. I could pull you out."

"Oh, Raymond, I long to."

"Then do it."

She began to undress. Shivering in spite of the warm air.

The water was warm but the mud that oozed between her toes was cool. She stepped carefully remembering the bottom dropped off suddenly.

"Mrs. Dobryn!"

She stopped.

"Lily Dobryn! Are you down there?"

It was Steve Roddin, the sheriff calling to her from behind the store. Mrs. Burnell must have called him. She could see the white of her slip on the bank. She still had time to get back to dress. If Steve came down the path to the river, he wouldn't find her naked with a young stranger. Behind her she could hear the soft regular ripple of water. Raymond must be treading water, waiting. Maybe just feeling the water, looking at the sky, being.

"Lily!" The voice was nearer. Steve was coming down the path. Another, closer voice, old Jack's—stern and harsh: foolish woman. The sheriff's flashlight cut jerky swaths in the velvet dark.

"Come on, Lillian." A whisper like wind on the water, "Let go." The boy? New Jack's voice? Or her own?

She turned and reached for the river, surprised at her own grace, and stroked her way towards the center. The moon slid behind clouds and with the deeper darkness came fear.

"Raymond?"

Silence.

She jumped when he swam up behind her; his fingers caressed her shoulder. At the gentle touch, she relaxed. He moved to face her, his eyes dreamy, studying her from afar. Raymond closed his eyes. "Taste that night air," he whispered. "Feel it touch your skin."

She felt in spite of herself and shivered.

His hands closed around her throat then slid to her shoulders. Leaning towards her, his weight pressed her down. The water closed around her neck and lapped at her chin. Opening her mouth to speak, "Raymond . . ." she tasted the river—dense, full of mud and decay.

Lillian! Her own voice. She gasped and began to flail, her hands slapped the water then found and pushed hard at his relentless hands on her shoulders. She fought to keep the dome of sky overhead, the sensual touch of the breeze on her wet skin, and the soft lapping tongues of the river. She fought for her life.

His hands relaxed, and she surfaced gasping for air.

"I just give you a present." His lips were against her ear. Exhausted she let her arms rest on his shoulders. "Not pretty and wrapped up with ribbon, but the best present anyone ever give you." He opened his eyes to look at her. "You know that."

"I might have drowned." She insisted.

He shrugged. "That would have been a different present. You picked."

A flashlight beam raced across the water searching for her, falling short, then touching her. The light seemed harsh to her, painful.

"Are you all right, Lily?" The sheriff called.

"I'm all right! I'm fine. Turn the light off, it hurts my eyes!"

The light went out. "You come on in so I see you're okay."

Guided only by moonlight now, she turned and began to stroke to shore, stretching and turning, all of her body aware of the water's touch. The soft sounds of water and her name, Lillian, sounding like water. The voice, her mother's? Jack's? Her own.

She expected Raymond was following her, gracefully without a sound. As she waded out of the river, the sheriff held out a hand to her. "I'm all right really."

After a quick glance at her nakedness, he turned his back, took off his jacket, and handed it to her without looking at her. Its warmth and roughness felt good against her skin. She turned to stare at the river, looking for Raymond, deciding not to tell that he'd nearly drowned her. Had he really meant her harm? "Where is he?"

"Where's who?"

"Raymond. The stranger. Didn't Mrs. Burnell tell you?"

"I ain't seen Mrs. Burnell. What was she supposed to tell me?"

"I thought she told you to stop by."

"No one told me to stop by. I just thought I would. Saw your house dark at this early hour and heard splashing in the river. Just wanted to be sure you were all right." He stared hard at her, wondering. "So what about this person who was out there swimming with you?"

Lillian heard the humoring in his voice. "Raymond. A stranger stopped by the store."

"And you went swimming with him? Buck-naked, if you'll excuse me, Lily?" The voice gentle now, soothing, "There was only one of you out there. And that one was you."

Lillian stared at him. Did it matter?

"Maybe I could make you some tea. Maybe you should get to bed." As he spoke, he picked up her clothes.

She looked out at the river. Except for moonlight highlighting the moving ripples, it was dark, still, silent.

"I don't need any tea, thanks. Or maybe I do but I can make it myself." She wanted to be by herself but his kindness pleased her and she put a hand out to touch his, to soften her refusal. The warmth in touching another human shocked her.

She started back up the path with Steve behind her.

"You shouldn't stay by yourself like this, Lily. Mind does funny things."

"Lillian."

"Huh?"

"My name's Lillian. Call me Lillian."

"Sure. Lillian."

Humoring again, she thought. It didn't matter. What mattered was the moonlit leaf shadow, the soft cushion of pine needles underfoot, the rich full smell of woods decay, the night air, cool and soft and the thrill of joy it gave her, being there, being alive.

Far off, she could hear a diesel motor on the upgrade—the nine o'clock Greyhound to Memphis.

POETRY

Catherine Doty
The First Time I Was Told To Fuck Myself

If he was playing possum
he played well—cupped paws
curled in self-reference,
orange tusks in a head
shaped to divot the very air.
There, I'd been told, was a meal
for a smart black family,
with possum gravy, buttered grits
and biscuits, and something green,
long-stewed with salted pork.
And so I presented him (he was a him,
playing possum on his back
in the tallest weeds) to Roscoe,
our neighbor, kind Roscoe
who dragged home iron
and lengths of pipe,
and could be seen sinking
his dark hands into our trash cans.

Long after the ugly words,
the flying bottle,
long after this shame
grew blunted by other shames,
I carried with me that meal
I had envisioned, the fear
as I lugged that creature
by his tail, not that he might
be dead, but that he might
not be, might thrust up
his punishing head and slash
my hands, then zig into the traffic
of Marshall Street, never to waken,
headless, skinless, gutless,
in a perfumed and oily pan
on a bed of sweet roots,
to be praised and divided,
to be divided and praised.

Breathing Under Water

Florida's just a thumb on a jigsaw puzzle,
but under water the Weeki Watchee Mermaids
pour their tea, cook, exercise, iron clothes, guzzle
with muscular skill their Grapette soda,
with only occasional surreptitious sucks
on an air hose hidden in shell-studded scenery.
They grin, open eyes afloat in their blue-lit skulls.
Holding my breath was a skill I practiced, too,
like when I was ten years old and woke to a body
lowering onto my body, and a breath that put me in mind
of a rotten leg, a thing I'd seen in a book once
and which scared me, but not as much as this body
on top of my body, these jabbing fingers. I was wildly aware
that the room I was in was a pigsty, and I was a pig to be sleeping
in my clothes, and I wanted to blame it on someone, which
would have meant speaking, which I could not do—
it would have been too real—and I was too old to blame anyone
anyway. I closed my eyes to make the black world
blacker. The lamp was within my reach, and a railroad spike
I could easily have lifted, and also a bowling ball I'd found
on the tracks, but all I could think of was being ashamed

and dirty, and grateful the whole thing was happening
in black and white, like those mermaids on TV, their lips
and nails a black I knew was red, their long white legs
safely fused in their glistening tails.

Behind Bars

Look, the lion likes you,
was all I needed to hear,
that what drew him to the bars
was my good smell, me
in my string-shouldered playsuit,
little plaid sausage.

Today I read about my chiropractor,
how he stalked a forty-one-year-old
female patient, and threatened to ruin
her life with lies to her husband.
He didn't stalk me at all.
Or did I miss it?

How awful to squander attention—
the unresponsive so cool in their
tasty flesh, so vastly ungrateful.
I remember Doctor Byrd leaning hard
on my shoulder, leaving me at dusk
on a manic couch, under the vinyl
of which waves of punishing thuddings
might just be going to the root
of all of my pain.

It was not my meat that the lion's
gold eyes grew great for,
but the horse chunk in the tub
being hoisted past me, glittering
flies, I recall, in bright song
on its surface.

Sweet Ants

November 12, and still the ants are here,
still skirt the butter searching for the sweet—
a swarm round a drop of syrup draws a crowd
like a lynching did in my namesake great grandma's
time, when she fought to part the crowd to reach the rope
and pluck it for good luck for her unborn child,
but was elbowed aside and trampled and great uncle nameless
was born there and then in a pile of yellow leaves and dead
as the ants I thumb-smash or squirt with Windex, the ants
in their martial tracks on the kitchen tile, dispersing
like a family and its stories, thinning and reaching the cracks
where they disappear, an elapsed-time shot of the culprits,
an aerial view, in which each apocryphal tale equals every other
so that the great grandpa who somehow caught his manhood
on a plow and so bled to death is equal to the one who fiddled
square dances, or the aunt who first employed pink toilet paper,
and the nieces who could not resist its delicate beauty
and wrapped it about themselves and thus festooned climbed
onto their towel-draped chairs at Christmas dinner, or the Iroquois
ancestor dropping off her high cheekbones, or the many more
Irish with asses as flat as their faces, or those with religious

visions, or Uncle Jim, behind whose chair I lingered to study
his head, in which, I was told, there was planted a plate of steel,
which I thought might have matched the steel bowl
with its silly strap in the newspaper photo, which he wore
in the war in France except once when he didn't, because of which
now his heart was purple too—or my mother tripping on the dog
as she runs to the table, a pineapple upside-down cake
in her arms, which she hugs as she rights herself and how we
howl at the sight of her bulls-eye, pineapple-cherry-tipped tits, as ants
sweep in waves to the still-warm sugar-caked pan, drawn
like a hastening crowd to a flaming tree.

SHORT STORY

Ron Savage
The Cave at Elgon

He blew a full breath into the elephant's raised nostrils. Willie told me this dream on the morning he had left for the war. The elephant nudged his chest with its trunk and blew its own warm breath back at him. A grassy breath, Willie had said. Then he said, That elephant smelled better than you would think, Raye Ann. Dry mud was clinging to the elephant's legs and its gray palm leaf ears. The trunk became a hook and Willie climbed onto it. Riding an elephant is like being an old ship in a bad sea, Willie said. His dream had clouds that were dark and thready and lined the moon. These clouds became shadows along the silver ground. His legs straddled the elephant's neck while the gray palm leaf ears twitched against his knees and tanned skin. Willie told me the elephant followed sandstone footprints to a cave in the mountain. The footprints are a hundred thousand years old, he said. Africa is where everything starts and ends, Raye Ann.

Two Baluyia tribesmen just finished rigging a large white canopy with mosquito netting. This will keep the insects out while Willie and I have our breakfast. The Baluyia come with their own elephant, who is now eating dried grass in the shade of a nearby fig tree. It's an enormous but gentle creature named Imami which is Swahili for Faith. The original owner gave Imami to the Baluyia for killing the cheetah who killed the man's wife. Imami likes to wrap her trunk about my waist. Sometimes she gnaws gently on my forearm but she never hurts me. Willie says elephants raised among people enjoy the company of people.

We arrived at Mount Elgon two days ago. Willie always wanted to visit Africa. That started when he was a boy reading his dad's *National Geographic*s. The magazines were stacked in tall yellow piles against the garage wall. One of the Baluyia has begun setting up Willie's tan metal folding chair and a straw pillow for his feet. The Baluyia is a teenager and very thin and very dark and has a gold front tooth that can startle you when he smiles.

Willie and I don't speak Luwanga and the Baluyia don't speak English but I let them know what we need through the tour guide or I draw pictures for them in the loose gray dirt with my walking stick.

The canopy and mosquito netting stop the sunlight and the rain and the bugs but nothing can stop the humidity. The long rains come to Kenya this time of year, the cooler months of July and August. If you want the heat you have to come January through March. Nothing about Africa should be assumed.

Willie and I have been together since we were babies. Who else would we love and turn to but each other? Our mothers had been college chums at Swarthmore. They had married two Savannah men. These boys knew how to sell real estate, get drunk, and build homes; any order would do. Our moms rocked strollers and pushed swings on more Savannah playgrounds than either Willie or I can recall. I know the story of every scar on Willie McCray's knees. And he knows my scars and stories. We have gone though childhood diseases together and coughed on our first cigarette together. We endured grade school Christmas plays together and helped each other remember the words. You don't let that person get away easily.

Six months ago I thought Willie had been killed in Fallujah or Baghdad or somewhere. We had been married only a year. For half that time we were on different sides of the world. The army said he was missing in action. This is what the army tells you when a soldier doesn't show up for his or her mail and they can't find the body. I wrote them back and said, What do you mean you can't find my Willie's body? He is six foot three and a hundred and eighty-two pounds. How can you misplace a person that big?

Major Burgess D'Amico of the 72nd Airborne answered my letter. He thought my case was both sad and typical and promised to keep me updated weekly. The major told me Iraq was a confusing place and people got lost there more than anyone knew. He also hoped I would correspond often and write about whatever was on my mind and in my heart. At first I wrote to thank him and then I wrote to tell him what was in my heart. Most of my letters had to do with how lonely I felt without Willie boy. Burgess wrote back and told me he was a thirty-two-year-old career officer and a recent widower who lived in Asheville, North Carolina. The man is a born caretaker.

The two Baluyia tribesmen have also started a campfire with dried grass and cedar next to our canopy. There is coffee and the sizzle and snap of frying bacon, or something that smells like bacon. I have learned not to question the tour guide about the food we eat. I take Willie's advice and pretend I'm eating food I know.

Imami likes to wrap her trunk about my waist. Sometimes she gnaws gently on my forearm but she never hurts me. Willie says elephants raised among people enjoy the company of people.

I am imagining Willie sitting on his chair in front of me. His narrow, tanned face, his brown hair thick on top and clipped close to the sides, his delicate hands and long skinny legs, Willie will be handsome forever. He has on khakis and a white, open-at-the-neck shirt with the sleeves rolled just below the elbow. Sunglasses hide most of his face. I breathe in the smell of his spiced apple cologne.

The elephants go into the caves at night, Willie says. His slender finger points beyond the mosquito netting and beyond the blond kikuyu grass and the shrubs and the cedar and olive trees. He is pointing to Mount Elgon. This is an extinct volcano that the Maasai tribe calls *Ol Doinyo Llgoon* or Breast Mountain. And if that's what they think of breasts, I would not want to meet their mothers. Elephants go there for the salt, Willie says. They break the walls with their tusks and lick the rocks.

Elephants go there to die, too, he says. The cave is a graveyard, Raye Ann. Baluyia believe the cave is a gateway to an afterlife for the elephants. The salt is supposed to nourish them for the trip.

Tell me you're happy, I say. I am dressed for jungle comfort as well as sun protection. I wear big round sunglasses and a white straw Panama. Only my bright red lips and a narrow chin are visible. I say, Don't you love being here? Tell me this is the best surprise you've had since you don't know when.

I know what Willie would say. Absolutely, he would says. You know it is, hon.

We were upstairs in the bed when Willie told me his elephant dream for the second time. Or that's how I remember it. This was a good two months before coming here to Africa. Willie was looking at the white ceiling and smoking a morning cigarette. His face and arms were very thin and he hadn't shaved in two or three days. I remember this because Willie is usually a fussy person when it comes to his appearance. He was holding his cigarette between his index and middle fingers and the tips of his fingers were quivering.

Willie talked about the dream, what it was like to ride an elephant, the roll and sway of it, and what elephants were like up close. His elephant was in a herd with seven others. Willie said the herd smelled of hay, sweat and urine. Fine hair grew in tuffs on their heads and the rims of gray palm leaf ears. Mud from the morning baths had dried and cracked on the elephants and by the evening the mud became dust that lifted with the breeze and blew off each animal's back and sides. Willie's legs hugged the thick wrinkled skin. Every few minutes the elephant's trunk would appear and curl around Willie's arm or leg to calm and reassure him. Or that's what Willie believed. The herd was following the sandstone footprints to the cave.

Different elephants go to the same cave night after night, Willie said and took another deep drag off his morning cigarette. He said, I had to go with them, Raye Ann. That was the deal. I didn't get a vote. These particular elephants were going into the cave at Mount Elgon and I was going with them and that was that.

Why didn't you run or put up a fight? I wanted to know. Willie has a delicate look but that look has never fooled me. I said, You're a Savannah boy and Savannah boys know how to take care of themselves. I have seen you go at it five or six times, schoolyards when you were a kid, bars when you were older, at a bus stop and a bowling alley, and once behind First Baptist. This isn't like you, I said.

I knew what Willie would say. I knew it before he had said it. His words came to me too easily. You can't run from some things, he said and reached over to the amber tinted ashtray on the nightstand and snuffed his cigarette. Then he said, Some things you can't fight. Willie had a half smile that seemed more sad than happy.

What was Willie's life and what was Willie's dream had become confused in my mind. But I did not feel confused at the time. A person can look back and see how she or he could hear a dream as more sinister than the loved one intended. Or we might even believe a stranger's concern is a flirtation. Isn't that what we do? Don't we reinvent this or that to suit us?

I am under our canopy and looking through the mosquito netting. Sunlight comes and goes with the drifting clouds. Imami is still under the fig tree. The younger Baluyia has been feeding the elephant raw cabbage leaves. Imami will curl the tip of her trunk around the leaf. Twice the elephant has tapped the boy's head with a leaf before eating it. The younger Baluyia rubs Imami's trunk then shakes a scolding finger. I have no idea what the boy is saying but I'm guessing he wants her to eat her vegetables and stop fooling around.

The grassland is vast in all directions and ends at the base of Mount Elgon. The ground colors are green and gray and tan. Dense clouds are filling the sky. Rain may be coming down by the afternoon. The dust rises above the thornbrush and swirls in the humid air. That breeze brings the smell of feces and urine mixed with cedar and the hay scent of the blond kikuyu grass. My throat feels gritty from the dust and aches each time I swallow. Not too far off, maybe fifty yards, water buffalo graze beside a muddy pond shaded by bamboo. Animals and insects are everywhere.

Yesterday I saw a small dark bird perch on the snout of a water buffalo and pick insects from its nostril. This morning two female lions are laying on the grass under a Jackalberry tree. Their tails twitch away the flies. The lions are watching the water buffalo like two hungry old women. Africa is nothing a person can get used to.

Since Willie came back to me I try not to think about Major D'Amico, but the Major is on my mind today. What can a person do? Burgess is another good man, much like my Willie. I have burned all of Major D'Amico's letters. Well not all of his letters but most of them. I have burned what I saw as the inappropriate ones, the ones that pushed me to question my heart and the person that I loved. How could I begin caring for anyone else while my husband remained a misplaced body? Willie and I had gone through too much together for me to dismiss him when things were so undone. No, those particular letters from Burgess, the inappropriate ones, have become ashes inside our patio gas grill.

In Major D'Amico's last letter, or the last letter I had allowed myself to read and keep, the major had written, My dearest Raye Ann, please do not take this the wrong way but I have a confession. You remind me so much of my recently departed wife. Emily died of breast cancer last year. She had fought what my dad would have called, The Good Fight. She did it with more courage and poise than I could have ever managed. Both our fathers were soldiers, and I wish those two old boys had been alive to see Emily do battle, to see what she had in her. That battle lasted five years. The cancer would pretend to leave just to lure us into thinking her life was her own again. It pretended to leave to give us hope. We have a special hatred for our best enemies. We say they are bastards, or some name like that. This one had been the king bastard of all the bastards. It had its job and it wouldn't quit. Emily was such a tiny thing, five-two, a hundred and three pounds. In her college days she had been a U.N.C.

cheerleader. The girl the others cheerleaders loved to toss into the air. And God she was a beauty, curled, rust-colored hair, lavender eyes, a complexion pale and clear enough to watch the blood rush through her veins.

The cancer first took the flesh from her ass and her breasts. Then it turned her body into skin stretched on bone. I won't let this beat me, Emily had said to me. You will see, Burgess, she said. You know I'm not a quitter.

One of the Baluyia has set a wooden breakfast tray on Willie's chair. There are two fried eggs with large, dark orange yolks and four thin strips of charred meat and something that might be slices of yellow squash. Coffee in a tin cup is balanced on the chair beside the tray. Steam from the coffee goes thin and dissipates in a breeze. The young Baluyia places a tray with the same breakfast on my lap. He bows with his fingertips pressed together like it's a prayer, and grins. His gold tooth is still a surprise. I mimic his bow by nodding back to him and touching my fingertips together. People should try to get along. I look at the wooden breakfast tray on Willie's chair. My chest swells with a sadness I cannot name.

Six months ago I thought Willie had been killed in Fallujah or Baghdad or somewhere. We had been married only a year.

That morning in bed, when Willie told me his dream again, that was our first morning together since his return from the war. I had trouble listening to him talk about going to a cave on the back of an elephant. I kept picturing Willie standing on our front porch in his tan uniform and his black beret. A canvas duffle bag leaned against his leg. My lost and found Willie. The late afternoon sun hovered low and behind him. Our lawn was still wet from an earlier rain and the grass sparkled yellow. Willie looked as if he didn't belong to his clothes, the pressed shirt, the pressed pants. He was too small and too thin and too washed out. A veiny redness showed beneath his eyes. I kept saying, Willie. Willie. Willie. I said his name like it was a question I had to whisper. I couldn't stop touching him. My fingers were on his arm, his cheek, his hand. I felt tears on my face before I knew I was crying.

I thought you were lost, I told him.

*

The breakfast is good but I am not hungry. I eat a small bite of the meat and some yellow squash. The meat is charred and crisp and has a bacon flavor. The squash was fried in the pan with the meat and doesn't taste the way squash tastes in Savannah. I pick and poke at the sunny-side eggs. I finish with a sip of the coffee which is hot and bitter. My mother used to say I was the world's worst eater. She does not have to show herself this morning for me to hear the words.

What I want to do is go see the Baluyia's elephant who is still eating dried grass under the fig tree. I want to look into Imami's beautiful black eyes. I want to feel her warm trunk wrap around my waist. I want to inhale her grassy sour breath. This is a strange feeling for me but if I am close to her I know I will be safe. Even lions back away from Imami. She is the true queen of this grassland, this jungle, this Africa.

The moment I approach Imami, she offers me her trunk. I grasp its leathery tip in both my hands and blow a long breath into it. The trunk lifts then caresses my cheek. Grassy breath rushes over me. Hello there, old girl, I say and rub away the dried mud beneath her lower lip. I tell her, Why don't you take me to that cave. What do you say, old girl? I have things I need to see for myself. Imami's trunk becomes a hook and she extends it to me.

You have that same courage, Raye Ann. That's what Major D'Amico wrote. He said I had the same courage as his wife Emily. He said, I can tell this by your exceptional letters, what you have revealed of yourself. I would be honored to meet you in person and have a cup of coffee and maybe a sandwich. We could talk about your Willie and my Emily. Savannah isn't that far away. I have enclosed a photograph of myself and my cell phone number. I wait for your reply. With much affection, Burgess.

The photograph was of the major in his dress uniform. He had a round puffy face but a strong jaw. His eyes were a severe blue and stared right out at you. His eyes also had different emotions. I could look at the photograph and imagine Burgess angry, or sad and tearful, or lost. Sometimes I saw my Willie in his eyes.

Sitting on top of an elephant is frightening. I am shaking and I can't find my breath. My knees grip Imami's neck. My chest leans flat against the back of her head. I am holding the rims of her gray palm leaf ears. Imami's rocking stride is directed toward the mountain as if she has a sense of the urgency. Willie is so right, riding an elephant is like being an old ship on a bad sea. The two female lions under the Jackalberry tree see Imami passing them. The lions lift their heads for a good view. Imami curls her trunk and gives a bray that vibrates my chest. But she does not slow her gait. The two lions settle themselves back into the tall blond kikuyu grass. I hear the Baluyia behind me and calling, Missus! Missus! I don't think I can loosen my hold of Imami's ears to look or wave at them.

I want to go to the cave in Willie's dream. I don't know what is there for me but I know when I must do something and I must go to that cave. How can I not go? Willie and I have been together since we were babies. Who else would we love and turn to but each other? I know the story of every scar on Willie McCray's knees. And he knows my scars and stories. You don't let that person get away easily. The Baluyia are calling to me again. Missus! Missus! they say.

I loosen the grasp I have on Imami's ears and turn to look at the Baluyia. They wave their dark thin arms over their heads and shout to me in a language I will never understand. I see behind them, too. The scalloped flaps on the rim of the white canopy twist in a breeze that is warm and sandy. Beyond the mosquito netting are two metal folding chairs facing each other. Willie's chair is still empty, his breakfast untouched.

POETRY

Mary Rose O'Reilley
The Last

Not even a decrescendo, much less an ovation:
people die with the TV on, nurse changing channels,
the popular shaman-psychologist set to divulge
meaning after the next commercial.
                                    You look
over your shoulder: *why was it all such a fever?* you ask,
wanting to lie down again on the grass next to the boathouse,
old men fishing for sunnies, the dog beside you
smelling lightly of things she's rolled in—
but the nurse in green scrubs, yellow cord at the waist,
picks up the remote and, *nothing*. Think: the release
bodies offer: just home from the office, feeling
through silk office blouses distended veins over the milk ducts,
symbiosis of mother and child, resting at last
cosmic as Buddha, as if we just came here to feed.
What did God know of breaking the body? Something asleep
in the white cells of his human brain told him to eat.

And the dip of a red bobber, the pull of the fish,
algae splitting its millions of hairs in the lake, sun,
your skin hot: maybe you sleep with the line loose
in your hand.   The last time, I didn't know it was over.
Weaning is slow work; one day, without tears, the child's steps
bend away but you don't notice. You think there will be
another smell of her damp sparse hairline, another day.
Another child, maybe. Even last night, in a dream,
I thought I was bleeding again.

Who on the Greyhound, crossing Wisconsin,
has not envied the line of hill, lights from the barn,
love's body: the moment he gets into bed and files his long
frame into the rim of her ruining self?
                                What he remembers is
all that is left in the world. What she herself
has forgotten or not known: flesh landscapes he paints
in a mind she can't enter. Before they knew each other,
there were cloak rooms, galoshes, pencil sharpeners,

irregular verbs. Still they were moving toward sleep
in each other's arms, thinking they wanted some other thing,
maybe a cocker spaniel. Not marriage, close as one breast
bone can get to a spine, what they cannot remember
and, just as they slide into sleep, what they will not say.

Reading *Anna Karenina* on the Empire Builder

Just west of Williston, sky's the actor.
Buttes: prehistoric shrug of animals
letting it go, silt sifting down til
farm after farm climbed them and broke in its turn.

Nothing can live here: his voice in the dining car.

The border. My father's assessing glance
values each gold wire of my braids.
Twenty horn buttons fasten a wool coat
behind each button a coin.
No diamonds in my ears; they are sewn
into the pintucks of each sleeve.

Geese fly out of the slough. He regrets
the waste of space in their bodies
air sacs unoccupied; as they ascend,
their free flight. In the old photo, my sister's
querulous baby gaze. Holding her hand I felt
each pearl in her mitten fingers. Loud girls
on the playground talk softball, not watching
their things: what luxury. I look for hinges wherever.

Arithmetic books deliver the codes of Swiss banks.
Running for base, toes flinch from gold rings
under the pads of my shoes.

A junkyard full of old woodies, wrecked
school buses, double-wides. I want to stop here,
live in a burnt car. Spend each year a button.
Pheasants get up from their corn, flaunt tails
they've earned. The Empire Builder burns
its long face into the smoke of the high plains.

Rain opens the next act. Cattle clump
under thunderheads, heifers walk in a line
resolute, as though one has a grip
on what might be fitting to do. The train
wails its Doppler. After awhile
rusty cars driven or dragged their last
cough's length to the end of the field
become lovely. Holiness enters again
into turquoise fins and the Cessna's carapace
lifts on its wind.

On the roof of the Tip-It Bar in Havre, Montana,
Santa—in March—still on the roof. Maybe
that's where he ran out of luck. Last child
of this world growing old. Blizzards begin
out of Cutback, gulleys and sloughs white.
Sudden as mountains things change. In 1887
avalanche closed the tracks and the travelers
picnicked. Bored youngsters descended the slope.
Curtains of snow slid over the lives of others. *Here
is their willow cross.* Rounding the bend ahead
the engine, blind as a worm, makes it,
heads into miles of tunnel. Red lights blink
go. We emerge into black spruce, granite,
streams frozen in mid air over the gorge.

My life was that way a long time: now it runs free.
When the engineer enters a tunnel, still does his doubt
begin? How long can he ride through the dark
without screaming? Has he begun to know?

Where the slope is sleek and perfect
there you get slides.

Tolstoy, like God, could not help creating Levin,
a good man to walk with him.
Vronsky imagines nothing
but Anna undressed. She, the foil of his eyeballs,
thinks of her velvet clothes.

Confession

Last night, I ate a soup bowl of ice cream
with butterscotch sauce. My basement
is full of trash I paid too much for.

I did not love my mother
and though I loved my father
I did not please him.

I take naps. For fourteen years
I couldn't forgive my ex-husband,
only hardened my heart.

My drawers are a mess.
I own too many shoes.
I don't give much money away

There are light bulbs I ought to replace.
I don't understand foreign policy.
I've let my languages slide.

I throw out the mending.
Sometimes I pretend
to care, to listen, to be working.

I read stupid mystery stories,
criticize. Also the dog
does not obey me.

SHORT STORY

Polly Buckingham
Monster Movie

"Make me really scary," Hiram said, gripping the edge of the kitchen counter with his hands as if he were prepared to be scared of himself.

"I'm doing my best, Hi," Melanie said, the Kids Paint in an arc on the counter—red, black, white, yellow, green. The yellow and green were Hiram's idea—*pus, Mom, or like rotten flesh*. But when she tried drawing a gaping red hole on his jawbone, *like a zombie took a bite outta me*, and lined it with yellow and green, it looked more like a Christmas ornament than a zombie bite. Hiram's feet rested on either side of her, occasionally and uncontrollably kicking her hips.

She wiped the fake wound clean with her rag. "What about a scar across your forehead with stitches in it, like Frankenstein's monster? And then we could put corks sticking out each side of your head."

"Who?" Hi cocked his bird-like head and looked at her.

"Frankenstein," she said. "Dr. Frankenstein who brings a man back from the dead." Above Hi's head, a large flake of flowered wallpaper had come loose from the wall.

He held a pink plastic mirror to his face and rolled his eyes. "That's not scary." She, too, looked into the mirror's tiny silver circle, and for a moment saw nothing in his sockets but the whites of his eyes. His pupils and pale blue irises had disappeared completely. Her sister's face rose up before her, as it had done for the past six years. She saw it in the whites of his eyes, how her sister's eyes would disappear and only the whites would shake with seizure. "Okay," she said. "No scar."

"What are you doing?" he asked as she squeezed out small worms of white and black then mixed them with her finger.

"A little blue," she murmured, not so much to Hiram, because for the moment he hardly seemed to be in the room. She saw only the face, so small the eyes looked twice their normal size, and though later she'd understand her sister had been blind, now the clear eyes rimmed by surprisingly dark, luxurious lashes stared unblinking into hers, penetrating, beautiful and haunting.

"What do you need blue for?" Hiram's hands began to shake, like they did when he got nervous or impatient.

"Hold still."

"They're gonna be here soon. What are you doing?"

"Trust me, Hi," she said as she ran her gray index finger in half circles under his eyes. She put a dab of blue on her finger and wiped one thin line under the half moons of gray then worked the blue in so that it seemed only a sheen of color, not a stripe, but as if the gray had the faintest bluish cast. Out from these circles, she continued with gray, which grew more white the further away it got from his eyes. She held his shoulders and looked at him from a small distance.

"What am I?" he asked, his hands fluttering at his sides.

He needed dark eyelids, almost black, with maybe a tint of brown. The rest of his face should be the waxy yellow of terminal illness. The cheekbones would protrude sharply from below the eyes, and around the temples the skin would fall in, accentuating the shape of the surprisingly small skull; the enormous eyes were sunk in dark pools of gray, the lips pale and almost gone, such that a row of straight, tiny brown teeth were always visible. She stroked his quivering eyelid with her finger. "Keep them closed," she said and stroked the other eye.

His eyes flashed open, and for a moment she saw the gaunt, shriveled body, the ribs fully visible under the stretched skin, the abdomen a deep depression, a body that should have been dead weeks ago, even months ago. Something that no longer appeared human. She set to the yellow cast in his face.

"What are you doing?" There was a whiny edge to his voice now, an impatience. His fingers shook franticly, snapping soundlessly. "You're pressing too hard," he said as she rubbed the paint into his cheek, holding his chin firmly in her hand.

"Momma," he said. "What AM I?"

She stopped rubbing and studied his face. "I don't know," she said finally. "But you're scary."

The minute she let go of his shoulders, he ran into the bathroom to get a full look. Wind hit the glass. Tree branches rattled. Outside the back window, warped with clear plastic, the remaining light of streetlamps and porch lights captured the triangles of roofs. The rest of the roofs disappeared into darkness.

When Hiram emerged from the bathroom, his mouth hung open; she did not recognize him as her son. His tiny skeleton hands hung from the hollow sleeves of the black shirt she'd loaned him. The shirt hung down to his knees. Below that he wore jeans. "Scary," he said, almost in a whisper. "I'm very scary." A faint fire shadow from the woodstove door, partially opened, flickered across his face.

"Mmm," she said, surprised to hear his voice, expecting instead raspy unintelligible sounds, psalm-like and distant.

"What am I going to wear?"

The doorbell rang, and she turned toward the candy bowl, a yellow Tupperware bowl she'd found in an abandoned house beyond the road blocks. Once it had seemed voyeuristic to explore this area, this destroyed neighborhood beyond her own where squatters were beginning to take over the houses others had left behind, but recently she'd grown more cautious; both the security force and the gangs of children had increased such that even someone like herself, someone who only half cared about being here, thought twice about rummaging through the left behind belongings of unfortunate circumstances. That and Hiram kept asking her if he could go, which clearly would have been inappropriate.

Often her choices as a mother boiled down to what would and wouldn't seem appropriate to the people around her, other parents, like her brother-in-law or the neighbors. She never could identify herself as a parent—she hadn't been prepared for motherhood, she'd barely been able to take care of herself before the pregnancy, and there was her sister's death—so she looked toward people who did identify her this way and followed their lead, whether she trusted them or not, which she didn't. Her brother-in-law, in particular, was not trustworthy. She stood motionless before the unopened door behind which her brother-in-law and nephew waited. Did she really have to let them in?

"I want to give the candy." Hiram jumped in front of her.

The bowl rested between his arms like a giant pumpkin. She opened the door for him.

Hiram's cousin Max, in a store-bought Mopface Mobster wig and Mopface's signature black and white striped tee shirt, held out a black pillow case, something Melanie had not allowed Hiram to carry—"Too much candy," she'd said. "No kid needs all that." "But Max has one," he'd protested. "Max is older."

She stared at the bright orange knots that stuck out in all directions from Max's head and not for the first time speculated that Mopface was a rip-off of Sideshow Bob, a cartoon character she'd seen as a child who had long since disappeared from television. She never imagined herself as the person criticizing "what kids watch now" as if things had really been better when she was a child. But she couldn't help but note the difference: Mopface had the spindly legs and sallow face of a crack addict, which he was, and when he killed, there was real blood, not cartoon blood, but real horror movie blood spliced into the cartoon. There were real shots of dead and decaying bodies, computer generated images seamlessly merged with cartoon graphics. It was hard to tell anymore what was real and what was not. She tried to imagine this as part of her Saturday morning routine as a child, but couldn't.

"None for me," Steven said as Hiram held out the bowl of candy. Steven was dressed as a robber. He had a thick, coiled rope with a silver grappling hook hanging over his shoulder. How appropriate, Melanie thought.

She wondered if he'd recognize what she'd done. But no. He smiled blandly at Hiram—it seemed the vision of his dying wife, gone six years now, had disappeared from his memory while daily the face resurfaced in Melanie's mind. It was as if she'd had a deck of cards and kept removing the joker only to have it reappear every time she sat down for a good game of solitaire. Of course, there was a reason Steven hadn't recognized the apparition of his dead wife. He hadn't been around for her death. You could speculate in his favor, as most people did, such as her mother: there was Max, there was work, how difficult it must have been for him. Or, if you were Melanie, you could see it otherwise: there was cowardice, abandonment, denial, refusal. She'd been eight months pregnant with Hiram, tired, sluggish, the muscles in her back burning, the long nights she'd sat beside her dying sister, helping her to the bathroom, turning her over in bed to apply cream on her bed sores, and still she'd been there. What did that say? The pantyhose thigh that had been pulled over Steven's face was now bunched together on his forehead. He's obscene, Melanie thought.

When the door to his aunt's house swung open revealing Hiram in what appeared a state somewhere between the living and the dead, Max felt pain, a tenderness toward his tiny cousin that always surprised him, a need to protect Hiram from his fucked up life with Aunt Melanie. Max liked Hiram. And that was saying a lot, because Max didn't like most people. He hadn't grown out of the habit of punching kids at school, maybe because his father and grandmother over and over again stood up for him—*this is healthy*, his grandmother would say. Max knew better. He'd waited to get in trouble with the people who mattered the most, and when this didn't happen, it only made him want to hit more kids. His father's denial of his problems with other kids infuriated him. When Max was pulled from the home school group, his father blamed the other parents. And at the Bible school with the horses, where Max went for a year, his father blamed the administrators. Max was in the fourth grade now at the Regular school, the same school as his cousin Hiram. "I always thought you should go to the Regular school," his father had said, "but your mother . . ." and then his voice had trailed off. So now it was his dead mother's fault that he hit kids.

He knew he'd loved his mother, though he remembered very little of her. His father told him she used to take him to the Crystal River when he was a baby, just the two of them for sometimes weeks at a time staying in a lean-to she'd made of wooden stakes and canvas tarps. His father said Max and his mom had planted a garden on the shore of the river—his mother called it her Garden of Eden. These trips had worried his father. But his mother was stubborn. She never wanted Max out of her sight. She never hired babysitters. She never let his father take him anywhere without her. She was fanatic about this, at least that's what his father said.

But these are not things he remembers. He remembers the hospital bed parked next to a sliding glass door and a swimming pool on the other side and how he used to ram his body into the bed and how she would moan and how his father would drag him out of the room. He remembers tired, pregnant Aunt Melanie who seemed to ignore his presence altogether. He remembers the police coming when his mother threw a phone at his grandparents and how he hollered for her and beat at their uniforms with his fists when they tried to pull him away. He remembers how one day he was there in the room of a house he lived in but didn't really live in where his mother never left the hospital bed, he was there playing with Greenback Fighters, toys his mother hadn't allowed, on the wood floor, and then he was at his grandparents for weeks, maybe months, until the party at the church and the talks with his dad about what death was and about Heaven. He remembers never wanting to be without her, as if his body were attached to hers and whenever that attachment was severed, he'd wanted only to hit, punch, kick, ram himself into people. He remembers his grandparents' house with air conditioning, something he'd never before experienced—he used to put his cheek against the vent—and the TV, which he'd also never seen, and how he'd sit in front of it for hours, watching cartoons, his still body surging with an energy over which he had no control. Later he would understand that just down the street, his mother lay dying in a hospital bed beside a swimming pool in a rented house, and he had not been allowed to be with her.

In the doorway, Hiram's small body was illuminated by the dim lights of Aunt Mel's living room. He balanced on thin legs, the candy bowl just about overwhelming him. It was ironic, really, the size of the candy bowl and the size of Hiram. It didn't take long for Max to do the math: there was the candy, and there was the smallest kid in the kindergarten, in fact, the smallest kid in the whole Regular school. He wore one of Aunt Melanie's long sleeved black tee shirts (she had a lot of them) and jeans. It seemed like he was only half in costume. He was barefoot, and it was cold out. The make up job on his face was downright creepy and accentuated that constant sense of starvation that marked him as a person. What was Aunt Melanie thinking? She stood behind Hiram staring off through a darkened, plastic covered window, her hair stringy, long, unwashed. She's crazy, he thought. It was Max's theory that Hi was starved of attention, and all the doctors (he'd seen plenty) couldn't fix that.

"I'm scary," Hiram said.

"Damn scary," Max said.

"Don't swear, Maxy," his father said, but Max knew he didn't mean it.

"Got any shoes?" Max said.

Hiram looked down into the bowl of candy.

"I can take it." Max took the bowl out of Hiram's arms, and Hiram ran to the kitchen. He came back wearing red rain boots, a blue zip up sweatshirt with a hood and a black watch cap.

"Where's your bag?"

"I can't have one," Hiram said. "I'm not old enough."

Aunt Mel held out a plastic pumpkin. "You make it sound like I'm starving you," she said. She turned to Max's dad. "I just didn't want him having a pillowcase. It's too much."

His father nodded, but Max didn't think he was really paying attention. Hiram was a chore for his father. And that made Max like Hi all the more.

"You should have a skeleton costume," Max said as they turned away from Aunt Mel's front porch and walked into the streetlamp lit night.

"I'm scary," Hiram said.

"Okay," Max's dad said. "Down this side of Maple, not all the way to the road block, then back down the other side."

"That's it?" Max said.

"Yeah."

"Can't I go on my own later?"

"No, Max. You heard what the committee is recommending."

A family of cats passed them. The mother held her tail in her hand, and the little girl's dragged on the cement behind her. The father had taken his off and strung it around his neck. Hiram meowed at the little girl, and she shrieked. He turned to Max and grinned. "Very scary," Max said.

Most of the houses along the way had lights on. Hiram wanted to ring the doorbells. Max liked to watch him run up the steps, hit the ringer, and stand with his tiny hands shaking furiously.

"My goodness, aren't you a fright," said an old woman dressed as a fairy princess. "What are you?"

"I'm scary!" Hiram screamed.

"You certainly are," she said and handed him a popcorn ball wrapped in orange waxed paper.

"We're dumping those when we get home," Max's dad said as they walked down the steps.

At the next house, Ms. Weeks, dressed as a valley girl, greeted them. "Did you hear about the committee lowering the gas limit?" She hardly noticed Max and Hiram, though Hiram was staring intently at the candy bowl. Everything in the bowl was Nestles. In fact, except for the popcorn ball, Max guessed everything he'd received that night had been Nestles. Nestles Butterfly Bites, Toffee Melts, Gummy Bears, Spastic Apples and the old standard, Nestles Crunch. He had imagined something special, but why? Who would drive out of town to buy Halloween candy? And then there were the road blocks.

"Shit," his father said.

"I was going to give my mileage to my parents. I haven't seen them for like five years. I'd been saving to move them here."

"Have you been to that site that sells miles?" He placed his palm against the doorframe as if he might stay awhile. "Mostly it's from other towns that don't have such strict limits."

"I can't afford that," she said, the fine hair on her arms raised from the cold. She was wearing a black mini skirt and red stockings. Behind her, flames pressed against the woodstove window. "That's a great costume," she said to Max's father.

He shrugged. "Can't be on the streets without one."

"It's good for the kids they still allow this."

"I suppose," he said. "Still, we had so much more freedom."

Max could see the toilet paper and eggs story had been invoked, and he didn't want to hear it. Ms. Weeks leaned against the inside of the door as though Max and Hiram had no place to be but her house. Hiram's hands were shaking again.

"Dad," Max said.

"Go on, I'll catch up," he said absently.

Max grabbed Hiram's hand and quickly descended the stairs, quietly so his father wouldn't think about what he'd just said and take it back.

"Can we?" Hiram said.

"You heard him."

Hiram ran ahead and spun around under the streetlamp. He held his hummingbird hands above his head and threw his head back. Max felt a surge of love for him. He was such a weird kid. You had to love that. Hi rocked his head back and forth and snapped his fingers in the air. Again the apparition of the skeleton rose before him as he watched Hi dance, the dark around his eyes accentuated by the fall of streetlamp light across his face so that for moments at a time he appeared to have no eyes at all. He could be a tiny shriveled old lady, or he could be the undersized six-year-old boy he was.

A damp wind rustled the leaves of the maple trees that lined the street. Branches clicked above him. He felt a jolt of energy from the dark wind, from the freedom. It brewed in his chest like a storm. They were only supposed to go as far as the road block (*we should turn around well before*, his father had said) but now the block was just two houses away, and both were dark. He and Hiram passed the first house. Hiram's hand in his felt cold and bony. The next street light was broken. The graffiti on the cement road blocks looked like dark flowers or lily pads.

A group of homeless boys sat on the porch of the last darkened house, smoking. He looked back to see if his father had noticed them. But his father was still talking with Ms. Weeks. He could see her shape curved against the doorframe, her arms motioning something in the light of the doorway. He could see the shine of his father's grappling hook. None of the boys were in costume, which is how Max knew they were homeless, though their burly coats, ripped pants and ski hats also gave them away. If you ever saw homeless kids, this is where you'd see them. A lot of the houses beyond the neighborhood had been bulldozed, but the city ran out of money to bulldoze more. Even the big corporations had given up on these areas. People squatted in houses without electricity, without plumbing, and occasionally appeared on the edges of neighborhoods like the one on Maple Street.

Three of the kids looked around Max's age, and two looked like teenagers. Now they were passing around a half smashed Pepsi can and smoking out of it. Max was close enough to smell the waxy scent of crack rocks burning. He stood just out of the streetlamp light, Hiram pressed up against his side, gripping Max's hand with both his hands, his sharp fingers pressing into Max's palm. Then another kid, a teenager dressed in desert fatigues, bowling shoes and a striped wool hat, appeared from behind the building holding a girl no older than Max. The others ran to the girl and crowded around her. The girl screamed, and suddenly she was naked, the boys pushing her up against the dark wall of the house. The scream rolled down Maple Street. Max felt the collective intake of breath, the phones dialing in nearby houses, the waiting.

The storm in him surged through his muscles. His body twitched with that familiar uncontrollable angst. A light switched on in a window across the street. He turned to look at his dad who was standing now beside Ms. Weeks, both of them facing the sound of the scream. A little witch and her sailor father stood still on the sidewalk, hand in hand, staring. Max wanted desperately to chase the punks into the darkness, kick, punch, throw them to the ground, pummel their faces into the dirt. The scream repeated itself inside him. He wanted to break through the stillness of all the people staring. There was nothing like action, nothing like motion, nothing like forcing yourself against whatever adversity you came up against. He'd had years of practice.

Hiram clung to his hand and planted his feet on the sidewalk. Max turned to look at him, and in that look he saw his mother, pleading. No Max, she said. And he remembered the face in the bed, the naked, shriveled body, the hands the size of a child's, the tiny wrists and ankles and calves, the peach fuzz of her hair making her look like a bug-eyed baby bird. It was as if in this moment he had a clearer picture of her than he had ever had. She appeared before him in all her monster movie gruesomeness, the single person he'd loved most in the world. Hiram, with her face, pleading. They hadn't let Max see her those last weeks. And no day of his life had passed in which he didn't think of her. He broke loose and ran, the glimpse of the girl's naked body setting in motion the only series of actions he understood. The first drops of rain flew into his face, and the street shuddered with the weight of large vehicles, but he didn't turn around to look.

"Maaaaaaaaaaax!" Hiram screamed. Even as he ran he could hear the sirens; the pavement in front of him was bright with the light of the security force Hummers, except for his own shadow which stretched out before him like a black ghost.

Melanie gave a little witch a handful of candy. "That's an awful lot," said her sailor father. Melanie just shrugged while the witch did a small dance ending in a full circle twirl on her doorstep. The father frowned. Melanie was not looking forward to a night of parents and their children, a night of feeling like the imposter she was.

When her sister was diagnosed with the early stages of breast cancer and given a ninety percent chance of recovery with treatment, she got off of her antipsychotic meds and chose to cure her cancer with diet and prayer. Her husband supported her choice up until the last six months of her life, at which point, as Melanie saw it, he'd abandoned her. A month before her death, there had even been plans for a divorce. Corey's death was nothing short of suicide. A long, agonizing suicide where the people who were supposed to love her most did nothing but sit back and watch, praying for her death sooner than later. Melanie, Hiram kicking inside her, had spent those six months beside her sister's bed, watching her naked body grow smaller and smaller, naked because even clothes hurt her skin and bones, and the cancer like a scab the size of a grapefruit occasionally popped, pussed, and bled. Corey had refused all medication, including morphine in the last weeks. She fasted regularly, and in the last few months ate nothing but tiny ice cubes of grape juice—God's cure, she'd said.

She died at forty pounds in a rented house, murmuring unintelligible prayers, bottles of Trinity water stowed under her hospital bed in case a hospice person should try to poison her. She died weeks, if not months, after the hospice volunteers had predicted or hoped. So late that even the hospice people, who would normally suggest a child be with a parent near or at the time of death, recommended Max be taken away. Their worry and terror were palpable. None of them had ever seen anything quite like this. The moment after Corey died, Melanie crawled under the living room table of the rented house, placed her cheek against the wood and bawled. She stared past people's confused feet at the triangles of bright blue light moving across the swimming pool and then at the darkness behind her eyelids, the dead weight of the baby like a rock inside her not two weeks from his birth. She'd grown up a shadow of Corey, wearing her clothes, choosing the same favorite color (blue), the same favorite animal (monkey), the same favorite dinner (macaroni and cheese, bratwurst and artichokes). How could she possibly follow an act like this?

After Hiram left for trick or treating, Melanie sat in a rocker she'd picked up at the dump and got stoned. A young woman in a hot pink clown wig peeked in through the window when Melanie didn't answer the doorbell. A child's tiny fingers gripped the edge of the window ledge. Melanie and the mother made eye contact just as she was lifting the joint to her lips. The bell didn't ring a second time.

She opened the woodstove doors completely and stared into the flames bouncing against the grid of the chain. They twisted and turned, the coals humming a brighter and brighter orange like a strobe. The heat whirred in the black piping and roared when a wind rose up. Over and over again, she replayed the events, as if rethinking them might change them, how she had protested Corey's choices, had called doctors, psychiatrists, even child protective services, anything to get her to stop the course she was on and get real treatment. But at every move, she was stonewalled not just by Corey, who stopped speaking to her for over a year because a nonbeliever would prevent her from God's cure, but by Steven. By the time Steven stopped believing—those last six months when Corey and Steven and Max moved into a house with a swimming pool next door to their parents and Steven commuted into the city to work where he eventually rented an apartment—the cancer had progressed far beyond any cure short of the miracle Corey felt certain would come. That was when you could still commute. And that was when the swimming pools in the wealthy section still had water in them. Some people with enough money had since built patios on top of them, but most were now dry and cracked.

The bottom of the joint burned the tips of her fingers. She stared at it absently. Her fingertips were stained brown where this had happened before. She felt nothing more than the usual dull pain. It wasn't like she'd even had her shit together before Corey's death—a college stoner who'd have sex with whomever on drunken nights and then never remember. Still, as much as she tried to follow Corey's lead, she hadn't been psychotic. She put another piece of wood—a remnant from someone's old porch—into the woodstove, went to the kitchen, and poured a glass of wine. She held the bowl against her palm and wandered from window to window looking out, smoke from the woodstove twisting across the cones of porch lights. Into Hiram's room, into her room, each set of roofs just like the last, except for the way the plastic over the windows uniquely warped each view. In Hiram's room, she stepped on a crayon and felt it crack under her stocking foot. She didn't bother to pick it up. Instead, she stared at it despairingly, wondering how anyone could have ever allowed her to be a mother. The window in Hiram's room was cold, despite the plastic. The pane had cracked; she'd wanted to cover the window with a square of insulation but hadn't gotten to it. Perhaps she never would.

In the bathroom she stared at her face in the mirror and saw her sister's blue eyes in hers, the worry that had crowded those eyes throughout her sister's life, as if her sister could see ahead of time where her life was headed, or perhaps such an end was the only place such worry could lead. Anything that was her sister, Melanie wanted in herself. Just to keep her here. She plugged up the bathtub and filled it with water. She rolled herself another joint, lit candles, poured another glass of wine, then slipped naked into the tub. The tiles were cracked and moldy, and plastered with clumps of her hair where she'd pulled it out after each bath. Twenty-six years old, and she was losing her hair. What did it matter? Maybe there was a cancer growing in her, too. She could not imagine how she would hold up against such a thing; she only knew she would not stake her life on a miracle as if to say, "God, if you love me you'll save me," as if to say, "See God, I can prove that you don't love me simply by dying." Still, hadn't she had her own way of proving she didn't deserve to be alive—drugs, alcohol, anonymous sex? Even now as she slid to the bottom of the tub and looked across the candle lit water, she could see her sister, months before her death, sliding into the unnaturally blue swimming pool, Melanie guiding her into the water, her tiny head, bird-like slipping under the warped surface. The doorbell rang, and she ignored it.

Melanie lay naked on her bed, her sheets gritty with dirt from walking outside in her socks, heat drifting in from the living room, cold emanating from the window. Strings of dust hung off the blades of the ceiling fan. It wasn't a room at all, really. Just an alcove with enough space for a bed and a small closet she had to take the door off of because there wasn't room to open it. She'd meant to hang a sheet or a tapestry but had never gotten around to it. The reflection of the fire flickered against the ceiling. Finally, she put on a long blue corduroy robe, another treasure from an abandoned house, and rustled through Corey's old DVD collection of monster movies. It was Halloween, after all. She remembered a film she'd seen as a child where a woman is buried alive, but she could remember nothing more than the hand coming up out of the dirt. As a child she'd imagined herself as this woman: the sound of the dirt hitting the coffin, the loss of air. She'd imagined herself in some sort of stasis for years, the coffin slowly decaying, the constant state of suffocation, and ultimately, still alive.

Her sister's collection included *The Shining*, *The Other*, *The Little Girl Who Lived Down the Lane*, *The Omen*, *Damien*, two different versions of *The Exorcist*, *Rosemary's Baby*, a handful of zombie movies, and multiple versions and variations of *Dracula*, *The Wolfman*, and *Frankenstein*. All movies her parents would have seen when they were little. She loved that about her sister—Corey liked old things, things most people had long since discarded. She liked old music and old tools and old books. Melanie pulled out *Frankenstein*.

Just after Corey was diagnosed, she told Melanie the world was going to end. Locusts had swarmed a Middle Eastern city—"just like in the Bible." Melanie had rolled her eyes. She wondered now.

Shortly after *Frankenstein* started Melanie drifted to sleep. She woke to a tiny hobgoblin screaming unintelligibly and waving its stick-like hands in the air. It was her dead sister, covered with the thick hair of the dying and holding up her tiny fingers with their long fingernails, and she would die all over again, as she did in so many of Melanie's dreams. Then she noticed that the little face was smeared with tears, and the Kids Paint had run down his neck. "Hi?" she said, one eye still pinned shut with sleep.

Hiram stood over her and shook her shoulders. She was surprised by the force of his small hands. It was almost impossible to understand him, his voice was so high and frantic. She sat up, the blanket falling off her. Rain pelted the windows.

"Slow down, Hi. I can't understand you."

"Max," he said, choking on his tears, choking so she worried he'd lose his breath.

"Take a breath," she said, fully awake now, but groggy from the pot.

"He's shot, the hummers, shot." He'd wiped at the make-up with his sleeve which was now covered in gray Kids Paint; beneath, his face and ears and neck were bright red. He began to scream.

"Hi, calm down, it's okay. I'm sure it's fine," but she could tell from the stiffness of his body and his weirdly animated face that it was not fine. And she knew Max. She knew the trouble no one wanted to look at.

"He's dead!" Hi hollered.

"Honey, how do you know that?"

"I saw him." Hi squinched his eyes shut, opened his mouth wide, tipped his chin to the ceiling and howled like an animal.

"Let me call your uncle, okay Hi?"

As she dialed, Hi walked into the kitchen like a crazed zombie, crawled under the table, his cheek pressed against the linoleum, and bawled. There was no answer at Steven's house. Surely he'll call, she thought. She sat stiff on the couch, listening to Hi's sobs, watching him as if he were miles away from her, alone with his cheek to the ground. The fire roared in the woodstove piping. Hi fell silent; his small body heaved as he sucked in panicked breaths as if he recognized how quickly they could become unavailable to him. Everything about his behavior was familiar, so that watching him as if through a series of years, her doubt disappeared. Max was dead. There was no other explanation. Rain slammed against the windows and roof.

One miserably hot day, a summer storm had risen up and blown across the hospital bed and across the bed beside it where Melanie sat reading aloud. "That feels good," she'd said. "Mm," Corey murmured, lifting her chin slightly to the breeze, her eyes closed, a small smile on her face. Both fell silent listening to the rain's onslaught until both drifted into sleep. No matter what changed in the world, the sound of rain would always remain the same. It was like the relief on her sister's face as her head rose up out of the swimming pool. How wonderful the cool water must have felt against her dying, stricken body. How wonderful the rain's breeze had felt against the sweat that had collected around the space where baby Hi had slept, curled up, waiting to come into the world. At the moment of drifting into sleep, she'd felt him relax inside of her, as if the time between that moment and her sister's death were equal to the time between that moment and Hi's birth, as if death and birth had collided. For six years, Hi's very existence had reminded her of Corey's gruesome death. On the TV, a little girl was handing Frankenstein a daisy. The sound of rain surrounded her. Melanie lifted herself from the couch, crawled onto the kitchen floor and lay on her stomach looking at Hi, suddenly grateful for the life that flickered across his stricken face, the jittery movement of his eyes beneath his closed eyelids, the tenderness of his worried forehead. Perhaps he should remind her of her sister's life, not her death.

"Hi. You can come out if you want." No one had come for her when she lay under the table watching the weird light on the swimming pool after her sister's death. Hi opened his eyes and looked at her. His eyes were open wide as perfect circles, and his pupils were huge. He looked as if he were in shock. She worried he wasn't breathing; this fear was sudden and sharp, a panic that made her feel alive, a moment in which she asked herself, Am I too late? Have I been gone too long?

"Hi?"

He crawled out, climbed into her lap and strung his arms around her neck. When Max was little, and Corey was dying, Max had slammed a half eaten peach into Mel's bare leg. She'd yelled at him—surprised and dismayed to find herself yelling at a four-year-old. They'd glared at one another until Corey had made him apologize. She was thinking now about how his violence must have finally done him in when Hi said, "He didn't have a mother."

"Honey?"

"He didn't have a mother, but I have you."

SHORT STORY

Jamie McCulloch
Roman Holiday

Two steps above Mother on the downward escalator to the express track, Melville notices for the first time how thin and frail looking the nape of her neck has become. A split-second image of his hands around her throat, knuckles rotating in opposite directions—how easy it would be, he thinks—just one quick motion. Naturally, the idea unnerves him a little, but it is only a passing fancy. Doesn't everyone entertain strange thoughts from time to time? Still it puzzles him how unsettling images can suddenly rise up out of the depths, so to speak, as one thinks about something else entirely—in this case, "Exhibit 53" of the EvenFlo litigation. What also perplexes him is the fact that he isn't even angry with Mother—they breakfasted together on toast and marmalade quite amicably this morning, even discussed the Science section of the *Times*—the heretofore undiscovered mating ritual of the sperm whale.

Slowly they descend, the two of them with different destinations: for him, court; for her a colonoscopy—her hunched posture indicating just how tense she is about her procedure, a tender distraction as he mentally sifts through the details of the EvenFlo case, doing his best to ignore the charred smell of electricity endlessly wafting up from the bowels of the lower level tracks along with the pungent stench of urine; and before he knows what he is doing, little by little, his eyes begin to settle on the nape of Mother's neck. How has she gotten so old? he wonders. *Why* has she let this happen?

Although it is only a passing fancy, after the escalator ride, to avoid approaching her from behind, Melville takes considerable precaution around the apartment that he and Mother share; but sometimes he is caught off guard—rounding the corner just as she is bending over to retrieve her reading glasses—or ambling into the kitchen with an armload of groceries to find her washing Brussels sprouts at the sink, the soft, white skin of her neck bared to him. Her chin-length Louise Brooks haircut doesn't help, either.

When he dreams of strangling Mother for the second time in a week, he makes an appointment to see a psychiatrist on east Ninety-Sixth Street.

Elevators, of course, pose a challenge—standing behind her to hold the door to let her in or out. Most of the time he remembers to fix his eyes on a spot somewhere over the top of her head, which isn't hard to do, as she is a good six inches shorter than he. But on occasion a woman enters and distracts him—women always fluster Melville—and he forgets to avert his eyes when Mother exits. And there it is—the soft, inviting, white flesh.

When he dreams of strangling Mother for the second time in a week, he makes an appointment to see a psychiatrist on east Ninety-Sixth Street. A beady-eyed, rodent-faced little man with a silvery goatee and an outer borough accent scribbles a few notes as Melville outlines the particulars of his life and describes in detail the latest of his strangulation dreams. When he finishes, Dr. Norstein, peering over his reading glasses, says, You want the expensive solution or the inexpensive one?

The inexpensive one? The expensive one? I don't know—is this some sort of trick question? I just want to stop dreaming about killing my mother.

Let me be blunt. You're thirty-nine years old, you live with your mother. Your mother's suicidal and controlling. You don't need a doctor, your mother does. Dr. Norstein adjusts his reading glasses and presses the intercom button on his phone.

Dolores?

Dolores provides a number, which Dr. Norstein scrawls on a blue prescription pad. Here, he says. Make an appointment and get yourself your own apartment. You'll be glad you did. Not married?

Melville shakes his head.

Oh—I envy you. I really do. Dr. Norstein grips his small head with both hands. Anyway, he continues, suddenly raising his head and smiling, that's the inexpensive solution—apart from the cost of the apartment. *Hah hah hah*, he laughs, three tight bursts like rounds from a machine gun.

Melville stares at him.

It's possible this man is even crazier than he.

Dr. Norstein shrugs. Okay, you want the expensive solution? Make an appointment for next week with Dolores. Here's a prescription for Klonopin, he says, scribbles and tears off another sheet from the blue pad, and hands it to Melville.

Melville gazes at himself in his full-length bedroom mirror and sighs, the starched tips of his white shirt collar pressing against the sides of his jaw. Measuring and adjusting the length of his tie, he doubts he will ever get to Rome for New Year's. Mother will pull one of her stunts, and he'll have to cancel his trip last minute. Like the time she chased a bottle of Valium with a bottle of Tanqueray. Already on his way to the airport, he had to tell the driver to turn the car around. He'd nearly called her bluff and flown the ten hours to Greece anyway. But instead of basting himself on a beach in Mykonos for seven days, he spent the week in the stale, acrid air of Bellevue Hospital waiting for Mother to be discharged.

Melville sighs and swings the wide end of the silk tie clockwise around the thin end, pushes it chin-ward, and feeds it back down again through the opening to knot it. There in the soft Manhattan morning light of his bedroom his mind drifts as he performs the most routine of actions. Half intent on his reflection, half on his mother, he is nearly oblivious to the action of his hands. But something about the arrangement of his hands—the proximity to his neck perhaps—dredges up an image from his latest strangulation dream—him falling and falling into a terrible white void—but he is determined not to go there, not fully. His attention slipping back and forth between the mirror and the dream, first he sees his hands and then the whiteness. Hands, then whiteness; hands then whiteness. For a moment he feels detached, outside himself—a stranger looking in—and when his hands appear and disappear again, he feels himself letting go. His fingers appear to crumble and dissolve like powder in water, then reconstitute and reform. Everything in the room suddenly tilts, and he places a hand on the mirror to steady himself. Afraid he still might fall, he mentally scrolls over his itinerary for Rome again: Touch down at Leonardo da Vinci, 7:45 AM, check in at the Hotel Scalinata di Spagna, "Rome's most famous boutique hotel" (so says the guide book). He briefly considered staying at the Hotel Duca d'Alba, near the Roman Forum and the Coliseum, but in the end decided upon the Spanish steps. The prospect of sleeping a few hundred feet from where John Keats spent his last night proved more enticing than lodging so close to where gladiators bled to death before crowds and emperors. The Trevi Fountain, dinner at Il Drappo, "a favorite of the local artsy crowd"; next day St. Peter's, *Capella Sistina* (the Sistine Chapel—doesn't everything sound better in Italian? For months he's secretly been listening to Berlitz' *Italian for Beginners* on the treadmill at the gym)—has it all planned out, every last detail—even the wines he plans to purchase—Chiantis, Orvietos, Sangioveses, Frascatis, Brunellos.

New Year's Eve in Rome. *Melville* in Rome. Roma. It's all too wonderful—he feels a little out of breath—revelers drinking from fountains, bathing in them like Mercutio in Zeffirelli's *Romeo and Juliet*, knocking back the Brunello by the case—a wild, lecherous bacchanalia! A golden swirl shimmers before him, and all at once, he thinks of the gold lamé shirt hidden at the top of his closet.

Two months earlier on the way to a restaurant in Greenwich Village, his taxi slowed and stopped for a light. By chance he turned and looked into a shop window, and there it was; an item so alive and full of color that at first glance he mistook it for a living, sentient being—not the shirt itself but the mannequin wearing it. Even now when he pictures it boxed and hidden under his father's old army blanket at the top of his closet, it is not as something still or inanimate but as something dormant, ready to wake—ready to come to life.

It was quite unlike Melville to buy such a flashy item of clothing. In fact, in the two months he's owned it, he never once dared wear it, except to try it on in the store. He hid it from sight the way a teenage boy might hide his first pornographic magazine. During a three-hour deposition last week, the mere thought of it aroused him to such an extent that he now blushes to recall the intensity and duration of that erection.

Mother is still in her bath. Perhaps he has time to try it on again now. She will be in the bathroom for another fifteen minutes. Not only was it not like him to buy a gold lamé shirt with sequins, but also it is not like him to keep a secret from Mother. The shirt, however, is something of which she must never know. Yes, it would enrage her, but that is not important. What matters is that it would give Mother the upper hand—give her a reason to act hurt, ashamed of him. Give her a reason not to come out of her room, not to talk to him—to be cruel, to sabotage Rome. He cannot risk that. Rome is too important now, too close.

Melville lacks nerve and he knows it. The very fact that he can't even bring himself to sit in Mother's paisley chair, when, on the rare occasion, Mother does go to dinner with her best friend Marianne or Aunt Delilah, is all the proof he needs. From time to time an odd, inexplicable urge to sit naked in her chair washes over him as he crosses the living room en route to his bedroom or the kitchen. (Mother prefers he use the hall, of course, but has turned a blind eye of late—no doubt because he pays the taxes and maintenance on the apartment—not to mention the cost of reupholstering the sofa and both chairs—the only two reasons he has the upper hand now.) Yes, it is a strange urge—and it shames him at least as much as it excites him.

Intermittent images of himself in Rome—sometimes surrounded by men and women at a table or at a disco, sometimes alone, weeping over the grave of Keats—always clad in gold lamé—excite him even more. Mother often speaks of self-indulgence as a slippery slope, and doubtless she is right. Always having taken great pride in their ascetic existence, she relishes any opportunity to point out where others have strayed from the path of virtue. Naturally, the fewer occasions he affords Mother to find fault with him the better. He saw what she did to Father. By resisting all sorts of little indulgences, Melville has attempted to immunize himself from her words. Next to money, self-denial is his greatest defense against her.

Still half in his imagination, he can almost feel the shirt, cool against his torso. The hair on his arms stands, and once more he tightens the knot around his neck. In the mirror his hands shimmer and dissolve again.

> **Let me be blunt. You're thirty-nine years old, you live with your mother. Your mother's suicidal and controlling. You don't need a doctor, your mother does.**

Mother will never let him go. Rome is simply out of the question. And yet— perhaps it isn't. Like a thief rotating a jewel in the light, he turns the idea over in his mind, letting it dazzle him. He holds his breath, half afraid he might burst if he draws another. From the bathroom down the hall he can just make out a few bars of *Otello*. That's a good sign, Mother listening to Verdi. It means she is in a good mood. All yesterday she stayed in her room after he arrived home too late from work to pick up the kippered herring. Mother can be cruel.

But today she is happy, and the morning has all the makings of a good, peaceful Saturday. Tie straight, shirt pressed, hair parted, his pale eyes reflecting back at him, he wonders whether he couldn't just go—say he was away on business. Seven blissful days. Villa Borghese, the Catacombs. Mother could manage without him, couldn't she? Seven days all to himself—the notion causes his mouth to curl; but when he remembers the crooked tooth behind his upper lip, his incipient smile quickly becomes a frown. On a whim he removes the pink and blue striped tie and casts it upon his unmade bed. Mother does not like unmade beds—nor does she like him to go out "open-necked," as she puts it.

But it is Saturday and there is no good reason why he should wear a tie. Besides, Mother is still in her bath. He has at least fifteen minutes while she "soaks."

Another glance at himself in the mirror, throat bare, and all at once he feels naked, incomplete. His face looks drained of color, his sandy hair as washed out as his skin, and the stark whiteness of his shirt beams back at him. The necktie, a gift from Mother who each year on his birthday gives him a white shirt and a striped tie from Brooks Brothers, came on his thirty-ninth only three months ago. It is one of the small ways in which she attempts to take possession of him; the way she did with Father, little by little, until one day there was nothing left of him. One morning while Mother and Melville ate jam and toast and drank tea out of the brown betty that Father and Mother brought back from their honeymoon in England, Father quietly asphyxiated himself in the shower with a plastic bag. Since then, Father is only mentioned obliquely in conversation.

The last time Mother mentioned Father, he recalls, was also on his thirty-ninth birthday. Each time she presents him with the annual white shirt and striped tie, she tells him with a curt smile, If I have to lose you *too* to the world one day, you might as well be properly dressed. Mother stubbornly clings to the idea that he will marry; Melville isn't so sure. Women seem to despise him, and his awareness of this fact, naturally, makes him nervous around them.

Last week Celia, his secretary, brought him the Merganzer brief and shot him a look of pure rage. While her words were respectful and polite, her eyes frightened him. Perhaps it wasn't rage but merely coldness. Whatever the case, he can't deny it—women behave differently around him—something about him puts them off.

The stark whiteness of Melville's shirt reflects back at him. How he would love to feel its fibers rip and fray until it was reduced into some amorphous, white mess. What would Mother do, if one day, upon receiving one of these white Brooks Brothers shirts, he began to savagely rend it to pieces? What would she do?

He doesn't know. There is really no precedent for such behavior. On his last birthday he remarked, as he always does, "Oh Mother, how wonderful—a white shirt!" Another white shirt. Staring at himself, open-collared now, Melville can feel himself being swallowed up by whiteness. The urge to pierce it, to bleed himself into color, into existence, washes over him. The terrible whiteness. It seems he isn't just looking at a shirt now but at his whole life. His whole life lacks color. Color is what he desperately needs. A big, dazzling, dizzying wave of color! He's always secretly loved color, but Mother never allows him to indulge in a liberal use of it outside of his large collection of neckties—which she inexplicably tolerates, even encourages. He almost wishes he were Italian—Italians live for color. In Italy a man can be unabashedly flamboyant.

To keep from being swallowed up by the terrible whiteness, Melville recalls the image of the gold lamé shirt. He still has at least ten minutes. He could put it on, press its coolness to his skin—feel it breathe. He could . . . frolic—a word Mother doesn't use, except derisively. Frolic. Sounding fun and light upon his lips as he says it silently to himself, the *f* aspirates off his lips; his tongue bends down with the weight of the second syllable, *lic*, like a diving board getting ready to fling it far out into the air. He says it again a little louder and laughs. To stand in front of a mirror without a tie, saying a silly word—the absurdity of it makes him chortle.

Oh, to frolic in gold lamé—to shimmer in sequins in Rome! The thought is too exhilarating—it almost doesn't seem real. So remote, so inaccessible—the idea almost dirty, lascivious. Two months ago, when he saw the shirt all aglitter in the shop window, and on a whim, bought it, he felt so alive—so much so that when the salesman with the flip in his hair and tight pants boxed it for him, he felt a sadness akin to loss. Rather inexplicably, he thought of his father's polished coffin in the pouring rain. Never having dared wear it but that once in the shop with the salesman looking on and nodding with approval, he's kept the shirt well hidden at the top of his closet where Mother will never see it. His senses heightened with anticipation, Melville can almost hear the knock on the dressing room door, see the hand on the other side, hear the voice ask if he needs any help. Politely, he declines. Blushes. Feels nervous, excited, and ashamed all at the same time—like when he found that magazine in old Mr. Smegly's trash all those years ago, the one that he tucked neatly away in his father's bowling bag.

The hair on his neck and arms on end, he still has time to try it on—the shirt only a few feet away. A little light-headed and short of breath, he wonders if he isn't having another panic attack. He swallows, takes several deep breaths.

Mother's door is still closed.

A turn of the knob and there it is—exactly where he placed it. With shaky hands he reaches into the velvety, illicit darkness of the box, and traces his long fingers over the smooth, rounded sequins. He removes it from the dark closet and carries it to the open window to let it ripple and undulate in the sun. It is too colorful, too dazzling, too wonderful.

It blazes.

There's a tightness in his chest and he can't catch his breath. He feels dizzy, a little intoxicated, sinful.

Even though he can hear the running of the bath, he glances over his shoulder toward the doorway to make sure Mother's door is still closed before stripping off his button-down and undershirt.

Enveloped in gold, he is overcome. In silence he stands, feeling its cool silk lining brush against his skin. Closing his eyes, he imagines himself deplaning in Rome, tanned and brash, dazzling and alive—a man no one knows, capable of anything.

Just what the hell do you think you're doing? A voice cuts the air. Melville opens his eyes: Mother's scowling, bloodless face before him, instantly he is a child again. He wishes he could evaporate: Poof! A spontaneous combustive escape. But no such escape comes. Instead Mother's sharp voice. Take that repulsive shirt off at once! You look like I don't know what—.

Her face is ghastly white.

No, actually I do, Mother continues. You look like one of those men—those men in that filthy magazine I found in your closet. Men on top of men—

Stop it! Melville shouts and covers his ears, Stop it! Stop it! Stop it! His voice cracks, and for a moment he can't breathe. Hoping that he might be dying—perhaps suffocating—he closes his eyes. In a minute it might all be over and he won't ever have to face her again.

Then something in his head shifts, and after a time—he can't really say how long—he finds himself lying on the rug, hugging his knees to his chest, no recollection of how he got there.

At the sound of Mother smoothing her dress and exhaling in disgust, Melville opens his eyes. She is speaking, offering him the white shirt he threw on the bed. He wipes his face and swallows. Avoiding eye contact, he slowly rises, pads over to the dresser, and pulls a clean white shirt from a drawer full of identical white shirts. Something about his vision isn't right. Mother, a torn image, nods at him, one hand extended, offering him the pink and blue necktie. Silently, he takes it from her, buttons the top button of the shirt, swings the wide end of the tie clockwise around the thin end, pushes it chin-ward, and feeds it back down again through the opening to knot it. Mother is close—only three feet from him—close enough for him to see the blue veins on her pale white throat.

Mother smiles a triumphant but understanding smile, and his vision dissolves into two separate images. Then nearly everything goes white. Melville can just make out Mother's hard, mocking, lipsticked mouth. A moving red oval that seems to encircle and corral every word it utters, every object in the room. Light-headed and unsteady on his feet, he begins to fear that he might fall and never hit the ground—like in the recurring dream he told Dr. Norstein about—the one in which he spiraled endlessly into the soft, white folds of Mother's neck while she laughed with lascivious abandon, over and over. In his mind, the contorted face of his father, his hair dry beneath the clear plastic bag, water still raining down on his naked body; in front of him, Mother's mocking red mouth encircling and prodding him into the terrible white folds—and then the floor begins to give. Not wanting to fall that endless, desperate fall, he reaches out to the soft, delicate, white flesh—and this time he will not hear. This time he will not fall.

SHORT STORY

Martin Ott
Sugar, Wine, Smoke and Glue

SUGAR

I wasn't sure what to make of it when my daughter sat at the breakfast table with a cigarette butt in one hand and a Skittle in the other. Karen had attempted to hide them from me, clenching her tiny fists when I tried to pry open her fingers. Her stubbornness already surpassed both Francine's and mine: nap time was a war of wills, latched doors a minor inconvenience, and she threw a fit if there were even the remotest chance she might land candy out of the deal.

Sweets were poison in my book. The cough syrup I guzzled as a teenager to get through the monotony of high school ruined candy for me as an adult. I never knew what would trigger my violent reactions, but I made sure to avoid the following: Jujubes, candied apples, Jordan almonds, yams, cotton candy, apple cider and toothpaste.

The only thing that seemed to help me from throwing up when I smelled sweets were the cigarettes I started chain smoking soon after I married Francine. I don't blame her for my habit or for my inability to feel comfortable with a woman and, later, a child in my home. The fault was mine—I'd fallen into some sub-basement of fatherhood, where my Dad had spent his entire marriage drinking homemade wine in a combination rumpus room and workshop of his own creation. My own escape involved a deck off the kitchen that my wife and exuberant daughter quickly learned to avoid.

This wasn't to say I didn't love Karen. She meant the world to me—bright, energetic and wise beyond her four years and two months should have made her. She had an openness that made me question everything about my own existence. In fact, she downright scared me at times.

Many of the memorable events in my life were foreshadowed by things my daughter either said or did. Just before my boss, Mr. Yancy at the insurance company, was fired for embezzlement, Karen said "Bossman Yancy take my candy," even though she'd never met him. And the morning before my fender bender with, of all people, a litigation attorney, Karen said, "Car go boom, Daddy." And so did my wallet. Francine and I stopped trying to spell out words around her. For example, my wife's recent suggestion: M-A-R-R-I-A-G-E C-O-U-N-S-E-L-O-R, led to Karen bawling for six straight hours.

My daughter looked on the verge of tears now as I massaged her knuckles and gently eased open her fingers. I snatched the Skittle and cigarette butt from her and walked away as the first sniffles started, tossing her "treasures" in the trash, but not before Fran noticed.

"Dan, you're ruining her childhood," she said before leaving the kitchen and joining Karen back at the table. Francine's own parents had been stern and unforgiving, something she made sure never to be with her daughter.

We were supposed to be Fran and Dan, the perfect Midwest couple with an open door and inviting smiles to welcome our child's future friends into our home. A couple with the singsong names that would roll off neighbors' tongues at barbecues. A couple that was not supposed to argue in whispers, first about finances and domestic roles, then about everything else.

WINE

I remember when my wife started sniping at me in earnest—the trouble rolled into our home the morning after last Thanksgiving. I'd argued with her parents all day and had ducked out from the festivities early to hang out on the deck. My lack of commitment to her "friction-free" holiday plans had made her angry beyond tossing the salad tongs into the stuffing. She glared at me and edged her chair closer to Karen, farther from me.

The next evening at dinner I noticed that Fran had decided to switch from beer to wine, not a dry cabernet, but a sickly sweet sherry she knew would nauseate me. She said nothing as she downed first one glass, then another. Even Karen noticed, saying, "Mommy mad." I took my dinner to the deck, the first of many to follow.

Perhaps this was her way of keeping me at arm's length. I wanted a big family that would invade every room and force me bubbling and effusive into the middle of it, but she was content with just a daughter—being an only child herself. Fran was also a career woman with no patience for losing ground to those around her who were less talented. An opinion I suspect that she was forming about me. She continually shifted from job to job, pitting her employers against one another for titles and salary. I was blatantly loyal and lacking in ambition. She called me her "starter husband" with mock affection.

Francine and I stopped trying to spell out words around her. For example, my wife's recent suggestion: M-A-R-R-I-A-G-E C-O-U-N-S-E-L-O-R, led to Karen bawling for six straight hours.

There was no middle ground in our home divided between sugar and smoke. I couldn't stand to kiss her anymore, even after inhaling most of a pack before bedtime. While I attempted to stoically accept the tension, Francine threw herself into a revolving door of hobbies: yoga, macramé, kickboxing, wine collecting and, most recently, feng shui, which involved redecorating the house to maximize our "love" zones and tacking crystals above the mirrors in our bedroom.

She was creating a different "energy" in our home, and part of this involved setting up separate twin beds in our room to give ourselves "space." Distance in close proximity, a foreign concept to me, even under the auspices of an ancient Chinese belief. But I agreed to the change, dope that I was, and Karen gradually distanced herself from me and her mother.

SMOKE

One evening Fran visited me out on the deck after we put our daughter to sleep. She had an intense look in her eyes—one I'd seen often during the early years of our marriage when she nuzzled next to me on the couch.

"What are we going to do?" she asked, pulling up a lawn chair next to mine.

"About what?" I looked at the planks of the unfinished pine deck, littered with leaves from the late October Indianapolis night.

"Karen deserves better," she slurred, taking my hand in hers. The wine on her breath was heavy, but not as sweet as usual. "Remember how we used to sit out here together?"

"Yes." I should have told her that I thought about it practically every time I was out here—muggy summer nights, freezing winter afternoons, rain-soaked spring mornings. Back when we were still Francine and Daniel.

"Do you smell that?" she asked.

"It's old man Hanson. Burning leaves."

"This time of night?"

"He doesn't have anyone," I said. "He can do whatever he wants."

"I can feel the heat from his backyard even from here."

"We're becoming our parents," I said, twisting the brittle body of a leaf, the dry husk separating in my fingers.

"Let's go to bed," she said and dragged me up from my seat, the end of my cigarette still curling smoke into the cool autumn night.

GLUE

It's surprising how some memories stay with you like a mole you hate or a scar you grow to love. When I woke that morning next to Francine in my bed, I knew that something was wrong. I immediately thought of the legendary starling that had flown into my parents' house when I was a child and got stuck in my sister's hair. I opened my eyes and stared directly into Francine's thoughtful look.

"You want another child, don't you?" I said, smiling. "Why else would you come to bed with me?"

"You're an asshole."

She tried to roll over and yelped. I felt a sharp tug on the roots of my hair. We were somehow attached.

"Jesus Christ," I said, running my hand up to where our hair was joined and feeling her own fingers patting an impossibly large wad of bubble gum.

"You're a pig," she said. "This doesn't surprise me."

"You can blame the liquor at least. I went to bed with you sober."

"Mommy? Daddy?"

We tilted our heads and saw Karen leaning against the foot of the bed with gum wrappers strewn at her feet. We tried standing, but it was too painful. We couldn't manage to work together well enough to reach our feet. Finally, we collapsed back on the pillow, attached from forehead to neck, her shoulder-length strands enmeshed in mine.

"Karen, honey, can you get Daddy's beard scissors from the bathroom and bring them out here?"

"Dan, she's only four."

"Do you want to get out of this or not?"

We tried not to look at each other as we waited for Karen to return.

"I'm growing bald. It won't grow back," I said.

"I just got a hundred dollar haircut."

"I've got a meeting on Monday."

"I'm a woman. Besides, yours stinks like smoke."

Karen crawled in bed with the tiny scissors and wiggled up to the headboard between us.

"Go ahead, Karen," I said. "Cut away."

"Karen, honey, why don't you decide whose hair you'd rather cut. Mommy's," she said sternly, shaking her head, "or Daddy's," she said sweetly.

The longer Karen paused the more it forced me to notice the nearly forgotten fragrance of my wife underneath the smoke, wine and lingering musk of last night's lovemaking. She smelled like home.

Fran smiled. "Cut Daddy's hair, honey. Won't he look funny with weird hair?"

Karen reached up and snipped away at the smoke and wine in equal measure until she was the only thing left between us.

POETRY

Renée Ashley
Where Does the Mind Go When It Refuses To Leave

You had thought of something Then that too was gone A dark involution took its place The shed skin of a snake Too bad: the twins flushed away Too bad the husband soaked in wine—so sad the soddened husband And the girl too Homely as a wasp's nest Head in a book What's that? Dead dogs Dead brother Poor brother! Dead man Bang bang like that Back to back Go back further Make yourself cry Then do it again Do it every time the girl lifts her head until she no longer lifts her head Sad the rum grunts in all the loud nights the restaurant with the whores upstairs You locked the white door from the inside What were you eight? Nine? Then all of the above Even a new name: *Dolores* You've got no one They all go away Poor you Poor victim of all that occurs and all that will not before you—who has no fault at all—go too

Contemplation within the Framework of the Dream

Consider the custom of likeness or unlikeness fit as the moon to a sky: let one point light up let it be relative to that The speed of that Let something quite real cry out The dead making themselves known their bodies ill-fit and mostly self-inflicted They change the story A pattern of escalation Of furthering and backing off Embellishment! There is no space big enough for me to speak into about this Any little human thing might act as balm What's your confession?

My Father Is Ashes

We are electric I know our conductor He is a very sad man We are not in a field of cosmos We are not in a field I'm only telling you that when the message leaves the body I do not know what to make of the world I make you up from the little I know with almost with soon Is it possible the thing I love most is guilt or that you are gone We are such pain and we are utterance We are a strange thing in the air You are so imperfectly dead

All My Suicides Have Been Men

It's no one's bed we're lying in & from it we can hear the almost-ocean in the eaves of the house behind the other house There is the whisper intrusion makes There the four low steps *Here Rest yourself before* There the cherry plum its red-black leaves sweeping the green roof The incense of sweet pea climbs the trellis You had the gun You the belt The belt! & the cliff face took you middle boy You left & I do not pretend to gainsay blame The sky was deep blue tulle & there were other skies but I was my center Always I am my center & everywhere the ghost text appears in waves in sheets in trifles of thought no longer than a trifle's worth I claim to be changed Come back I am grown I know nothing now & am willing to tell you

SHORT STORY

Matthew Salesses
The Last Seal Pup

That morning, before the egg shop closed—and before Sally ran across the beach and saved a seal pup from the killer whales—Dad took us out to pancakes, Loosey Goosey's family and ours. I ate quickly and then got up to leave. When Mom asked where I was going I said Sally (the girl I loved then) wanted to see me before her mother might die. Mom looked at me like I'd suddenly changed into someone else. LG, two grades above me and half-Argentine, mouthed, why don't you go fuck yourself instead, because I was going down the block to Sally's house to show her she should choose me over him.

Indeed I'd been chasing Sally ever since I started choosing a person to masturbate to. She was gymnastically thin, with hollows under her cheekbones that could fit an egg (we'd tried as children). And she was tougher than most boys. A couple days ago I'd told her she was losing too much weight, and while she'd smiled and covered her stomach she hadn't blamed it on her mother's cancer. That denial: she was growing up, already putting her parents behind her.

Now I knocked on her door with my bruised knuckles, from building resistance to pain. She opened up only to block the way. I knew she wanted a boy as grown-up as her. I moved in close enough to kiss her. She brought her mouth down to my shoulder and bit me.

A little oval of red tinted through my shirt. In her recent habit of hurting people it was the first time she'd made me bleed. She was exacting this pain for her mother.

You owe me, I said after the shock wore off.

At first she shook her head. I rolled back my sleeve. Her teeth marks corrugated my shoulder.

I told her in return she should drive us out beyond the walls of our American community, into the rest of Argentina, someplace dangerous and more romantic. Like the bay, a wide quarter-moon of sand on the far side of a small forest, where the Argentines went to have sex.

She unlocked her mother's car without a word. She wanted escape even more than I did.

She drove wildly through the forest, almost ramming into the trees. Simian cries followed us. Monkeys lived somewhere in the forest, though I'd only ever heard their voices, sad for wilder times. The adults said the Argentines, who lived in shanties a half-mile from our community, believed you could see your future in nature. Our community believed in raising their kids abroad, not believing in what other people believed.

I didn't know until we arrived at the bay that the killer whales would be coming and going among the seals. We listened to their annual hunt from the parking lot. They sang as they murdered, vacuuming romance from the air.

I looked out onto the beach. Alan, a squat, sad boy with a transitional mustache, stood beside his father. His father was pointing out the alpha male. Alan rubbed at his lip. He was my grade in school (ninth), and I decided I would enlist him as my wingman, to help me keep LG away from Sally.

Let's go out there, I said. The bigger whales kept nudging their babies onto shore to learn how to attack.

One bite, one favor, Sally said. You used yours up. She turned on the music. The whales crashed into each other in their hurry to eat.

I walked out and told Alan to meet me later. This time, I said, whatever LG's planning isn't going to work. The seal pups kept returning to the ocean, stupidly, like they'd forgotten what happened to their brothers, or believed it was just a test. Sally was in a mood because she didn't want to be reminded of death, of her mother's cancerous ovaries.

The whale chief pushed past the others, snapping his head back to throw the seal pups he caught into deeper water, where the rest of the pod waited. Alan slumped where he stood like a punching bag cut from the ceiling. I showed him where Sally had bit me and said I was keeping the scar as evidence she cared enough to hurt me. He said my scar wasn't a scar. Beside us his father watched through binoculars: the seals were crying like dogs and dying with exasperation.

Last summer Alan's father had gotten Dad to bring me down to the bay, and had told us that the males have the biggest fins, that they hunt by the season and know the best times to catch certain foods, and that a killer whale could catch anything it chose. I figured if you were that feared you didn't need to choose; things just offered themselves up to be eaten, like the seals.

I remembered that day and wanted to break Alan's father's nose. He was sort of the head of our community—Dad had come down to Argentina at first just to interview him—and he thought he was everyone's father. Sally hadn't been at the beach last year. Back then no one noticed her absence, or presence, but me.

Now Alan's father tried to give me the binoculars and I walked past him back to the car. I wondered when Alan would murder his father the way I understood psychology said you had to. Alan rubbed his lip and stared into the ocean.

When I opened the car door Sally pulled me in hard, leaving scratches with her bitten nails. I turned to her and rested my first three fingers on her cheek.

Your time's up, she said. I hoped she would bite me again, but she didn't. She punched me in the diaphragm. I coughed out a few professions of love.

Through the windshield I watched the whale chief re-beach and push a last seal pup out into the water, where the pod slapped it into the air with their tails, calling to each other. Then the whale chief brought the seal pup back to shore, unharmed, like some sort of offering, and the killer whales swam off.

Look at that, I said. Redemption.

Sally put the car in reverse and said we better get back before she got in trouble for taking it out, let alone escaping. The fact was she was an underage driver and I was younger, and Alan's father, when he wasn't patrolling our community, was a doctor (slash aspiring marine biologist) at the hospital where her mother was treated.

I'd missed my chance.

During the drive back Sally asked did I think we could choose whether or not to become adults and I knew she was thinking about that seal pup after all, taken out and returned like the dying guy who sees God. She looked out the window at the denseness of nature. The monkeys chimed in with their usual pathetic dirge. I gave her a list of things we couldn't choose: shoe-sizes, rain, what time it is, where you're from, who your parents are. I didn't say death. I said she should admit she wanted to kiss me before we got to the egg shop, which took up the bottom floor of my house. I knew Mom would be hollowing out the eggs like every Sunday and I'd think of Sally's cheekbones.

Years later I would push an egg up against a girl's cheek and she would crack one over my head, misunderstanding.

When I walked into the shop Mom said someone had come in and put every egg on hold. All two thousand: fifty a shelf, ten shelves high, on each wall. She was taking down the window display with the Three Stooges, eggs she said people could better relate to—I'd helped her paint them, pasting the hair onto Curly's shell. Sally had helped with the shop until she decided the eggs were childish. A day full of rain and confessions.

Don't tell your dad, Mom said, but this man wants me to start painting eggs for a gallery. Dad was out having a cigar with some of the other community leaders.

Mom climbed up to pull A Storm's Coming down off the top shelf, and I pictured her dark-swirled egg next to a nude sculpture.

No fucking shit, I said. Who in Argentina would want a shelf full of Audrey Hepburn eggs, her favorites?

Mom sighed, came down the ladder, and gaveled my head with her fist. Do I have to tell Dad you've been swearing again? Her fingers were brittle and on the slap they hurt like five little reeds. I was surprised she could still hurt me.

As I considered revenge, LG came strolling along the sidewalk. He was bigger than me, not muscular big, but bigger like an over-sized dog: hair falling over his eyes, nose jutting out, body taking up more space than his legs or arms. He'd told me a week ago that when it came to Sally he would take what he wanted, but I knew eventually I'd figure out how to burn down the house of his plan.

Only three months earlier, during the rainy season, LG had organized a group of us to have some fun and I'd let us into the egg shop. We'd thrown Mom's labors of love at each other. Pieces stuck to our cheeks. The next morning she found shelves covered with eggshell and chipped paint, and I cried so she would believe it wasn't my fault. Dad cleaned the walls and repainted quietly, not looking at me. He'd probably known what I'd done from one of the neighborhood kids—though I was sure he hadn't told Mom.

After the break-in LG offered to help out in Sally's stead, pretending to be such an angel. We bought wax and paint and blew the yolks out of dozens of eggs. Mom let LG do the real work; I got stuck helping her do the girl things Sally had done. Dad hovered around the shop and I considered telling the truth, but maybe I'd already blown the yolks out of so many eggs that the truth was obvious. Once Dad had told me that to parents kids were a lot like clouds—when you were sad they rained, and when you were happy they took shapes and drifted across your life—he'd said this like it was advice. He liked to talk like I was about to have kids myself. He said the first time your child suffers, you know he'll end up, after all, a human being.

Now LG came in and immediately helped Mom pack up the eggs into, what else, cardboard egg cartons; they'd hit the big time. What's happening, I asked. The egg shop's closed, LG said, mouthing, the fuck do you care. She must have told him everything, like he was her real son. I wasn't going to lose to him. I said, I was asking my mom. The egg shop's closed, Mom said.

> **They sang as they murdered, vacuuming romance from the air.**

Maybe she had sold all the eggs. I didn't know what else to say so I told them both about the killer whale attack. Guess what, LG mouthed, I'm meeting Sally on the beach later. Mom said the guy from the morning had told her she could make a million dollars.

When Dad comes home, I said without conviction, he'll straighten it all out; he'll say no for sure. The man of the house. I figured selling Mom out to an Argentine gallery man would never fly. Mom said to make a relationship work you had to win a fight or two. She gave this advice more to LG than me.

I couldn't stand another minute of everyone falling for his act. Crushing an egg in my hand I felt the shell slice into my palm. I started to bleed for the second time that day. As the yolk and blood dripped onto the floor I said, I let LG into the egg shop, and he and me and the others busted all your precious eggs.

He whispered, you little shit, I'll fucking drown you.

Mom stroked the last Audrey Hepburn's yarn hair as she placed it in the carton, and said, I think you boys can go. She said it just like that. LG gave me a sick grin, as if he'd already told her. Then Mom said she was closing a chapter of her life. She turned to LG and said, take him with you, and his grin faded. I heard her crying as she picked up all the cartons she could and carried them into the back.

In the car LG punched messages into his cell phone, taking deep breaths and grinding his teeth—but I didn't notice, too surprised he didn't hit me or swear at me or anything. I didn't realize he was putting his plan into action. As we pulled into the bay I saw Sally's small body squatting among the seals. She started away from them and LG got out of the car and headed toward her. I watched without knowing that Sally had made him a deal—if we got in a fight and he kissed me instead of fighting back she would choose him over me—or that she would break it, moments later, after he pushed too far. The seals bobbed their heads and groaned. They had sex as if to replenish the lost bodies.

    I remembered a game Sally and I used to play when we were younger, which she called "honeymoon." We would set up all the chairs in her house like rows of seats in an airplane and fly off to Hawaii because we were married. Then she would make us roll around on the floor next to each other. Sometimes I crashed the plane and we floated on a raft in an endless ocean and decided who should live and who should be eaten. She called the game "honeymoon" because she said a honeymoon was when you became an adult, and we both wanted that.

    When we got older my parents often had her family over for dinner. Twice a month until the cancer diagnosis. Then they stopped coming. Only once would Sally talk about her mother in the five months between then and the killer whale attack, during a long stretch of rain. A half-drowned bee stung her as she tried to rescue it from a puddle, and as I sucked the poison from her finger she said her mother didn't act like her mother anymore, she acted like a sick person. Adults should act like adults, she said. It wasn't her job to save or condemn her mom.

    That was the kind of toughness that impressed us. When she bad-mouthed death. That same beautiful girl then but different, ready for the inevitable change we all sensed.

    Now, as I slammed LG's car door shut, Sally started screaming from the beach. I ran to her rescue. LG's two-years-older body loomed in front of me, and I put all of my run into my right hand. I slugged him in the gut. Hard. He doubled over. He lay on the sand like a monkey fallen from a tree, and I even thought maybe I'd killed him. Sally just laughed her recently crazy laugh, so finally I asked if he was okay. When he pulled me in close and gave me a fat kiss on the lips Sally started really laughing. She crawled over and kissed him with tongue and everything, and said, so you really love me. He reached for her boobs. But at this she drew back, snapped in like a cobra, and bit him on the chin. He howled and pushed her into the ocean.

I ran after him, thinking I might still win. I grabbed him around the waist as he followed her. Pulled him in tighter and tighter. Sally cursed and kicked the both of us. I laughed with victory, thinking if she hurt both of us I was winning. I knew her and what violence lurked in her heart. LG fell on top of me, sinking us underwater. I tried to push back to the surface. I struggled against that wet-flour lump of my enemy, as if his big fat-for-muscle body was all made of dough. I looked around for Sally, but she was gone.

I don't know why I was so surprised, months later, after her mother's death, when she and her father returned to America—I must have known already that she was leaving us behind.

Back at the house (slash abandoned egg shop) I thought about why Sally had made LG prove his love to her by acting gay. I asked Mom if she was still angry, and she sent me straight up to the second floor, only pointing at my wet clothes. When Dad got home I heard him accuse her of chasing a pipe dream. For some reason I put my faith in Dad's maxims. I was sure that he was in charge. I stopped thinking about how I could pay LG back and listened to my parents, in the egg shop below me, my ear pressed to the floor. Mom said Dad's only reasoning seemed to be she hadn't had it hard enough to become an artist. Dad said her work didn't have enough pathos, a word I looked up later. And then Mom said what about their marriage, she'd come to Argentina because of him, because Dad had wanted to write about this experimental expatriation, because his book proposal turned into a permanent stay. Five years after that summer the Argentines would graffiti the walls in a war of propaganda that would bring about the community's end.

I stared at the Ansel Adams posters on my wall and lay down in the same bed I'd had since I was five. I spent seventeen minutes like this before Dad knocked on the door and said he'd negotiated permission for me to come to dinner. He sat beside me and said, your mom and I are not getting a divorce, in case you were worried.

I said I hadn't been worried but now I was. He sat on the edge of the mattress and I could feel his weight tilting the bed. I didn't want to lose them the way I felt I should.

How's Sally, he asked.

She bit me on the arm.

Your mom used to do that, he said. Don't worry, it's a phase.

I couldn't tell if he was joking.

As we sat down to eat our Argentine duck the intercom buzzed. Mom pushed the button and Alan's voice shimmered with static. I'd forgotten he was coming. Mom said I was grounded for losing whatever heart I was born with, but Dad stuck up for me, as if our conversation had changed something between us. He said, at least our boy admitted it: admitting your mistakes is something to be proud of. I think he just wanted to win a fight. I remembered a time when I was young and Mom said I'd hit my head if he carried me on his shoulders. He'd done it anyway, and when I got hurt he'd bought me a bicycle to make up for it.

Mom buzzed Alan in, returned to the table, and tore off a piece of duck between her teeth. Alan came up the stairs into our dining room. She said he could only stay if he helped out with the eggs, and he agreed. With his help we finished the Argentine duck, and the bacon carbonara, and the fruit salad of melon cut into little flower shapes, and the fresh-baked apple pie, and the peach sorbet, and then we went down to the shop to finish packing. Rubbing his lip like an idiot Alan helped Mom think of new ideas for eggs, like Elvis and Early Easter, which sounded like naming hurricanes. When we ran out of the things to say that avoided the things we wanted to say but couldn't it was time we said the things we meant. Do you think Sally's mom will be awake when they cut her up, I asked. Will she see what she's like inside? In a rare moment Alan said, I bet her mom will be awake all the way up to her death.

I didn't understand it when Mom cried for the second time and said to stop acting tough. I'd bled twice. Mom had cried twice. She said men were always pretending. You can't get girls by pretending, she said. I didn't point out that she was a girl and LG had fooled her easily. Tears stormed down her face. She said boys were rotten and they didn't get much better as they got older.

In the evening the killer whales attacked again—the strangest thing, everyone said, since they never went back to the same place so soon—and Alan's father called to say he didn't want his son to miss it and I could learn something too. In the end my parents agreed to drive us down there. Heading back to the bay again I felt like a guy with gangrened legs, trying to fit all his travel into the last day before they were amputated.

During the car ride Dad said we didn't have to look, but if we did we should look at the seals, like watching someone's hips to see where they'll go in soccer. Listening to the monkeys I wondered whether Sally's mother would offer Sally any last advice in the hospital. Mom rode up front with her sketchbook of eggs, refusing to talk. Whenever she turned around she looked at me as if her eyes hurt from having to love me. Outside the window Argentina could have been anywhere; I'd never been out of the country.

The whole community had shown up by the time we got there, even Sally and her father just six days before her mother's surgery. LG and his parents and a group of other Argentines had come, too. They stood off to the side, and I imagined the gangs Dad said ran their shantytown, boys wielding the teeth of killer whales as knives. The real marine biologists came in a speeding van, with camcorders, and talked excitedly in Spanish. They ignored Alan's father, who followed them around like a puppy that didn't know it wasn't wanted. Alan tagged after him, though I tried to stop him. He was useless after all, a hurt little lizard that couldn't grow back his tail.

I pushed Dad's hand off my shoulder and made my way down to the seals. They looked as shocked as if they'd just found out they were all adopted. The other Americans from our community stood around talking about making my mother famous. I told myself I would apologize to Mom if she broke off her conversation to wave to me. I remembered how she'd started the egg shop the year Sally and I said her eggs were our favorite part of Easter. The day of the bee sting I'd finally made the connection to ovarian cancer, why Sally had quit the shop. Now I thought, how pathetic that they gathered around Mom; the only way she would become famous was if one of her eggs hatched a painted chicken. I wanted to find Sally and joke with her. To hear her old laugh, the one with music, the one she'd either abandoned or lost.

The seal pups were still in the water, fishing among the whales. I couldn't believe it: they never figured out this would get them killed. The older seals must have survived this already, but they didn't do anything to prevent the deaths of their offspring. They did nothing but moan and low like cows. The killer whales hopped up in the air in a way that made it clear they were only a type of dolphin, though by their dorsal fins they could have passed for sharks.

LG saw me walking back and joined me. He pinched me in the soft back of my arm so no one would notice. I could feel a bruise bloom under my skin, but I didn't flinch. He asked Sally to come with us before I got the chance. Her dad looked so sad he must have been eager to give her up to us, making us three. He looked too weak to be able to hold onto her. As we walked down the beach away from the seal killings Sally threw up a little. That's okay, I said, they're just seals.

The stars were coming out, and LG said it would be more romantic without me. He said he wished they had some liquor, they could toast to tricking me before. I realized he was the one, the rainy night we broke into the egg shop, who'd left a whiskey bottle on the counter as an excuse. The smell of dead animals washed up with the tide.

A breeze blew in from the water and I felt the salt on my face. I knew keeping quiet was what Sally wanted. I could see her eyes darting around. I could see her wanting to hurt something.

After a while LG said he was better than me any day of the week but still I didn't say a word. He nudged me aside to get closer to her. I stumbled a little. Finally Sally said LG would never be anything near a boyfriend, that he was just a drunk like his old man. She said she'd made him do what he did on the beach just to see if he would, and he did, and that didn't make him anything but a slave. She picked up some sand and threw it in his eyes. Then she stared off at the seals. I rubbed her back when it looked like she would be sick again.

LG wiped furiously at his eyes—I almost felt bad for him. The sea air filled my lungs like smoke, and I remembered the time Sally and I coughed through two Argentine menthols and she said she didn't get it, like it was a math problem. She seemed too gentle then even to hurt herself.

We took a few steps and Sally tipped over, resting her hands on her knees. Then she talked about the hospital for the first time since the day of the bee sting. It's not fair, she said. Mom thinks she can back out of life if the surgery doesn't work. She thinks she can warn us now and it's all okay. It's only sixty percent it will spread after the surgery. I heard them talking about it. Debulking. They think I don't know what that is.

She looked off. I wanted to say it sounded like a diet for cancer. I wanted to make her joke, or bite me again. Or anything.

I know it all, she said. I looked it up. Cutting her open. Her ovaries. The internet says they're like two tiny onion bulbs.

Seeds that will never grow.

She moved my hand up to her cheek and I felt her heat. Her sweat. In defiance of the breeze. Things were leaking out of her.

They could have been sisters, she said. Possible other lives.

I held her up by the shoulders, as she seemed like she might fall. The seals were still there yet not. LG was wiping his eyes over and over again and washing them with saltwater like an idiot. Sally stopped talking. She looked at me with our shared childhood in her eyes. Then I leaned in and kissed her. She wasn't surprised and she didn't stop me. I got my tongue into her mouth and searched it like a cave. She tasted a bit like vomit and I could see she knew it. She didn't care.

I can't stop myself thinking, she said when I was done.

This all took a couple of minutes, no longer, and then she started running, getting her sneakers wet. The marine biologists filmed her running into the middle of the whales. Shit, I thought, she's going to kill herself. I tasted her sweat on my lips. LG yelled to stop. Her dad looked he was going to bury himself in the sand, already given up.

She dodged down and picked up the littlest seal pup, hugging it to her chest as it writhed awkwardly in her arms like a motorized doll, except slimy and brown. It was the size of a fat shih tzu. It yelped and kept trying to slip away from her. She kept holding it still. She was bringing it back to us. The whale chief let out a yawp and rested his tail on the sand, watching. The rest of the pod was nowhere in sight. She rushed back and up to the cars and all us kids followed her: LG and Alan and me and everyone else. I heard our parents give a few far-off shouts but they were nothing but the wisps of some remembered advice.

In the parking lot, cut off from the beach by our family cars, we gathered around Sally. She leaned against a telephone pole, weeping and cradling the barking seal pup. Her arms shook as it wiggled. LG bent to take it from her, his red eyes looking up at her in an eager way I'd never seen before, but she scowled back.

Please, he said.

I almost knew what he meant. He put his arms out, and she gave him a good kick. He fell on the ground. She kicked him again and again, the seal slipping up and down in her arms, struggling to get back to the water. Nobody went to help LG because they didn't want to get beaten, too, and maybe—I realized later—they'd begun to fear me and my blossoming hatred.

Then Sally turned on us. None of you is a man, she said. You're all so fucking full of yourselves but really nothing to write home about. You're stuck in your dumb lives.

LG kissed Peter today, she said. And she described the game she claimed we were all caught in. Our fake community and the fake community of our childhood.

She looked so convincing, standing there holding that seal pup and us knowing her mom was dying, that for a moment I thought it was true, none of us was a man. She was our alpha male. I stooped to help LG up before I knew what I was doing. Sally took a step back and collapsed again against the telephone pole, crying into the seal's wet fur. I think each of us secretly wanted to leave her there, alone; she'd broken our sense of what it meant to grow up, of how we could do it. We returned from small acts of rebellions to comfortable lives—her growth was a result of a depth of emotion, a terrible realness, we might never feel. Her pain could not be practiced or imitated or known. I think that image of her must have stuck somewhere in each of our youths, LG who became a straight-A student and a diplomat, Alan who became a doctor, and I who became a veterinarian and then, like Dad, a writer. The day after the attacks the news announced the whale chief had beached himself permanently, and we all went down to the bay again to watch the rescue efforts. He dried out and died inches from the water that could have saved him.

BOOKS

H. L. Hix
In Conversation with
Frank Bidart

This summer, esteemed poet Frank Bidart joined fellow poet H. L. Hix for a conversation about formal structures in poetry at Fairleigh Dickinson University in Madison New Jersey. Tears were shed as both interviewer and interviewee wrestled with the profundity of influence, mutual admiration and the sublimity of alienation. Then they moved on to craft and—not surprisingly—psychology. In 1975 Bidart wrote the long poem "Ellen West," based on a dusty old phenomenological psychology case history he'd read in college about an anorexic woman. Bidart explains here how he relies on intellectual structures to approach intimate emotional subjects, and narratological techniques to mimic the psyche. Somehow all of that adds up to one of my favorite lines of poetry ever written—from Frank Bidart's poem "Ellen West": "Only to my husband I'm not simply a 'case.' / But he is a fool. He married / meat and thought it was a wife." —M.P.

H. L. HIX: I'd like to start this interview by asking you about something you said in another interview. Your volume of collected poems, *In The Western Night*, includes an interview conducted by Mark Halliday, in which you say, "If you can create a structure that is large enough or strong enough, anything can retain its own identity and find its place there." You and I are speaking now before a community of writers. Do you think of your remark as a charge to all of us as writers:

---

*This conversation was recorded live at Fairleigh Dickinson University at Florham on August 5, 2009. Frank Bidart appeared as a guest at the MFA in Creative Writing summer residency.

to create structures that are large enough and strong enough?

FRANK BIDART: That's a kind of ideal. I grew up in the generation where the Mahler symphonies were first widely experienced and known. These first stereo recordings made Mahler more accessible . . . you could hear much more than you could in the mono recordings of the forties and fifties. Mahler is a kind of an aesthetic model. I mean, he could include folk songs, he could include a sense of nature, of cowbells, and yet build very intense emotional structures in which all these things seemed relevant. They're not local beauties; they're not distractions, or entertainments along the way. They are part of a vision of the world and a vision of one's own nature in which they have their place.

HLH: So it's a form of realism you are pursuing? It's not the way we normally apply the term "realism," but you describe the poem as letting things retain their own identity, rather than transforming them into something else.

FB: *Realism* applies because it starts with an experience of either oneself or the world or of oneself in the world that acknowledges the power of these things. For example, I love Maria Callas. She's my favorite singer. I'm obsessed with Maria Callas. In "Ellen West" I felt so lucky to be working on a poem in which suddenly there could be a passage about Maria Callas. In which I could say things that in fact I think are true, but I couldn't say in my own voice, because I couldn't quite justify them. Whereas if the person talking is Ellen West, who is anorexic, she has a certain drastic sense of possibilities, of the dominating issues, and this gives her a severe insight into Callas' life. I think what she says in the poem is true, though it's not the kind of thing you can put in a scholarly article. It's realism insofar as it grows out of an authentic experience. Not just an aesthetic emotion; not something made up; not an "as if"—even though there's a fiction involved. Ellen West as a person did exist—but the crucial thing is not whether she literally existed, but that she corresponds to my sense of human experience, and the nature of human experience and the possibility of human experience. In the distinction between fancy and imagination that Wordsworth makes, I hope she's an act of imagination, not fancy.

HLH: Ellen West's anorexia is an explicit subject of the poem. But if we're pursuing this version of realism, it sounds like the real stakes are that what is *real* in the poem and what has its identity there is not so much a *thing* in the world as a person, a value, an ideal. I'm thinking of the passage in which she is described as an uncompromising soul. That sounds like an obligatory ideal—we all should

be in some sense uncompromising—yet also a source of her self-destructiveness. Is that what you're trying to make real in the poem, what you want to retain its identity and find its place?

FB: Yes. The poem is based on a case history by Ludwig Binswanger, from the first collection in English of papers in phenomenological psychotherapy, called *Existence*. When I was an undergraduate at the University of California at Riverside, I belonged to a book club, the Reader's Subscription. As a member, I got this book, which I certainly had never heard of, in the mail. When I read around in it and read the case of Ellen West—there was a tremendous identification on my part. I had never been anorexic, but I was heavier before I began graduate school, and I had always hated it. I was certainly obsessed with food, and with both losing weight and eating. I found a mirror in the case of Ellen West. She was at the mercy of this desire not to have a body, in a way that I have felt too—but never with as imperious necessity as she did. I grew up a Catholic, with Catholicism's fundamental sense that there is a war between the mind and the body, between the spirit and the body. The case of Ellen West allowed me to see this more sharply. I felt it was profoundly common and human . . . not in specifically religious or Catholic terms. I right away wanted to write a poem about her, and had no idea how to, and certainly couldn't then. Fifteen years later, after I published my first book, I was writing a series of poems about the mind-body problem. And it suddenly occurred to me that I could understand the case of Ellen West in relation to the mind-body problem.

When the case of Ellen West was at the level of anorexia—eating, not eating, being obsessed with food or not being obsessed with food—I couldn't deal with it. Most poets start on the ground with very particular experience and details. I seem to need the opposite. I need an intellectual framework that allows me to move down from the large categories to specifics. Again, I'm not offering that as a model for anyone else, I think that's the nature of my mind. I'm a very bad observer of the world. After I leave here, if someone were to ask me what people looked like—I would be able to say something about the feeling in the room, perhaps the emotions. I couldn't *describe* anybody. I couldn't say, "Oh, there was somebody in a red jacket." I do not observe the world well. I notice eyes. I notice expressions, the way people talk, and their affect. One reason I'm not a novelist is I don't understand people and events through the clothes they wear and the literal actions they perform.

In any case, once I had the mind-body problem as a category, and I felt it as real, not simply a theoretical issue—then, I could go back to this material that I had read so long before and experience it again. I read it very, very slowly over months. Binswanger was one of the first people to apply phenomenological insights to psychotherapy. And so I tried hard to absorb not only the narrative in terms of the details of her life but in terms of the intellectual categories and central ideas. I felt I could embody them in the poem in ways that very immediately were dramatic and had to do with fate. . . . I was imagining a book that began with the narrative of somebody who loses his arm in an auto accident. The poems in the middle were about my mother, and the book was to end with Ellen West. The first poem, about the guy who loses his arm, in many ways ends very positively. There's a sense of his new understanding of himself, and his identity, as having been created by this event, this accident, his own sense that in fact it changed and deepened him rather than destroyed him. Whereas Ellen West kills herself in the end. She's somebody who enacts, lives out, these problems, dilemmas, and cannot resolve them, or resolves them by leaving the earth.

So the book I was imagining began and ended with two opposite embodiments of the war between mind and body. I wanted there to be something in the book about the mind-body problem and art. Ellen West was herself a poet, but she saw herself as a failed poet. Then it occurred to me, she can think about Callas—who in life enacted many of the same issues, but was a great artist. At one point, Callas lost sixty pounds. Some of her fans said she had swallowed a tapeworm. It radically changed her ability to perform certain roles. There are great photographs of her as Violetta in *La Traviata*, which would have been very different if she had been as heavy as she had been six months earlier. Her voice undeniably changed in the process. It was part of the progressive . . . diminishment of her voice, and her ability, therefore, to be an artist. . . . Though it also allowed her to communicate certain things that she couldn't have with more voice. Seeing this was thrilling; suddenly, making art was in the mix of the mind-body problem.

Let me add one more thing. As a graduate student, I had taken a course in Yeats, who talks about the "anti-self," about the usefulness of including an anti-self in the work of art—which is to say, someone who is all the things that one is not. By giving voice to what one is not, one understands oneself by confronting one's shadow. Embedding a small narrative about Maria Callas into a larger narrative about Ellen West, where many of the same issues are enacted, many of the same problems about having a body, one's relation to the body, the relation between art and having a body—yet things come out differently for each of them. It's what Shakespeare does when he uses a double plot. I think it hugely enlarged "Ellen West" as a poem. In fact,

I have used the double plot in every long poem I have written since. It is the most useful structural principle I have ever learned for a long work of art.

HLH: There's a connection now in my head between what you've said about Yeats' notion of the anti-self and your sense of the double plot. Going back to an even earlier poem, "Herbert White" . . . Herbert White, I trust, is not Frank Bidart?
FB: No, thank God.

HLH: Herbert White the serial killer is not Frank Bidart but an anti-self. Yet, there's a point in the poem where he says, "I wanted / to *feel* things make sense," which recalls for me an observation you made in the interview with Mark Halliday: you talk about using "the materials of a poem to think." Accustomed as we are to such definitions of poetry as "emotion recollected in tranquility," we typically think of the poem as a locus of emotion and feeling. But you're telling us it's a place of thinking, you're talking about the conceptual apparatus you bring into your poems, and you've had Herbert White speak of a thinking that's defined in terms of feeling—"to *feel* things make sense." Is that a web you can untangle for us, or should it stay tangled?
FB: No, no, no. I hope I can. Let me just go back. With my second book and "Ellen West" I realized the usefulness of the double plot, which I'd heard about, but never really understood. Then, of course, I realized that I had done this in my first book—without using, to myself, the term.

My first book begins with a dramatic monologue called "Herbert White," about a necrophiliac and serial killer. The rest of the book goes on to talk about Frank Bidart growing up in Bakersfield, California.

In the structure of the whole book, Herbert White is that double plot, the mirror, the anti-self, and in many ways I see him as the opposite of the son in the book, who *is* me. When the son feels contradictions and conflict, he doesn't go out and murder someone, he goes to a shrink, and reads Aristotle and Schopenhauer, he goes to school. And I think that's a better way! The world I'm from is full of people who have to think the world all by themselves, who don't have those kinds of structures—shrinks, college, books—to help them think their life. There's a wonderful line in Elizabeth Bishop's "Crusoe in England," "homemade, homemade, but aren't we all?" We are all homemade, but the elements we find at home are different. Herbert White has to do it all by himself without any apparatus from cultural history, or intellectual history. What he comes up with is profoundly destructive, and he can't live with himself. He has finally to believe someone else did it.

I think each of us craves the feeling that things make sense. We do things that make us *feel* things are making sense. But all of us experience all the time great contradictions in feelings. We love and hate the same person. We feel envy and scorn at the same time about the same things. How do we deal with these contradictions? Do we do something violent that seems to resolve them, or do we apply some set of ideas and structures that help us understand the contradictions and the cause of the feelings? Herbert White has no apparatus with which to do that.

The rest of the book is about the son trying to absorb such an apparatus. And after a series of poems about my parents and their lives, and my father's death, there is a translation of the opening of *The Aeneid*. Well, one of the things you find when you learn history is that it's not as if it is a series of triumphant apprehensions of how to live. History is a series of often catastrophic events. It is a vision of how terrible dramas were enacted, and that's partly what *The Aeneid* is. To gain a sense of history is *not* to live in a Disney World of solutions, but to enter into tragedy, into paradox, into histories of blood. In the process you are transformed, yet you still want things to feel as if they make sense, and you have many, many more elements that you bring to bear on that. At the end of the book, the son meets in a dream the monster figure, a stylized version of Herbert White.

HLH: If I may follow through on the notion of paradox and contradiction. Paradox is crucial, it seems to me, to many of your poems. Your versions of Catullus, for example, such as the one in your most recent book, *Watching the Spring Festival*, always pose in condensed form their paradoxical, contradictory, impossible question.

FB: Well, let me see. This is a two-line poem by Catullus, it's Catullus 85, that begins with "Odi et amo"—*I hate and I love*. And it's not—I hate this person and I love another person. But—I hate and I love the same object at the same time. This poem, which I first read in graduate school, compelled me tremendously, because it seemed to me the quintessential statement of ambivalence. My experience is that nothing is more fundamental to me than hating and loving at the same time. For me it is the great paradigm of my relationship to my mother, who I was tremendously attached to, and at war with. I think it's also true of the nature of the erotic objects of my life—to put it in the most antiseptic way I can think of.

He does it in two lines. Essentially, the Latin means: I hate and I love. You ask why? I don't know, but I feel it done to me. Then the last word is *excrucior*: and I am crucified. After Catullus, that word *crucified* has come to have such strongly Christian associations that it's a very hard word to use in English because the point here is not Jesus on the cross. It is something less everyday than a crucifix on the wall. It returns to a terrible sense of pain, afflicted pain, without any divine resolution or amelioration. And I immediately looked up every translation I could find. This is a poem that everybody fails at translating. I didn't like any of the versions I found! Ezra Pound, who's a very great translator—well, I don't like his version very much. It's quite good until the end, and then he just uses the word *ache*. "It beats me, I feel it done to me and ache." "And ache" just doesn't have any of the force of *excrucior*. And I felt, to do a version at all, I had to be very unliteral. It had to be what Robert Lowell calls an imitation rather than a translation. I've done three versions, and I hope that fact alone communicates that no version is adequate. It's got to be two lines. It's got to be short, epigrammatic, and cut like a knife. Yet, there's no single version in English that succeeds in that. Anyway, the third version I did is in my last book. It's not necessarily my favorite of my versions. Each version ends up emphasizing some different element of the two lines. What I think I'd lost earlier was the sense that what's tormenting Catullus is that he doesn't know *why*. How can it be that you both hate and love someone at the same time?

Anyway, this version is called "Catullus: Id Faciam":

What I hate I love. Ask the crucified hand that holds
the nail that now is driven into itself, why.

... But it's only *a* version.

HLH: Is there a correlation, then, between that experience—the contradictory, paradoxical experience—and our identity, itself paradoxical and contradictory? As in this passage from *Star Dust*, where you conclude a poem with italicized lines: "*We / are darkness. We are the city // whose brightness blots the stars from night.*" It seems as if there's both a paradoxical, damaging identity and a paradoxical, damaging force from outside. Is it the fact, the presence, of *both* of those that makes us need to *feel* things make sense rather than *think* things make sense?
FB: Of course the history of thought is a history of assertions about what is real. If thinking that things made sense was simply a question of speculation, there are all sorts of theories of why things are as they are. History is a series of postulates about

what is real and why we have the experience we do. I feel that any sense of what I am has to be built on an apprehension of these contradictions of feeling because that's almost the most fundamental thing I feel. The most intense attachment to my mother, for example. And the most intense sense that if I lived the life she wanted me to lead, I would be destroyed or devoured. Not everybody has that experience, but for me, it was fundamental. It could have to do with a lover—it could be any intense, grounding relationship that, I think, always entails some sense of contradiction and conflict. I can't build any image of who I am that isn't built on apprehending these states in my experience. It informs everything I understand about the world. I grew up a Catholic; I'm no longer, but I sense that the war between the mind and the body, the spirit and the body that is so fundamental to the Catholicism I experienced, is an analog to what I'm talking about. To emphasize contradiction is not to say that all things are fundamentally chaos. There are many ways in which we live with contradiction. We carry on, not just in the face of contradiction, but embodying the contradiction.

One reason people love poetry is that it is the arena in which such opposites can be held in a kind of suspension. There's still a theatre of feeling that is very strong and it is not blocked. Most dramas have to resolve everything by the end. Good poems don't do that. I think there's something truer about art that does not do that. It probably means that in the short run, it has a smaller audience, but I think people will keep coming back to it because they will find something truer to their experience.

BOOKS

Stephen Elliott
The Adderall Diaries: A Memoir of Mood, Masochism, and Murder

Reviewed by Jena Salon

In my husband's family if you're reading a book and put it down on the coffee table to go get a snack, your book is fair game. You hold no claim to what you're reading and you may never get it back. Fiercely protective of my reading, I have always been appalled by this. Reading a book is like having a relationship—I don't like sharing.

Two days into *The Adderall Diaries,* Stephen Elliott's new memoir of "moods, masochism, and murder," my husband found it lying on our coffee table and began reading it. I stole it back immediately. But strangely found myself, as I continued, wanting to push the book back in my husband's direction, just so that I could say "have you made it to the part where?" I don't like to ruin a book or give away big plot twists to someone who is trailing me by a chapter, but these interlocutions were never about what was actually happening in the book's plot, they were about the great lines, the true moments, the dirty sex acts.

Elliott's memoir is about him trying to write a true crime novel about the murder of Nina Reiser. It's not that the murder itself isn't filled with intrigue—Hans Reiser, her ex-husband, is accused of murdering Nina after she leaves him for his best friend, Sean Sturgeon. Sean happens to have just confessed to "eight murders maybe nine" (he's not sure if one was already dead), the names of whom, he refuses to release—but there are so many shocking moments from the author's life, and these carry a somehow truer, more voyeuristic thrill. Elliott writes:

Graywolf Press, Saint Paul, Minn., 2009

"[My ex-girlfriend] kept a knife by my bed. . . . It had a grip handle. My breathing would slow down when the blade opened my skin. I would close my eyes and feel my body lift from the mattress. It was like being on a raft. One time I was blindfolded and my chest was bleeding and I tried to kiss her while pushing up against the knife which she held to my jugular."

Using sex as escape: normal. Having sex while blindfolded: slightly less run-of-the-mill. Letting someone slice lines down the length of your back: scandalous. Voyeurism, of course, only goes so far, and these moments would seem cheap tricks and vapid transcriptions without Elliott's explanation of the emotions, the enjoyment. He wants his lovers to literally make him bleed. Yet, when his girlfriend follows his attempt to kiss her with the line, "You have no sense of self-preservation," you understand it to be true. Honesty of this variety is hard to come by—in life and in literature.

Halfway through *The Adderall Diaries,* my husband—an economist by trade—proclaims that he wants to write a competing book review to mine and that he doesn't need to finish the book to do it. He says the book is just a series of stand-alone anecdotes and uses as proof that up to page ninety-four, at least, all the internal monologues and reflective passages are not about Elliott's emotional world, but about how other people want to be written about. But "Nobody ever likes what's written about them." My husband argues that there is no reflection at all after the scene where Elliott, homeless, living in a car, ends up going home with a man who lets him stay in the spare room "where he kept a wooden cross with eyebolts and leather shackles drilled into the wall." The man says, "If you come home drunk I'm going to chain you to that and fuck you." Elliott's response, "I prefer if you didn't."

My husband has a point. There are many moments that are retold and then not explained fully. But there is an inner pulse, something vital embedded in Elliott's words, that makes me convinced he should read on. It's not just about each individual interaction or scene; it's about crawling into Elliott's mind and experiencing how he connects these moments, the circuitous nature of our thoughts. It's about watching him piece his life together.

Elliott writes, "I'm working on this book, which is supposed to be about a murder, but I don't know where I'm going with it. To write about oneself honestly one has to admit a certain inconsistency and randomness that would never be tolerated in even the best of novels." This is a manifest struggle by a person, a real person, to piece together the disparate parts of his life, and find a connection, a meaning. Elliott tries to connect his father's story of having allegedly murdered a boy, Sean's confessions, the murder of Nina Reiser, the trial of Hans Reiser, the orphaning of Reiser's children, Elliott's own orphaning and drug addictions, his need for S&M. He's endeavoring to tell the story of *him*.

At every turn, *his* story is torture and pain, and moments of random violence. He tells the story of two of his friends who as teenagers "spotted a homeless man in a loading dock, sleeping on his left side on top of a cardboard box. Dwight idled the car while Ted pulled on a pair of leather gloves, slid a razor-tipped arrow into the bow, aimed from the window and shot the man in the heart." Elliott is traumatized not by the fact that people are violent, but that in the midst of it, he never fought back—especially towards his father who was emotionally and sometimes physically violent. He reenacts this failure over and over, at one point literally laying himself out in front of woman who makes him call her "Daddy" as she threatens to shave his head (what his father *actually did*) and who hits him, and scratches the words "MY DIRTY WHORE" on his thigh with pins. He lays there and he takes it, and he loves it, at the same time that he hates himself for it. He hates his constant impotence in the face of power, and this, he tells us, is precisely why he does it: to torture himself because he hates himself.

Elliott writes about a post-coital moment when his partner leaves the room, to wash her hands: "'Don't go,' I almost scream, wrapping my arms around her leg. The panic shoots through me, turning to a cold, familiar fear. *I'll never see her again*. 'I'm sorry,' I say. I say it over and over and over. 'I'm sorry. I'm sorry. I'm sorry.'"

On the page I mark down: *this is how I feel*. Not meaning, I love my husband so much and this is how I feel after sex. Meaning, this is how it feels to be a survivor of sexual abuse. This is how it feels to hate yourself. It always strikes me that survivors of abuse talk about the same emotions, the same quirks: desperation, guilt, sorrow and a sense of being worthless. *You will leave me, and know I deserve it.* And I can't help but notice that his abuse and need to relive the pain manifests itself sexually, instead of, for instance, through getting in bar fights. Whereas my sexual trauma manifests itself not through seeking pain in sex, but in causing emotional pain, raging pain, to those I love.

I always earmark pages of books when I read them, even though some people say that it's disrespectful to the writers. And I always scribble notes in the margins, whether I'm reading for myself or for more academic reasons. But writing in a book in which someone is trailing you is different. When I scribble down "this is how I feel" I look down and consider scratching it out. I wonder if my husband will try to decipher my hieroglyphic handwriting and read what I've said. I don't want to let him see this because I am embarrassed to have written it. But in a way, I also hope he does read it so that maybe he can understand. Because I explain and explain, and my words never seem to mean as much to him as they do in my own head. For a moment I consider that where I have failed to explain to my husband, somehow Elliott—not knowing me at all—will succeed.

My husband is right in a way, Elliott doesn't explain. He simply writes that he doesn't want his girlfriend to leave. He *reports* what he said, "I'm sorry. I'm sorry. I'm sorry." He doesn't explain it because it doesn't make any sense. He hates himself enough, he is desperate enough to apologize for his very existence, but to those who love you, you are not hateable, and they can never understand, not truly, what you feel unless they too hate themselves. And then of course, you don't have to explain anything.

BOOKS

Valeria Parrella
From Grace Received

Reviewed by Cassie Hay

On Sunday, December 26, 2004, an earthquake shook the ocean floor near Aceh in north Indonesia. Hours later, two thousand had died in India, thirty-five hundred in Sri Lanka, four thousand in Indonesia, all indiscriminately swallowed by the rushing water. On Monday, August 17, 2009, at least eight people were killed when gunmen open fired in a bar at Ciudad Juarez, a town on the border between Mexico and Texas. It was just one more shooting—only eight more deaths—in a wave of drug-related violence that has already claimed over thirteen-hundred lives. There are precarious worlds such as these, worlds whose inhabitants are faced with death—sudden, violent, anonymous and close at hand. In Naples, Italy, treacherous and chaotic in the shadow of Mt. Vesuvius, crime is random and brutal and expected. It is in this precarious world, a world where a survivalist instinct is required but is not always enough, where Valeria Parrella's beautiful and haunting new collection of stories, *For Grace Received*, unfolds.

The women of Parrella's Naples live not on solid ground but on quicksand that slips away beneath their feet in an instant. Each of the four stories in this collection concerns itself with a different caste of Naples society, each with its own cadences and preoccupations, and though the stories are seemingly unrelated, in each the same undercurrent of anxiety exists. The author brings the anonymous women of

---

Translated from Italian by Antony Shugaar, Europa Editions, New York, 2009

these perilous worlds to life with honesty and integrity. Eschewing the earnest, faux-literary stuff for simple, subtle emotionality, Parrella creates characters who, faced with impossible choices and impending doom, passionately pursue their own happiness to the end, regardless of consequence. For these women, there is no guide. The anonymous protagonist in the title story "p.G.R.," (*per Grazia Ricevuta*, or, for Grace received), describes it this way: "Then one day, the Black Market came to an end. Since then, it's been so much more painful to go back home to my mother's. It's been like walking back along streets without landmarks."

Walking back along streets with no landmarks. It has become cliché nowadays to reference the events of September 11, 2001, but for an American such as myself, the innocent, assumed security I'd felt for much of my life was shattered at 9:01 that morning. The shocking vulnerability of my world was suddenly laid apparent. Parrella's portrait of Naples perfectly and strangely captures those same seismic anxieties.

In the story "Run," Anna's world collapses when her lover Mario is viciously stabbed and killed while walking home from work. Anna searches for clues as to the identity of Mario's unknown assassin, but even as she finds herself digging deeper into the search, she becomes more aware of its futility. After being sent to jail for selling drugs to make ends meet, Anna knows that searching for Mario's killer will not pay her mounting bills or care for their child. "One day, I had a son," explains Anna, "and another day, someone decided that it was no longer my job to raise him . . . and so I am no longer a mother." The price Anna paid was for blind obsession. She, too, has no landmarks to guide her, had no option but to move forward, ever forward. She musters on, grabs life by the *coglioni,* and continues to live. What else can she do? What else can *we* do? As Anna finally says, "I'm still alive. Can you tell? Can you feel I'm still alive?"

On Friday, August 14, 2009, four men tried to rob a store, a restaurant supply store named Blue Flame on 125th Street in west Harlem. They entered the store, pistol-whipped one employee and threatened the others. The owner, 72-year-old Charles "Gus" Augusto, pulled out his shotgun and fired four deadly shots. Minutes later, when the smoke had cleared at Blue Flame, two men were dead, and two seriously wounded. Violence, swift and devastating, had this time descended on 125th Street. It was the kind of death you saw during the tsunami, the kind that you saw in cartel wars, and the kind that takes place daily on the streets of the Naples of Parrella's stories. "It was Michele's good luck that, just when they . . . raided the shop, he was in the back, talking to Rosetta on the phone, because she had suddenly sensed that the baby was a boy, and had called, breathlessly to tell him," says Matteo in "Siddhartha."

In the past, I would have merely noted the devastation, but after reading *For Grace Received,* I was urged on to think about those were left behind. The employee who was pistol-whipped survived. The policemen who arrived on the scene moved on to the next case. Gus went back to work the next Monday. His bold stand reminded me of Anna. Tragic Gus, anonymous Gus, seemed to be saying, "Can you feel I'm still alive?"

BOOKS

Mahmoud Darwish
If I Were Another

Reviewed by Paul-Victor Winters

Dealing with any literature from a cultural tradition other than our own can be like hiking a trail at night with only the starry sky as a guide. When most of us encounter poetry in translation, or "world poetry," we recognize that something—some nuance of language or some cultural reference, perhaps—may be missing. Whether or not we ascribe to the philosophy of Contextualism, we tend to approach the literature aware that we lack a well-defined context in which to set it. The fear that we simply won't "get it" is the sort of thing that tends to keep readers from seeking out literature from outside the canon of their own traditions.

    Many of us, however, expect literature to offer us something of value beyond context; literature can explain the world beyond facts. Consider Palestine. CNN's finest graphics and most polemical talking heads cannot bring voice to a threatened people or illuminate the nature of life in exile the way the poems of Mahmoud Darwish can. His later lyric epics, translated and edited by Fady Joudah in the posthumously published *If I Were Another*, make relatively uninformed American readers—and I include myself in this category—see Palestine clearer. Even without a great deal of background information or cultural context, these complex poems illuminate not only the complicated mess of the Middle East, but the nature of conflict at large, as well as its influence on personal identity.

Translated by Fady Joudah, Farrar, Straus and Giroux, New York, 2009

Darwish asks us to consider a "land of words the pigeons carry to the pigeons" and "an exile of incursions speech delivers to speech." These lines come from the poem "Take Care of the Stags, Father . . . " in which the speaker addresses a father who soon becomes not an individual, but something more conceptual. The speaker says:

> . . . you're a land
> of mint under my poems, drawing near and going far
> in a conqueror's name, then again in a new conqueror's name, a ball
> snatched by invaders and fixed above the ruins of temples and above the soldiers.

To whom does the speaker speak these lines? His father? All fathers? A generation of fighters? It is fair to be concerned about context here. How *should* we approach Darwish?

Taking text out of its home context, forces us to consider its self-sufficiency. One might not necessarily want to approach a translated work as a New Critic would and expect the text alone to "do the work," but effective poetry is expected to, at least to some extent, transcend its origins, function even when context is missing and also actually provide context—historical, social, political—and, in so doing, provide a broader understanding of the world in which it was created. Poets, of course, were the world's first documentarians.

If New Historicism is correct in assuming that no piece of literature can be seen independently from the context in which it is written, it may yet be safe to say that a work of literature itself can provide an understanding of that context. That is to say, one need not take courses or read too many books on Ancient China to read Li Po and gain something from the poems. The act of reading Li Po may itself serve as a fair enough introduction to ancient China.

This is the sort of thinking one might do before even cracking the spine of a Mahmoud Darwish book. Considered the "National Poet" of Palestine, Darwish is as intriguing a political figure as he is a literary figure. A member of the Palestine Liberation Organization until 1993, when he resigned in protest of policy, Darwish spent the majority of his life in self-imposed exile and is said to have drafted a declaration of Palestine's independence. He spoke and wrote passionately about the need for a Palestinian homeland, insisted that Jews leave the West Bank and Gaza, and yet denounced anti-Semitism, and insisted on the possibility of peace in the Middle East. He was also a fierce critic of Hamas. Palestine's reaction to his death in 2008 made clear his importance to the people; President Mahmoud Abbas declared an official mourning period and delivered Darwish's eulogy and commemorative postage stamps were issued.

Readers uncomfortable with Darwish's political life may find themselves surprised at his work. In the US, it is sometimes too quickly seen as anti-Semitism to give any credence to the Palestinian plight. It's useful to remember, however, that one can criticize the nation of Israel without criticizing Judaism; the two are different and separate institutions. In considering the tragedy of the Middle East, one needn't point fingers; human suffering, injustice, and tragedy know no borders and ignore allegiances, affiliations, and tribes.

Throughout this new volume, there is a lot of musing on place and identity. he poem "Rubaiyat" might be read, in part, as a response to Israeli occupation, with its consideration of "nations looking for bread in other nations' bread." And there is surely something nationalistic in the poems; elsewhere in "Rubaiyat," the speaker says "the country within my hands is of my hands." Still, there is nothing too overtly anti-Israel; rather, the poems that investigate conflict, exile, and occupation tend to be broader in scope. The speaker of "Truce with the Mongols by the Holm Oak Forest" says "Each war teaches us to love nature more: after the siege / we care more for irises . . . " And Darwish is more inclined to allude to the natural world, to Western philosophy, to Gabriel Garcia Lorca, or to the Native American plight than to simplify the conflict in the Middle East. He uses a particular conflict to write of conflict as concept, as in these lines from "On the Last Evening on This Earth," a section of the long, wistful "Eleven Planets At the End of the Andalusian Scene," a poem at once about the history of the brutal treatment of Jews and Muslims in Spain and also about human brutality in general:

> . . . we contemplate . . . a conquest and a counterconquest
> and an ancient time handing over our door keys to the new time
> so enter, you conquerors, our homes and drink our wine . . .

While critics suggest that his earlier work places a greater emphasis on nationalism, these later poems seem set on establishing a collective cultural voice. Darwish is lauded for redefining modern Arabic poetry and for stepping away from classical Arabic tradition in many ways. In these later poems, however, he may be both redefining and nodding toward tradition. He is myth-making, lyrically story-telling, documenting, and, at least to a relatively uninformed American reader such as me, creating a greater Palestinian identity.

If in his earlier works he is working to establish a national identity, here he is working to create a cultural identity that can be both personal and collective. Salma Khadra Jayyusi, in her "Mahmoud Darwish's Mission and Place in Arab Literary History," the foreword to *Mahmoud Darwish: Exile's Poet* (2008, Olive Branch Press), a collection of critical essays edited by Hala Khamis Nassar and Najat Rahman, says "this personal/communal expression is the essence of Darwish's poetic address." The speaker of "Tuesday and the Weather is Clear," a section of the long poem "Exile," says

> . . . Give birth to me and I
> will give birth to you, sometimes I'm your son, and other times
> your father and your mother. If you are, I am. If I am, you are.

The poem, rich in point-counterpoint rhetoric, utilizes dialogue and memory in an effort to investigate the self and place. The speaking voice in the poem is clearly a personal one (and one often is tempted to read autobiography in these poems, perhaps justifiably), but that voice becomes united with others' voices, and the journey in which the speaker engages becomes the journey of all people, reader included, an expansive representation of what it means to struggle with identity.

If this represents something radical, Darwish's movement away from a more traditional Arabic poetry may be lost on those of us with only a limited understanding of that tradition. The poems in Joudah's volume come across as quite modern—lyric even while narrative, passionate without melodrama, both witty and poignant in their observations, both personal and universal, and incorporating varied diction. Most illustrative of this, perhaps, is the long, sectional "Exile," one section of which, "Like a Hand Tattoo in the Jahili Poet's Ode," is considered by Joudah to be a sort of *ars poetica*. In this sequence, Darwish contemplates love ("This heart, my heart, is small / and the love, my love, is large"), the relationship between identity and language ("My language, will I become what you'll become or are you / what becomes of me?"), and occupation ("He said: I'm not looking for a burial place, / I want a place to live in and curse if I please." He also examines a duality of self; in one section, he writes "I am two in one / or am I / one who is shrapnel in two?" and in another, "I have two names that meet and part, / and I have two languages, I forget / with which I dream." In the poem's final section, the speaker is joined by the writer Edward Said, Darwish's close friend. This final section may serve to memorialize a friendship but it does so in an effort to further a contemporary mythos and to continue an examination of identity; Said, as a character in one section of the poem, says "Identity is the daughter of birth, but in the end / she's what her owner creates, not an inheritance / of a past."

Nonetheless, many poems serve not just to memorialize a moment or event, but to create myths or serve as a sort of model of self-reflection, something, perhaps, not wholly new or modern. Jayyusi writes that Darwish "evaded a curse . . . the mad race toward innovation at any price, the passion for novelty" that is the undoing of many otherwise fine writers wrestling with concepts of modernity. Rather than leaving tradition in the dust, Darwish tries to carry it into a modern world.

There is something of the traditional at work within the modern; Joudah's introduction to his volume and the work of other critics suggest that Darwish utilizes elements of traditional Sufi poetry. Again, we must pause to consider the importance of context. For many of us, Coleman Barks's translation of Rumi's poetry is all we know of any Sufi tradition. That is sufficient, I think, to see these elements at work in Darwish's later long poems.

Barks calls Rumi's poems "a fluid, continuously self-revising, self-interpreting *medium*" [emphasis his] and suggests that Rumi seeks *ilm*, which Barks defines as "divine, luminous wisdom," through the *zikr*, "the remembering that everything is God." If no other 'Rumiesque' element seems present in *If I Were Another*, this aspect does. The long poem "The Hoopoe" is, according to Joudah, "based on the twelfth-century Sufi narrative epic poem *Conference of the Birds*, by Farid Addin al-Attar Nishapur." In it, a hoopoe (a type of bird) lives "within us [and] dictates his letters to the olive of exile." This epic is one of a transcendent, ecstatic, and inspired journey that seems inward (" . . . from our names we come / to our names . . .), perpetual (" . . . the road is the arrival at the beginning of the impossible road."), and instructive (" . . . all is His / and all is within Him, He's in everything, search for Him if you want to find Him."). The hoopoe is a guide, "search[ing] for a lost sky," who, eventually, finds an entire flock of birds whose "goal is the vastness," behind which is "vastness after vastness after vastness." Perhaps this is what Barks calls "a mind within the mind, the *qalb*"; perhaps this is the zikr, the realization that God is all things. In "The Hoopoe," the collective and the individual commingle and 'destination' is the journey itself. This is, clearly, not an issue of politics and the poem deals not with religion, but issues of personal spirituality and the mystical.

Joudah's previous translation of Darwish poems, *The Butterfly's Burden* (Copper Canyon Press, 2007), received more critical attention in the UK than the US. In an interview with Daisy Fried on *Harriet: A Blog from the Poetry Foundation*, Joudah calls the world of poetry "a world that eschews politics but is, nonetheless, governed by it." It may be that Darwish's American audience views him first as a political figure and only second as a writer who is, in Joudah's words, "a master of language, able to transfer between the gnomic, the absurd, the mythical, and the quotidian." Jayyusi says that Darwish's "primary incentive . . . is to consider the human condition," not politics.

In Fried's interview, Joudah notes, "whenever Darwish's work is 'discussed' it is not really his work that is discussed, but his circumstance and history (with a capital H), which does a lot of disservice to his art." Perhaps Joudah would agree that considerations of the context surrounding a work may be useful, but can also harm one's reading of a text. Najat Rahman, in introducing her interview with Darwish, "On the Possibility of Poetry at a Time of Siege," also found in *Exile's Poet*, says that the poet expressed to her his concern that a certain critic "only offers political readings" of his work. There, on the subject of critical reading, Darwish adds, "There is . . . a political, accusative reading of my poetry that reads . . . like a political prosecution, but I do not attach to it any importance or interest."

Perhaps, then, Darwish would hope that we read without becoming too concerned with historical or political context. The poems in *If I Were Another* do what they do, present readers with a magic both particular and broad in scope, and they do so beyond their time and place of origin, beyond politics. Sure, it is a book about Palestine, a book about turmoil, about exile. But it is also a book about struggle, about homeland and community, about the human relationship to the divine, a book about identity and resistance. It functions within and without context.

BOOKS

Eula Biss
Notes from No Man's Land: American Essays

Reviewed by Marion Wyce

"Even now it is an impossible idea, that we are all connected, all of us," writes Eula Biss in *Notes from No Man's Land: American Essays*, a provocative exploration of race in America. Biss is talking about telephone poles and wires, the massive project of connecting every home in the country following Alexander Graham Bell's invention of the telephone. But she is also talking about what enabled enraged whites to hang blacks from telephone poles in the late 1800s and early 1900s for "crimes real and imagined" and what continues to allow racial privilege to persist.

In the dazzling opening essay, "Time and Distance Overcome," Biss begins with Bell's invention, a fact your average elementary school student could recite. Less well known, though, is the "war" on telephone poles that followed; viewed as a blight on the landscape, the poles were often cut down as quickly as they were erected. Biss draws her readers in with these interesting, if benign, historical footnotes before punching them in the gut with a graphic catalogue of black men lynched from telephone poles. "Now, I tell my sister, these poles, these wires, do not look the same to me," she writes. This is a technique Biss employs throughout her collection, connecting the seemingly unconnected, making the familiar strange as she works to unsettle her readers' perceptions of race.

Graywolf Press, Saint Paul, Minn., 2009

Biss's undertaking, then, is to lead us into no man's land by uncovering how we're already there. Drawing upon stories from the media, historical records, sociological research, and her own keenly observed experiences, she demonstrates how the legacy of racism has left the U.S. a kind of disputed ground, a place of confusion where whites and blacks may find belonging within their own racial groups but struggle to belong together as Americans. In "Relations" she opens with a story of a white woman who gave birth to twins, one white, one black, after being accidentally implanted with a black couple's embryo. From a fundamental question—to whom does the black child belong?—Biss moves to other questions of belonging: famous "doll studies" in which black children expressed a preference for white dolls, a census-worker's puzzlement over how to categorize her mixed-race cousin. As a white woman from a multiracial family who grew up with African traditions, Biss interrogates her own whiteness and the privileges it confers on her but finds no easy answers. She writes, "perhaps it would be better if we simply refused to be white. But I don't know what that means, really."

Yet for all her questions and uncertainty, Biss doesn't leave us in no man's land. She sees a way forward in repentance, the possibility of our collective salvation. Her final essay, "All Apologies," is just that: a list of apologies made and apologies withheld, by Biss in her own life, by U.S. presidents on internment camps, Hiroshima, Abu Ghraib. In the act of apologizing, she suggests, we as a people may find the connection and belonging that has eluded us. So Biss ends by offering up an apology, for herself and perhaps for us all: "I apologize for slavery. It wasn't me, true. But it might have been my cousin."

BOOKS

Inger Christensen
Azorno

Reviewed by Christine Condon

Written in 1967 by Denmark's revered experimental poet Inger Christensen, the slim novel *Azorno* is arguably a work of poetry—or a maze-like puzzle for adults. Five female narrators are all pregnant by the same alluring man, an author named Sampel. The plotline, which rivals the most outlandish of reality TV shows, is relieved from the baseness of such drama through its depth and breathtaking language.

In the mixed-up world of *Azorno,* flowers are symbolic of people; voyeurs watch their neighbors while worrying about others' perception of them; and silence is compared to being surrounded by a huge bell: "I felt like a diver who finds himself on the bottom of the ocean one minute and on solid ground the next, unable to hear whether the others are saying he's alive or dead because he's encapsulated in a silence as vast as if he'd brought the ocean up with him. In that silence."

Christensen, who died in January 2009, is renowned for poetry that explores structure, form, and patterns within nature—elements she explores in this book, especially through color and language. In *Azorno,* she playfully writes:

> First I will work out a general explanation.
> Then I will explain everything to Xenia.
> Then I will explain everything to Randi in general terms. . . .
> Will then explain to myself.
> Explain myself.

Translated from Danish by Denise Newman. New Directions, New York, 2009

> Explain
> Plain
> In
> In the late afternoon at five o'clock I go out again.
> If I haven't already gone out at twelve o'clock or three o'clock.

Beautifully translated by Denise Newman, *Azorno* is a series of repeated events, sensations, and colors—a riddle that questions identity and individualism: Is Azorno a real person or the main character in Sampel's book? Which of the five female narrators is telling the truth and why do their experiences blur together?

Although each chapter is from a different character's point of view, protagonists Bet, Louise, Katarina, Xenia, and Randi do not have distinct voices—actually, they have startlingly similar ones. The women are writing to explain their situations, and yet they repeat each other's lines in a way that makes them seem interchangeable, each mimicking the commentary of the previous woman. For example, some share a quote: "He quietly licked my eyelids with his large rough tongue, and I was afraid that he would lap up my eyes." This, as with many events, happens to the characters in a different sequence and setting—turning the reader round and round in a web of obsessive thoughts about everything from writing and tulips to Sampel and the other women.

The details in *Azorno*, which can be as mundane as eating white bread with raspberry jam or as unusual as making note of a fountain "with a tone other than rain," are woven into the narrative as each next character adds something entirely new, which will then recur later in someone else's chapter.

There's another, more political, layer to this book: *Azorno* examines women's roles in society. The writer Sampel is known for seducing women in his rose garden, and the women are often likened to flowers. He repeatedly recites Latin plant names, eventually intertwining them with the women's names: "Rosa rugosa . . . Rosa Hugonis . . . then I at last reach my long-planned pet names, these improved rose sisters, Rosa Katarina, Rosa Randifolia, Rosa Louise . . ." Written in the sixties, this work criticizes a world where women are considered to be replaceable as evidenced by the rosa names and multiple pregnancies. In Sampel's only chapter—his single chance to speak—he watches the women moving through his garden. "There are so many that when you try to follow a particular woman's movement and then look away for a second, she instantly becomes confused with another; and in this way it seems you can see them opening . . . and then drooping, falling, shriveling up. They lie there in a multicolored heap, and you can see them turning into dust, you can smell them dying, dry and soft."

As the novel moves forward, the women explore their power as individuals, as writers. Multicolored tulips appear and reappear, and they take on a special significance for Katarina: "It suddenly occurred to me that I could write about the people I knew. I could make them dance around with each other here on the dining room table. Make them stretch out in all directions like the multicolored tulips that haven't had any light. Make them wither and die." In this striking manner, *Azorno* exposes the power of the narrator, making the reader subject to someone else's shifting portrait of identity. At one point Louise denies that she is pregnant, in love, or that she even knows Sampel. "Rather than preventing the whole story from living its own life, I simply began a new story. A different story." It is liberating that she can escape in her own story, whatever she chooses to make of it.

Like the women, Sampel also struggles with the truth, with reality, with secrets (and he is not the first character to say these lines, or similar): "How much have I told them? . . . thinking about how much I've told each person, how much I've told some and not the others, how much I've told one and not the others, and how much each one has then told the others and not me, how much they've told each other and not me." It is lines like these that hit at the heart of the intricacies of human relationships. With this repetition of events, impressions, and the similarity between each woman's interaction, we must also consider this interpretation: These women are not interchangeable, but are instead one single woman. This is where Christensen's genius lies—exploring the impermanence of character, how can a writer betray human complexity in the act of establishing persona? How, indeed . . . she makes them *many* women instead of one. There are moments when the maze of interweaving characters dizzying—bordering on frustrating. It's easy to become lost in the labyrinth of what is real and what isn't, but that is part of the intrigue—and enjoyment—in reading this truly unique play of twists, turns, and crisply vivid imagery. The payoff is worth it as the women find their voices.

Not your conventional read, *Azorno* is like tasting something for the first time—you need to make sense of its flavor and texture . . . and savor it.

BOOKS

Guillermo Rosales
The Halfway House

Reviewed by Abigail Deutsch

Disruptions ranging from schizophrenia to exile to suicide rocked the life of Cuban novelist Guillermo Rosales, whose first translation into English, the harrowing *The Halfway House,* takes interruption as its theme. William Figueras, the protagonist, composes a novel that never achieves publication. Driven mad by this failure, William voyages to the United States, where his aunt interns him in the titular halfway house—a home for the stymied, whose every detail hints at frustration. Sitting down to his first meal there, William can't swallow his food. A broken-down car lingers in the yard, never to budge again. Old linens perpetually stop up toilets. The other patients are as filthy as the clogs in their drains.

Through books and dreams, William manages to leave the house without leaving the house, but even his saving mental escapes cease suddenly. When he glances into his volume of Romantic verse and cites a fragment, he quits at the first diversion: "I open it at random, to a poem by Coleridge," William says, and quotes "The Rime of the Ancient Mariner" until "the door to the room suddenly opens." Later, he begins to meditate on the life of Coleridge, "but my thoughts are soon cut off."

Slipping without transition from the poetic exaltations of the Romantics into the prosaic despairs of his situation, William tells a story movingly fractured by distraction. He repeatedly denies himself the rewards of continuation: Citing only the

---

Translated from Spanish by Anna Kushner, New Directions, New York, 2009

first part of John Clare's "I am: yet what I am none cares or knows," he never reaches a later section describing "the living sea of waking dreams, / Where there is neither sense of life nor joys, / But the vast shipwreck of my life's esteems." Yet those lines resonate meaningfully for novel and character alike. The halfway house is indeed a site of shipwreck for those blown off the course of their former, more functional lives—victims of voyages cut short. (The original title of the novel, "La Casa de los Naufragos," means "the house of the shipwrecked.") Clare's mention of dreams likewise rings with relevance. Rosales interjects dreams as well as verse into the novel, fragments of narrative that end as abruptly as the poems, emphasizing how in the halfway house, to quote the lines William never provides, "there is no sense of life," no logic. If William could finish the poems, he might gain insight into his experience, and feel less isolated, less the "self-consumer of my woes"—but his great tragedy is the incapacity to finish anything.

Fittingly, he finds himself unable to pursue the one opportunity that appears at the halfway house: love, in the form of a batty woman named Frances. In a neat symmetry, she shares William's age, politics and artistic proclivities. Her portraits of the house's residents create stills out of the characters' lives, stalling them on paper—the painterly equivalent of William's more writerly descriptions. Throughout the novel, he grants characters epithets that never evolve—"one-eyed Reyes"; "Hilda, that decrepit hag"—thus highlighting both their predictability and his own. The residents of the halfway house appear trapped not only in the home, but in themselves; they suffer not only from the banal and filthy routines of the halfway house, but also from their own dull and dissatisfying rhythms. This internal entrapment may be the most effective, and affecting, element of the novel.

Frances prompts William to break his pattern, to move from dejection to anticipation. Yet his decades-old failure to publish an account of doomed romance foreshadows the fate of his love for Frances, which—abiding by the pattern dictating his own life—ends prematurely.

Quietly underlying these heartbreaks—the unsuccessful novel, aborted love affair, devastated mental state—is the grand heartbreak of Cuban politics, the Communist fervor that both William and Frances once espoused. Of another resident, William observes, "He will never desperately embrace an ideology only to feel betrayed by it. He'll never feel his heart go 'crack' in the face of an idea in which he firmly and desperately believed. . . . He'll never feel the joy of taking part in a revolution or the subsequent anguish of being devoured by it." In *The Halfway House*, hope inevitably implodes into disappointment, and love—whether of a regime or of a woman—curdles with the possibility of destruction. Danger laces William's sexual overtures: "I get on top of her gently. I put my hands around her neck and start squeezing." While they have sex, she asks him to kill her. "'Die!' I say, feeling myself dissolve between her legs." The failure of William's impractical dream to marry Frances mirrors the collapse of the communist movement, itself an optimistic, ultimately unrealistic labor of love.

William isn't the only sometimes-abusive character; a sense of criminality permeates the halfway house as insidiously as the scent of sweat, implicating even its staff members. One, Arsenio, bears scars "from being stabbed in prison, five years ago, where he was doing time for stealing." The ironically named Caridad ("charity"), who stingily ladles out to residents uncooked lentils, "also served time, back in Cuba, for stabbing her husband." Arsenio kicks, whips, and sexually abuses the residents, who attack one another in turn. Whether caretaker or patient, whether former Communist or former proletarian, nearly every inhabitant of the halfway house behaves like a thug. The novel blurs opposites, binding love and destruction, and collapsing political parties into a mad, monstrous mass—perhaps the ultimate communist aesthetic.

One element of William's experience, however, sets him apart from everyone else: his passion for literature. Early in the book, he declares: "My name is William Figueras, and by the age of fifteen I had read the great Proust, Hesse, Joyce, Miller, Mann." He claims his identity in the same breath as he establishes himself as a reader, and harkens to a period when he accomplished a great deal very quickly (whereas now he is unable even to finish a poem). His expertise still matters: A doctor offers to help William "because in this damned city, I don't think anyone has read Hemingway the way you have." Literature in *The Halfway House* suggests William's singularity and achievement, as well as his stagnation and failure. Most significantly, perhaps, it argues against his self-described "complete exile"—from family and society as well as from country—by orienting him with an international pool of authors, many of whom were themselves exiles. And so even in the halfway house, a place that is neither here nor there, William manages, subtly, to anchor himself; even as his environment blurs extremes, he maintains identity; even as he drifts in a sea of interruptions, a hint of continuity persists.

THERAPY!

Contributors

Renée Ashley (poems 175) is the author of four volumes of poetry; the latest, *Basic Heart*, was awarded the 2008 X.J. Kennedy Poetry Prize. She is the Poetry Editor for *The Literary Review*.

Karina Borowicz (poems 95) has recent work in *Bellevue Literary Review, American Letters & Commentary* and *The Southern Review*. She lives in Western Massachusetts.

Polly Buckingham ("Monster Movie" 147). Her work appears in *The New Orleans Review, The North American Review, The Tampa Review, Exquisite Corpse, Kalliope, Hubbub* and elsewhere. She is founding editor of StringTown Press and teaches writing and literature at Eastern Washington University.

Lawrence Cady ("Help Me, Christina" 43) is a writer living in Portland, Oregon. A graduate of the University of Wisconsin - Madison and Portland State University, Lawrence is finishing his new novel, *The Celebrated Dead*.

Bruce Cohen's (poems 30) have been featured in various journals, including *The Georgia Review, Harvard Review, Ploughshares, Poetry, TriQuarterly & Western Humanities Review* as well as being featured on Poetry Daily & Verse Daily. A recipient of an individual artist grant from the Connecticut Commission on Culture & Tourism, he has two collections of poems, *Swerve* and *Disloyal Yo-Yo*, which was awarded the 2007 Orphic Poetry Prize.

Christine Condon (Books 214) is a writer living in Jersey City, NJ. She is the copy chief at a Manhattan publishing company and earned her MFA in creative writing from The New School.

Linda Davis ("The True Definition of Fat" 12) received her MFA from Antioch University and attended Breadloaf Writer's Conference. She lives in Santa Monica with her husband and two sons.

Abigail Deutsch (Books 217) is a writer based in New York. Her reviews and essays appear in *The Village Voice, n+,* and on poetryfoundation.org. She's currently a journalism fellow for the Poetry Foundation.

Catherine Doty (poems 122) is the author of *Momentum*. She has been a featured poet at The Geraldine R. Dodge Poetry Festival, the Frost Place and other venues.

Karen Emmerich (Translator 69) has translated works by Margarita Karapanou, Vassilis Vassilikos and Miltos Sachtouris; her translation of Sachtouris's *Poems (1945–1971)* was a finalist for a National Book Critics' Circle Prize.

Chris Gavaler's fiction ("The Marriage of the Strawman and the Patchwork Girl" 51) appears in over two dozen national journals, including the *New England Review, Prairie Schooner* and *Shenandoah*. He received an MFA from the University of Virginia and teaches at Washington and Lee University in Lexington, VA.

Jeff Hart ("The Amazing Dreamer Stays Awake" 83) was previously named one of *The L Magazine* Literary Upstarts. He is an editor of the online magazine *Culture Blues*. He lives in Brooklyn.

Cassie Hay (Books 203) is an essayist and documentary filmmaker. She currently serves as editorial assistant for *The Literary Review* and is in development for a film based on the theft of the Quedlinburg treasures. She lives in Hoboken, New Jersey.

H. L. Hix (Interview 191) is a poet who teaches in the creative writing MFA program at the University of Wyoming. Recent titles include *As Easy As Lying: Essays on Poetry*, and the poetry collections, *Legible Heavens* and *Chromatic*, which was a finalist for the 2006 National Book Award.

Peter Kocan (poems 7) is an Australian poet and novelist. His most recent novel, *Fresh Fields*, was named one of the Best Books of the Year by the London *Times*.

Rand B. Lee ("Girl, Breastless, Dancing" 24) writes from northern New Mexico, where he has lived for twenty-two years. He is not currently in therapy.

Yonatan Maisel ("Self-Esteem, by-Proxy: On How Your Downfall Quells My Angst" 67) is a psychologist and writer. His most recent work, *Life After Death in The Bronx*, appears in *Review Americana, the Literary Journal of The Institute for the Study of American Popular Culture*. He lives in Jerusalem.

Jamie McCulloch ("Roman Holiday" 161) is a graduate of Fairleigh Dickinson's MFA in Creative Writing program. His work has appeared in *The International Fiction Review, Best New Writing, Storyglossia, The Redbridge Review* and *The Kelsey Review*.

Kyle McManus ("Other People's Boredom" 78) is an English writer. His short fiction has won two prizes, and has been published in *Flash: The International Flash Fiction Magazine*.

Robert Nazarene (poems 48) is founding editor of *Margie: The American Journal of Poetry* and IntuiT House Poetry Series publisher of the 2006 winner of National Book Critics Circle award in poetry. His volume of poems is *Church*. New work is forthcoming in *The Iowa Review* and *Prairie Schooner*.

Martin Ott ("Sugar, Wine, Smoke and Glue" 170) is a former U.S. army interrogator. His fiction and poetry have appeared in over sixty publications and have been twice nominated for a Pushcart.

Mary Rose O'Reilley (poems 138) is the author of *Half Wild*, which won the 2005 Walt Whitman Award of the Academy of American Poets, as well as five books of nonfiction, most recently *The Love of Impermanent Things*. She works as a potter, musician and gardener.

Gillian Parrish (poems 37) teaches writing at Washington University in Saint Louis. Her work has appeared in *Cimarron Review, Phoebe, Spinning Jenny, and Hayden's Ferry* and is forthcoming in *Practice: New Writing + Art*.

Faye Reddecliff ("The River" 110) is a native of Pennsylvania living in Northern California. A writer of short stories and personal essays, her work has appeared in various journals and magazines.

Robert Repino ("We Have the Answer to the Apocalypse" 98) earned his MFA in creative writing from Emerson College after serving in the Peace Corps. His fiction has appeared in *Night Train, Hobart, Juked, Word Riot, The Furnace Review, The Coachella Review, Ghoti, JMWW* and the anthology *Brevity and Echo*.

Matt Salesses ("The Last Seal Pup" 179) is the author of the chapbook *We Will Take What We Can Get*, and has stories forthcoming in *Glimmer Train, Witness, The Lifted Brow* and *Torpedo*.

Jena Salon (Books 199) is the Books Editor for *The Literary Review*.

Ron Savage ("The Cave at Elgon" 130) has published more than eighty stories worldwide. Some upcoming and recent publications include *Glimmer Train, North American Review, Shenandoah, The Magazine of Fantasy and Science Fiction, Film Comment* and the *Louisville Review*.

Ersi Sotiropoulos ("An Almost Guinea Fowl" 69) is a Greek writer. Her story collection *Landscape with Dog and Other Stories* has just been released from Clockroot Books. Her novel, *Zigzag Through the Bitter-Orange Trees* was awarded Greece's national prize for literature.

Paul-Victor Winters (Books 206) is a writer and teacher living in Southern New Jersey. Recent poems and book reviews have appeared in *The New York Quarterly, Tattoo Highway* and *The Literary Review*.

Marion Wyce (Books 212) has received an AWP Intro Journals Award in fiction and had her work performed in the InterAct Theatre Company's stage series Writing Aloud.

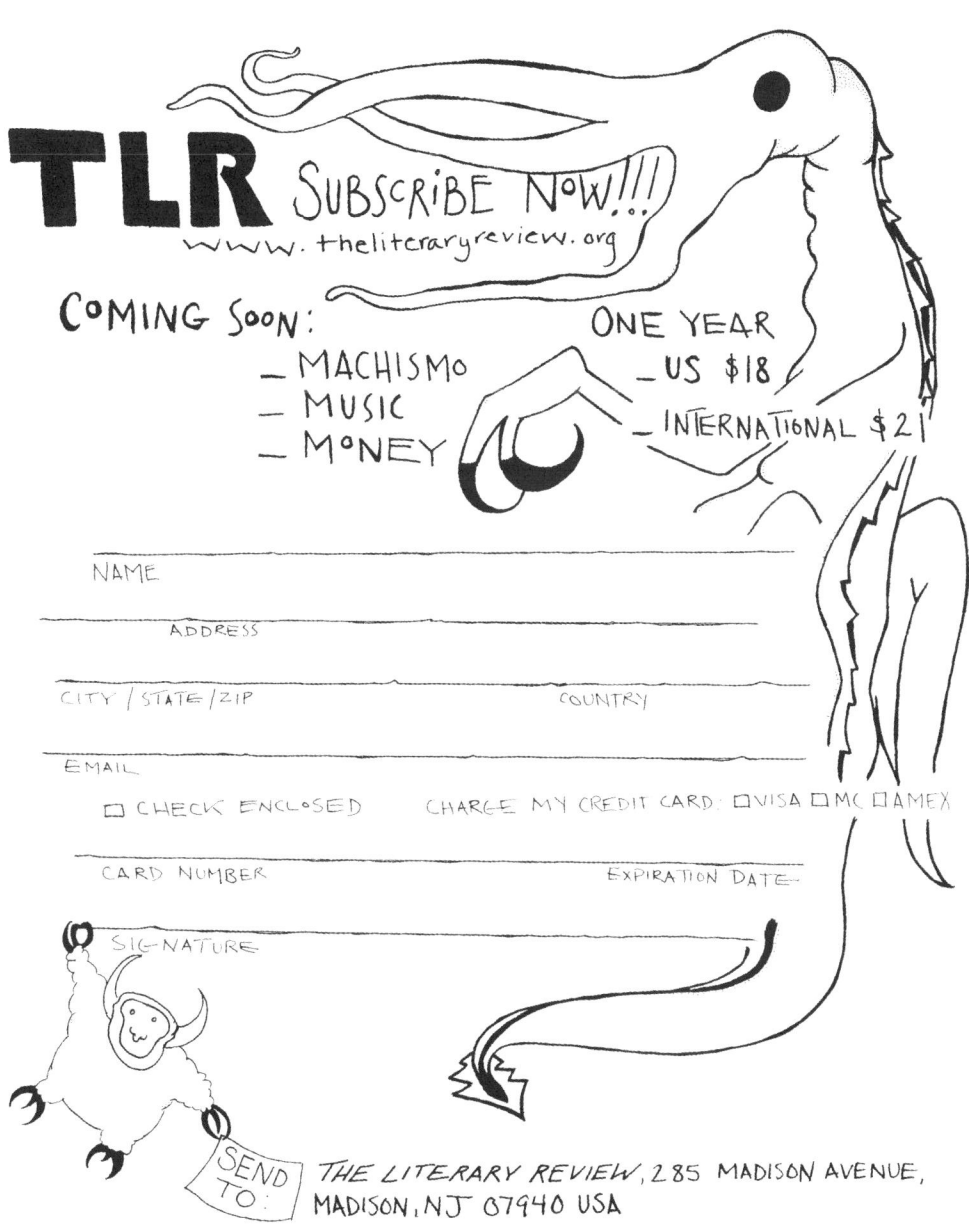

The editors of *The Literary Review* would like to congratulate Chris Arthur for having his piece "(En)trance," which appeared in TLR's Winter 2008 issue, selected for *The Best American Essays 2009*.

THE BEST AMERICAN ESSAYS
EDITED BY MARY OLIVER AND ROBERT ATWAN
MARINER BOOKS, OCTOBER 2009

Chris Arthur also deserves some attention to his own new book, published in June. In *Irish Elegies*, Arthur continues his experiments with the mercurial literary genre of the essay, using it in innovative ways to explore aspects of family, place, memory, loss, and meaning.

IRISH ELEGIES
BY CHRIS ARTHUR
PALGRAVE MACMILLAN, JUNE 2009